"NOW, WE ARE GOOD FRIENDS"

(Death of the Boer Republics)

WILLIAM MCDONALD

"Now, We Are Good Friends"

DEDICATION

To the innocent victims of war – in the past, and in the present, and in the future.

ACKNOWLEDGEMENTS

I am indebted to my wife for her encouragement and support during the writing of this book, and to my friend, Fred Calvert, who kindly undertook to proof-read my manuscript and correct the many mistakes.

Those remaining are wholly my responsibility.

Previous book by the same author:

The Lost Victory – Battle of Spion Kop

CONTENTS

HISTORICAL BACKGROUND

INTRODUCTION

GLOSSARY

MAPS

CHAPTERS

Title	Page
1. Battle of Paardeberg	24
2. Epidemic	37
3. Amanite/Josiah	44
4. The Last Stand - Battle of Dalmanutha	56
5. Gerrit Pretorious Returns	62
6. Railway Attack	72
7. Pieter	87
8. Kitchener takes Command	97
9. Interlude	102
10. Battle of Nooitgedacht	120
11. Guerilla Offensive	133

12. Emily Hobhouse   142

13. Scorched Earth   154

14. Blockhouses   168

15. Middleburg Peace Talks   173

16. Middleburg Concentration Camp   185

17. The Birds   194

18. Escape   200

19. On Commando   208

20. The "Joiner"   217

21. "Drives"   231

22. That Bloody Woman!   237

23. Night Raid   244

24. Flying Column Number 3   249

25. The Trial   269

26. Battle of Tweebosch   288

27. The Bitter End   295

28. Denouement   326

AFTER-NOTES

READERS' NOTES

Biblical quotations are taken from the Authorized King James' version and are in *italics*

Other passages in *italics* are extracts from contemporary documents.

HISTORICAL BACKGROUND

"There is no way out of the political troubles except reform in the Transvaal or war ... I should be inclined to work up to a crisis ... by steadily and inflexibly pressing for the redress of substantial wrongs ... It means we shall have to fight."

Letter from Sir Alfred Milner, High Commissioner to Southern Africa and Governor of Cape Colony, to Joseph Chamberlain, Colonial Secretary.

****

During their early mercantile voyages to the East Indies, the Dutch identified the need for a re-victualling station at the Cape of Good Hope. On 6 April 1652, Jan van Riebeck arrived with a party of settlers and orders from the United Chartered East India Company to build an earthen fort, plant a vegetable garden, and acquire cattle by barter with the local natives – Hottentots. Within fifty years of the landing there was a town at Table Bay, and a suburban farming population.

In 1688 these Dutch settlers were joined by a stream of French Huguenots, refugees from persecution in their home country, and a smaller number of German Protestants. They made common cause with their Dutch predecessors, and were quickly absorbed into an evolving race.

The typical Boer farm was six thousand acres, and most wanted two: one for summer and one for winter. Their numerous sons were sent to the limits of the settled area to stake out new claims, and in this way the settlement rapidly expanded eastward. This movement was untroubled by law behind or, initially, enemy in front. As the frontier advanced, the authority of Cape Town faded. Each Boer farm was self-sufficient with no need for outside authority. If the Natives were troublesome, the Boers would combine for action. They saw no reason to pay taxes or to render service to a distant

Chartered Company which provided them with nothing. Not unsurprisingly, they developed a unique individualism and a strong sense of personal independence.

During the Napoleonic Wars, British troops occupied the Cape due to its strategic importance, and then post-war Britain bought it for six million pounds from a bankrupt Holland. The Boers became British colonists without any consultation. They and the British authorities were soon at loggerheads, and grievances mounted as the colonists perceived more and more anti-Dutch laws being introduced: burgher councils abolished; the Dutch legal system swept aside; greater liberty extended to the black people. The crunch came in 1834 with the ending of slavery upon which the colonists' system of farming depended. Compensation was paid by the British government, but was only collectable in London.

The Boers looked to the vast interior of the Continent, previously only visited by hunters and adventurers, to set up an independent state. So groups of families set out in columns of ox-wagons which slowly trekked inland. Within a couple of years nearly half the non-British population had left the Cape. This migration entered the Afrikaner folklore as the "Great Trek".

Although the land was teeming with game and so food was not a problem, they did experience extreme hardships. Many died from disease whilst others were killed in skirmishes with hostile black tribes. These voortrekkers, or pioneers, began to see themselves as members of a chosen race escaping from unbearable oppression, and like the Israelites of the Old Testament, they anticipated their promised land.

Over time two Boer Republics were born on the high flatlands called the veld: the land between the Orange and Vaal Rivers became the Orange Free State; whilst that from the Vaal to the sleepy Limpopo River became the South African Republic, more familiarly known as the Transvaal.

10

A Boer attempt to establish a republic in Natal was thwarted when Britain annexed it in 1843. It became a separate British colony in 1856.

For the remainder of the nineteenth century the idea that Britain had sovereignty over the whole of southern Africa was a running sore in the relationship between the two sides. The Boers were determined to retain their own independent way of life, whilst Britain's imperial ambitions were running high. However, in 1877 the Transvaal was plummeted into financial crisis as it attempted to construct a railway from Pretoria to Delagoa Bay on the coast of Portuguese East Africa - a railway which gave the land-locked Republics an alternative line of communication independent of British territory. The Republic was also threatened by the belligerent Zulu and Pedi tribes.

British assistance came at the cost of annexation, however, after the British army had neutralised the external threats, the Boers took matters into their own hands and revolted. They besieged Pretoria and other British garrisons, and invaded Natal where they inflicted a number of defeats. The final British humiliation came at Mujuba Hill on the Transvaal - Natal border, when some of the most famous British regiments were put to flight.

The Prime Minister of the day, Gladstone, was not prepared to become embroiled in a difficult war in southern Africa, and quickly made a rather vague and ambiguous peace. So ended what the Boers call the War of Independence, and the British the First Boer War.

In 1886 the discovery of gold near Johannesburg in an area known as the Witwatersrand, brought unexpected riches to the Transvaal. From being a poor agrarian society it became the owner of the richest reef of gold ever discovered. This find heralded a gold rush which attracted thousands of foreigners, mostly from Britain. These became the despised "uitlanders".

From the British perspective the President of the Transvaal, the ageing Paul Kruger, deliberately obstructed their interests in his Country: he prevented the Transvaal from entering into a customs union with the Cape; he handed out concessions to Dutchmen and Germans giving them monopolies on essential goods and equipment; and he imposed a heavy tax regime on what he regarded as the licentious interlopers.

Whilst the uitlanders protested by sending a petition to Queen Victoria inviting British intervention, Cecil Rhodes, then Prime Minister of the Cape, surreptitiously supported and encouraged an uprising by despatching a private army led by his protégé, Dr Leander Starr Jameson. He hoped that in the ensuing chaos and instability, the British government would once again annex the Transvaal. However, this motley force was promptly surrounded and captured by the Boers, and the revolt fizzled out.

In 1897 the Colonial Secretary, Joseph Chamberlain, appointed Sir Alfred Milner as High Commissioner to Southern Africa. They both shared the imperial vision of a South African Federation incorporating the two Boer Republics and the two British Colonies. Milner imitated Rhodes by exploiting the grievances of the uitlanders. As residents in the country they wanted a say in the laws and taxes that governed them, and demanded the franchise. The uitlanders outnumbered the enfranchised Boers who were, not unsurprisingly, cautious about extending the franchise and potentially losing control of their country. The Boer President offered a fifteen year residential qualification whilst Milner demanded five. He and Chamberlain whipped up support at home in the press and amongst the public for the uitlanders' cause, and instigated the despatch of army reinforcements to South Africa drawn from Britain and garrisons in India, Malta and Egypt.

Kruger and Milner met on 31 May 1899 at a conference in Bloemfontein, where the latter refused to discuss anything but the issue of the franchise. Proposal and counter proposal produced no agreement, and in the end Kruger correctly declared in exasperation: *"It is our country that you want!"*

There was a stand off. Both sides prepared ultimatums, but it was the Boers who issued theirs first on 9 October - they were joined by the Orange Free State tied to them by treaty.
On a miserable spring morning - 12 October 1899 - the Boer forces launched pre-emptive invasions of Natal and the Cape. Their intended strategy was to capture the ports and so prevent the full weight of the British Empire descending upon them. Subsequently, from a position of strength, they would sue for a favourable peace on their terms.

At the outbreak of hostilities the Boers greatly outnumbered the British garrison. (Approximately 14,000 soldiers against 85,000 Boers: this including an estimated 13,000 Dutch rebels from the two British Colonies and 2,000 in foreign corps).

In the west, British forces were quickly surrounded by Commandant-General Piet Cronje's commandos at Kimberley, and by Commandant De la Rey's men at Mafeking.
    The main Boer thrust was made into Natal under Commandant-General Piet Joubert, with the objective of taking the vital port of Durban. After indecisive battles at Talana Hill and Elandslaagte, British forces retreated into the town of Ladysmith where they too were besieged.
    With a substantial element of the Boer forces tied down in wasteful sieges, the invasions lost momentum. The opportunity to strike deep into the Cape and Natal whilst British forces were numerically inferior, was lost.

On 31 October 1899, General Sir Redvers Buller arrived from England with a newly mobilised Army Corps of 47,000 men. He was met by the news that British in-country forces were invested in Ladysmith, Kimberley and Mafeking. This situation frustrated his original plan of launching an offensive up the railway line to seize the Republics' Capitals: Bloemfontein and Pretoria. Instead, he determined to relieve the besieged towns as quickly as possible and to this end divided his force into three. From the Cape, one column was to strike for Kimberley with its axis along the western railway line. Another was to attack the important railway junction at Stormberg and drive the Boer forces which had penetrated the Cape, back across the Orange River. Buller would take half of his Corps and relieve Ladysmith in Natal.

All three offensives failed miserably. In what is infamously known as "Black Week" (3 December – 15 December 1899) once again the British Army was humiliated at the hands of a citizen army comprised of Dutch farmers.

The British Government's response was not to follow Gladstone's earlier example and rush to capitulate, but instead to despatch further reinforcements under its most venerated and highly decorated soldier, General Lord Roberts, with Major-General Lord Kitchener as his Chief of Staff.

Roberts decided to follow the original strategy of invading the Boer Republics from Cape Town. However, he planned to use the western railway for a limited distance and then achieve surprise by launching a wide sweeping manoeuvre across the open veld to outflank the forces under Cronje which were besieging Kimberley.

INTRODUCTION

My earlier book on the Boer War was inspired by a visit to Spion Kop - this is the highest hill in a range of hills to be found in what is now Kwazulu Natal in South Africa. These hills lie about twenty miles to the south of the town of Ladysmith, and it was here that a British Army fought against a defiant collection of farmers in an attempt to reach the besieged town. After four bloody battles, they eventually broke through. Spion Kop was the site of one of those battles.

Having told the story of the attack on Spion Kop from the perspectives of generals and soldiers, both Briton and Boer, I determined to continue the war narrative after the relief of Ladysmith until its conclusion.

The war can be neatly divided into two parts: the conventional phase and the guerilla phase. After early humiliating defeats, a new Commander-in-Chief, Lord Roberts, with his Chief of Staff, Lord Kitchener, swept the Boer forces before them in a series of conventional battles. However, the newly emerging Boer commanders such as Louis Botha, De la Rey and De Wet, had already come to the realisation that a small agrarian country could never defeat the might of the greatest industrial country in the world with the seemingly limitless resources of its unprecedented empire. The answer was to take the long view: to wear down their enemy by attacking lines of communication, isolated units and vulnerable locations at times and places of their choosing; of dispersing into small groups for provisioning and secrecy, and combining quickly to achieve local superiority. These tactics were first apparent even as Roberts fought his way towards Bloemfontein, when De Wet captured large quantities of supplies in Roberts' rear, and cut off the water supply to the Capital by seizing its reservoir.

The Boers were pushed eastwards astride the railway line towards Delagoa Bay until they were trapped between the British steamroller to their front, and the Transvaal-Portuguese

East African border behind. After the holding battle of Dalmanutha, the Boer forces dispersed, each commando to fight in its home territory.

This sequel tells the story of the guerilla phase of the war from the Boer perspective through the continuing experiences of the Van den Berg family and General Louis Botha, and from the British side through a young Lieutenant in the Northumberland Fusiliers and the opposing general, Kitchener.

The war was projected as a "white man's war", but this is a fallacy. We glimpse the role of the African Natives through the participation of Josiah; or more correctly using his tribal name, Amanite.

This is an historical novel which relates true events told through the experiences of fictitious soldiers and real generals and politicians.

GLOSSARY

Afrikaans: Language used by the descendants of the Dutch in South Africa

Afrikaner: Name used for descendants of Dutch colonists in South Africa

Baas   Boss: used by non-whites to address a white person in a position of authority over them. Now regarded as offensive.

Biltong: Dried meat

Bitter-Ender: Boer fighter who remained in the field until the end of the Boer War

Boer: Dutch Farmer

Burgher: Male citizen of the Boer Republics

Commandant: Senior officer in charge of a commando

Commandant-General: Commander of a Boer Army

Commando: Boer regiment

Donga: Cutting made in the ground by water

Drift: Ford

Enteric: Typhoid

Hands-Upper: Boer who surrendered and took no further part in hostilities

17

Inspan: To harness/yoke draught animals (typically oxen) to a wagon

Joiner: Boer who actively collaborated with British forces

Kaffir: From the Arabic for "infidel". Term used by British and Boers for Black South Africans; now regarded as extremely offensive

Kop: Hill - Literally "head"

Kopje: Small hill

Kraal: Native village: group of huts and cattle enclosures

Kriegsraad; Boer council of war before battle

Laager: Fortified camp; often formed by a circle of ox-wagons

Outspan: To unyoke/unharness animals from a wagon.

Pitso;   Tribal public gathering

Predikant: Minister of the Dutch Reform Church

Schanses: Defensive post constructed by piling up stones – British Army equivalent is "sangar".

Sjamboks: Hippopotamus-hide whip; thong six foot plus long.

Spoor: A track, trail, scent, droppings etc by which the progress of human or animal may be followed.

Spruit:	Stream
Trek;	To move/to travel
Trektow:	Centre pole on ox wagon
Uitlander:	Foreigner
Veld:	Open country
Volksraad:	Boer Parliament
Voortrekker:	Pioneer

VOX MILITANTIS
(The voice of the Soldier)

On the wide veld, beneath the vaster sky,
The graves of battling Boer and Briton lie.
By day the sunlight watches o'er their sleep,
By night the skies their solemn vigil keep.

Cold, calm, and brilliant, from that awful height
They ask: "Were ye so weary of the light?
Ours the slow aeons, yours the flying day,
Why reckless fling its noon and eve away?"

And lo, the answer: "Nay, but life was sweet,
Death a grim horror that we loathed to meet,
But Duty spurred us to the foremost place,
And Honour beckoned with a smiling face.

Berman Paul Neuman

"Now, We Are Good Friends"

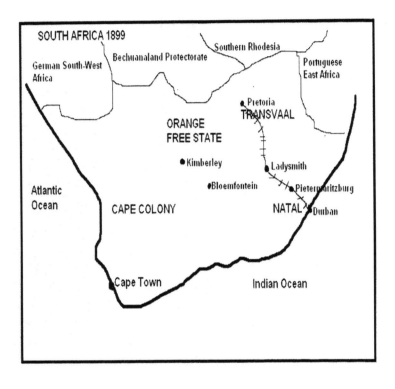

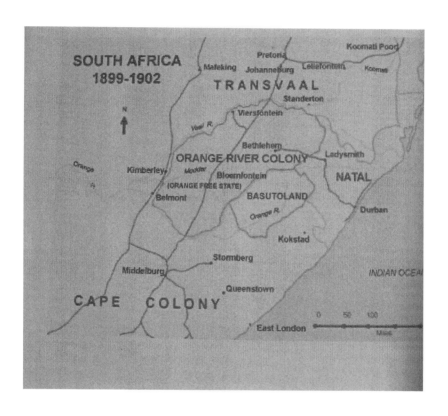

CHAPTER 1

"I beseech you, in the bowels of Christ, think it possible you may be mistaken."

Oliver Cromwell's letter to the General Assembly of the Kirk of Scotland, 3 August 1650

BATTLE OF PAARDEBERG
(18 February 1900)

Horatio Herbert Kitchener First Earl of Khartoum and Broome, stood on a prominent kopje intently studying the scene before him. At six foot two inches, his large, square frame and angular build were unmistakable. A man of few words; he said nothing as he half-crouched peering through his telescope which, for stability, rested on the shoulder of his young aid-de-camp (ADC). It was not yet seven o'clock in the morning, but already the summer sun was high in a cloudless sky heralding another scorching day.

About a mile to his front a thin line of willow trees and thorny mimosa bushes snaked across the otherwise denuded veld. It delineated the route of the Modder river. Here the waters flowed through a broad bed which only filled in times of heavy rain; its banks were twenty-five to thirty feet high and were intersected at right-angles by a series of small dongas. From his vantage point to this splash of greenery stretched a level plain shelving gently down to the river, absolutely devoid of cover. Not an ant-hill, not a mimosa bush scratched the tedious terrain.

His attention focused on the far north bank of the river and a conglomeration of more than three hundred Boer ox-wagons and mule-carts, plus numerous horses, which formed an untidy laager. They had been drawn to this place by a break in the steep banks which offered an opportunity to ford the waters, but they had been abruptly stopped from doing so by a British cavalry force with its accompanying artillery. The destructive shells had brought panic and a scramble to close up the wagons into the traditional, circular, defensive posture.

****

The patriarchal General, Pieter Arnoldus Cronje - a child of the "Great Trek" - had held the British Army at bay south of the besieged diamond town of Kimberley since the outbreak of hostilities four months earlier. During that period he had inflicted firstly a pyrrhic victory on his enemy, and then a resounding defeat. But a few days ago he had been outflanked by a reinforced and reinvigorated British Army under its new Commander-in-Chief, Lord Roberts of Kandahar. To avoid encirclement Cronje had been compelled to flee eastwards towards Bloemfontein - the capital of the Orange Free State - only to be blocked as his ponderous column sought to cross the drift near Paardeberg. His choices were limited: he could abandon his guns and ammunition and all the wagons with their vital stores, together with more than fifty women and children who had joined their menfolk during the leisurely siege, and attempt a breakout before the noose was pulled tightly; or he could take up a defensive position along the banks of the river, and once again give the British a bloody nose whilst awaiting relief from the nearby commandos - particularly those under General Christiaan De Wet. The wagons and guns were too valuable to lose. He decided to stay put.

****

Next to Kitchener stood the tall, venerable figure of Lieutenant-General Thomas Kelly-Kenny, the Commander of the 6th Division. Both were bachelors, both Irish born – though for Kitchener it was more an accident of residence, whilst Kelly-Kenny was a native who nurtured nationalist sympathies.

They were ill-matched. During the pursuit of the last few days, Kitchener had attached himself to the 6th Division and Kelly-Kenny had found him to be fussy and interfering. Now Kelly-Kenny was smarting from his recent humiliation. It was his Division which was in hot pursuit of Cronje, and as the inevitable battle approached he naturally assumed that, as the senior officer, he would conduct the fight. He had issued orders accordingly. But not so. Unbeknown to him, Kitchener had dispatched a galloper to Roberts, who was *hors de combat* due to a heavy chill and was resting in Jacobsdal, and had sought clarification of responsibilities. Kelly-Kenny had been surprised when, on the eve of battle, he received a private written message from Roberts pointing out that Kitchener was his Chief of Staff:

"Please consider that Lord Kitchener is with you for the purpose of communicating to you my orders."

He had been publicly subordinated to a junior; clearly, he did not have the confidence of the Commander-in-Chief. And Kitchener lost no time in making it brutally clear as to who was in command.

"I still believe that we should complete the encirclement around Cronje's laager, and use the guns to bombard him into surrender." It was Kelly-Kenny speaking.

Kitchener continued gazing at the laager where the smoke of numerous camp-fires swirled lazily upwards. He envisaged the Boers brewing their coffee and mixing their mealie porridge; enjoy your breakfast whilst you are able, he mused with a confident grin.

Kelly-Kenny again, "The men are utterly exhausted. They have been forced marching since five o'clock yesterday evening none stop in the heat and dust, existing on a couple of dry biscuits and little water. They need rest and food before beginning the fight."

Kitchener was irritated; he didn't need to be reminded of the situation. Had he not ridden with the marching troops? He was aware of the shortage of food following the capture of the Army's supply column by De Wet and his Commando with the loss of ten days' rations. He knew that water was scarce. Yes, the men were beat, but he must make one more supreme demand of them – the opportunity to defeat this Boer Army could not be missed.

"If we wait as you suggest then it gives Cronje the opportunity to break out or to be relieved by Boer commandos who are marauding around, or might even come from Bloemfontein. No, we cannot waste time. We will attack immediately," insisted Kitchener assuredly. He turned towards his rival and stared at him with his cold, azure-blue eyes set wide apart in a large moustachioed face, "From my experience in the Sudan, a defensive position is best overcome by a quick and aggressive assault. Cronje has what … four thousand men? We have fifteen thousand; the advantage is with us."

Kelly-Kenny could not hide his exasperation at what he saw as Kitchener's naivety and reckless impatience. He knew this to be Kitchener's first fight against white men, "A frontal attack against the Dervishes armed with breech-loaders and spears is a very different proposition than an attack on a Boer laager," retorted Kelly-Kenny. "We are up against a new form of warfare: expert shots armed with the Mauser rifle and fighting from well-constructed trenches. With the smokeless cartridge it's almost impossible to pin-point their positions. We have fought in these same conditions only months before and suffered very heavy casualties."

"This is not a frontal attack!" defended Kitchener. "It is an all-round attack! Your Division will hold the Boers with an attack from the south, whilst the 9th Division, on arrival, will split its forces to attack simultaneously from east and west astride the river. The cavalry will block the north."

"Our recent experience shows that the balance of advantage has swung decisively towards the defender; we shall suffer heavy casualties," protested Kelly-Kenny. "Surely it is better to bombard Cronje into surrender and spare the troops?"

Kitchener reflected that apart from Roberts himself, Kelly-Kenny was the oldest serving officer in the British Army. Perhaps this explained his lack of aggression and over-caution. "My plan is set. You have much to do." He curtly ended the discussion.

"Send a cable to Lord Roberts," Kitchener addressed an ADC:

"We have stopped the enemy's convoy on the river here. General Kelly-Kenny's division is holding them to the south, enemy lining bank of Modder River, convoy stationary in our immediate front." He outlined his battle plan, then, *"I think it must be a case of complete surrender."*

Kitchener looked at his watch and expressed confidently to his meagre staff, "It's now seven o'clock. We shall be in the laager by half past ten."

The orchestral guns began their deadly overture: field artillery, 5 inch howitzers, naval 12 pounders. The roar filled the still, baking air. The laager disappeared under a cloud of greenish lyddite smoke: pieces of wagon were tossed into the air, ammunition exploded spectacularly, the shredded flesh of oxen, mules and horses was scattered indiscriminately.

From his kopje Kitchener examined his front as the small brown figures of the infantry moved in lines across the bare plain towards the objective. He searched anxiously through his telescope; he was rather bemused; there was no sign of the Boers.

****

The white sandy banks of the Modder river made just as effective trenches here as they had thirty miles downstream where the British had previously been mauled. Working furiously through the night, and with their usual ingenuity, the

Boers had dug a network of rifle pits along the south bank of the river concealed in the bushes, and on the north bank in a protective half-circle enclosing the laager perimeter. Tunnels had been excavated horizontally into the high river banks, and flanking trenches were provided by the numerous dry dongas.

In their practised way, the Boers waited concealed until their enemy drew to within a few hundred yards, and then they poured out a veritable wall of death. Rapidly and firmly they drew back the bolts of their rifles after each aimed shot, before pushing it forward again, driving a fresh bullet into the breech. In this way they emptied their magazines into the reeling soldiers to their front. The first wave of Khakis went down; the second wave faltered before crumbling; the third wave came on before the depleted survivors dropped to the ground desperately seeking cover amongst the writhing maimed, and the still corpses. And over the tumult and the carnage of the confused battlefield, the burning rays of the pitiless sun beat down arbitrarily upon the living, the dying, and the dead.

****

Kitchener eagerly scanned the battlefield excited by the prospect of a quick and easy victory. To his front Kelly-Kenny's Division charged across the open plain. He watched the brown dots advance by short rushes, but each time fewer and fewer rose to dash forward, until the attack petered out. Forward movement ceased. Survivors hugged the dust several hundred yards from the unseen Boers; the slightest move on that cover-less ground invited a deadly retribution.

He turned his scrutiny to the left flank; there the West Ridings and the Oxford Light Infantry had made some headway. They had succeeded in reaching the southern river bank a couple of miles downstream of the laager, and had swung right in an attempt to roll up the defences, but they too had stopped. Even the blood-curling charge of the rugged Highlanders had come to nought.

Supposedly attacking from the east and downstream on the

southern bank was the 1st Welsh and the 1st Essex, with the Mounted Infantry (MI) under Colonel Hannay, similarly attacking along the northern bank. But he was alarmed to observe the infantry facing away from the laager and skirmishing in the hills – were they fighting off probing commandos? He did not have sight of the MI.

It was midday. The sky suddenly darkened, thunder clouds gathered, and a tremendous storm broke directly overhead. Sheets of rain cascaded down - a boon to the thirst-tormented men lying in the open. An aide held out Kitchener's mackintosh; he slipped into it never taking his gaze from the battle below. He stood like a dripping statue.

The roar of the thunder-peels mixed with the dull boom of the artillery to create a discordant cacophony; the intermittent brilliance of the jagged lightening played over the veld, accompanied by the lesser flashes of fire from the forty British guns. The flames from burning wagons illuminated the momentary gloom.

Kitchener surveyed this awesome spectacle of terror and grandeur - God and man in perfect harmony. What he could not see were the Boer trenches flooded by the gushing waters of the Modder, which rose to engulf the rotting corpses of man and beast, and to swallow the excrement of thousands.

Gradually, the storm passed; the dark, rain-filled clouds rolled eastwards; the sun once again exerted its dominance.

The stalled attack must be renewed. Kitchener mounted his horse, and accompanied by his aides, galloped to the headquarters of the 9th Division commanded by Lieutenant General Colvile.

"What about making a more determined assault?" prompted Kitchener.

"I only have a few fresh troops: the half-battalion of the Cornwall Light Infantry who are guarding the baggage," explained Colvile.

"Then the Cornwalls must go at once!" insisted Kitchener. "They must ford the river and rush the position!" With that he rode off to find Kelly-Kenny.

Colvile felt dispirited at the thought of ordering a hopeless attack. With heavy heart he summoned the Commanding Officer of the Cornwalls, Lieutenant Colonel Aldworth, and relayed the orders.

"The men are exhausted and just about to eat their meagre rations," pleaded the Officer.

"Postpone the attack till afterwards. At least the poor devils will not have to attack on empty stomachs."

"My men are either pinned down or exhausted; I have no reserves," reported Kelly-Kenny to Kitchener.

"I'm sure one more rush will carry the day," insisted Kitchener.

"You don't understand," reiterated Kelly-Kenny. "To rush the Boer position held by four thousand determined men entrenched and armed with the finest modern rifles is impossible." His neck veins grew taught with anger, "My Division is in no state to renew the assault."

Kitchener was furious at the lack of drive and cooperation of his Divisional Commanders which was frustrating his attack. He turned his attention to the remaining flank wherein lay his only hope of success. He dictated to his aide:

"The time has come for a final effort. All troops have been warned that the laager must be rushed at all costs. Try and carry the Essex and Welsh with you, but if they cannot go the mounted infantry should do it. Gallop up if necessary and fire into the laager."

It was his final, desperate throw; "Deliver this to Colonel Hannay."

The Commanding Officer of the MI was a large, courageous highlander. He sat on the damp ground and leant back against a tree-trunk, careless of the rain-drops still dripping from the sodden foliage. All around him sprawled his weary men: some brewed tea, a few cleaned weapons, others slept the sleep of the exhausted. Since daybreak they had fought off Free State commandos desperate to break the siege of their encircled countrymen, and then they had fruitlessly attacked the laager. Their horses were tethered to trees; the animals stood quietly, calmly, bone-weary from debilitating activities, hunger-weak from lack of fodder, sweating profusely in the uncomfortable heat – some had already succumbed to the testing conditions, their carcasses rotting on the veld, a banquet for the ubiquitous vultures.

"Over there!"

Hannay looked up. A young, smartly dressed officer carefully picked his way through the prostrate bodies.

"Colonel Hannay?"

"Yes."

"I have orders for you from Lord Kitchener." He handed over a sheet from a signal pad.

Hannay remained seated. He stretched forward and took the paper; he unfolded it and read … "What the hell!" Mounted infantry use horses for mobility, but fight on foot like conventional infantry, not from the saddle like cavalry with lance and sword. The idea that they should charge entrenched Boers firing from the saddle was ludicrous, nay, suicidal! The ground in front of the enemy positions was already littered with Khaki dead, witness to their earlier hopeless, bloody attacks. But to disobey this insane order, to refuse this quixotic idiocy, would forever expose him to accusations of cowardice, particularly as seemingly it was part of a wider coordinated action.

The aide looked at him expectantly.

"You can inform Lord Kitchener that I will do my duty."

"Sir." With an affirming nod the young officer returned to his horse and trotted away.

Hannay hesitated. He could not restrain a resigned,

phlegmatic grimace:

> *Theirs not to reason why,*
> *Theirs to do and die ...*

He rose to his feet and instinctively slapped his slouch hat against his trousers before placing it on his head. He paused and looked about. His senses absorbed the surroundings with the heightened intensity of a man on his way to a firing squad: once again the sun commanded the blue sky; white puffy clouds skipped along shooed by an invisible breeze; rain drops glistened on lush leaves; the damp after-smell of rain mixed with the musty odour of steaming horse. It was a beautiful world.

He slowly mounted his horse, withdrew his carbine from its leather bucket, and declared to his men who were watching him quizzically, "We are going to charge the laager." He said it matter-of-fact, more an observation than an order. He pulled the reins turning his mount towards the Boer lines, and with a kick of his heels urged his horse forward from a trot to a canter and finally into a full gallop.

His bewildered men - perhaps fifty in total - scrambled to their feet, hurriedly mounted their horses and chased after their Colonel - he was already riding full-tilt towards the laager. It was not a structured, cohesive body of men which surged towards the Boers, rather a confused horde, anxious to follow their respected leader.

****

The Boer defenders were astonished to see a lone horseman racing towards them, outstripping a disorderly group in pursuit. They hesitated to fire at a man so blatantly inviting death. Was he berserk? Was he some kind of decoy or distraction? Reluctantly they opened fire; rider and horse collapsed. The rider painfully extricated himself from beneath the convulsing animal; he was badly shaken. Dazed, he staggered to his feet and searched for his discarded carbine; there was no sign of it. He drew his pistol and lurched forward on foot shooting ineffectually until, riddled with bullets, he keeled over in the dirt. Empty-saddled horses thundered by his body, until finally the survivors swerved off to the left, fleeing the singing metal.

****

The half battalion of the Cornwalls charged with a ringing cheer; their line wavered; paused; disappeared. Colonel Aldworth died leading his men in a futile gesture.

....

With sunset came stalemate. The bombardment of the laager ceased through the utter exhaustion of the gunners, and only the intermittent explosions of ammunition and the crackle of burning wagons disturbed the cool of the evening. In the chaos, some units dug-in where they were, others raggedly withdrew. The wounded were collected - the dead would have to wait.

Kitchener was disappointed. He felt thwarted by the lukewarm support of his fellow generals and their lack of drive and enthusiasm for the fight. Tomorrow would bring success. He cabled Roberts:

"We did not succeed in getting into the enemy's convoy, though we drove the Boers back a considerable distance along the river bed. The troops are maintaining their positions, and I hope tomorrow we shall be able to do something more definite ... Our casualties have, I fear, been severe."

....

Roberts was unsettled by the reports of the battle which filtered through to him during the day. Despite feeling quite unwell, he left at four o'clock in the morning and made for Paardeberg. En route he met the convoys of wounded heading to Kimberley. In order to lighten the baggage train, he had conceded Kitchener's request to leave most of the ambulances and field hospitals behind; now his men were paying for that decision. Bereft of ambulances, the wounded were being transported in the back of spring-less bullock-wagons across atrocious tracks torn up by the passage of countless vehicles and horses. Their subdued moans and occasional shrieks tore at his guilty heart.

It was about ten o'clock when he arrived at his headquarters' wagon with its sheet of tarpaulin stretched out to make a shaded lean-to office. This diminutive man displayed no sign or badge of rank, and wore a plain khaki coat with ordinary shoulder straps, cord breeches, putti gaiters and issued pith helmet. He looked more like a private soldier than the Commander-in-Chief. His staff greeted him enthusiastically – nothing could go wrong now.

Roberts threw his helmet onto a table and sank into a canvas chair, "What are the latest casualty figures?" he asked anxiously.

"Returns are still coming in, sir, but over one thousand killed and wounded so far," reported the officer.

"So far?" Roberts was alarmed.

"There will be more, sir. Not all units have submitted their casualty lists."

A thoughtful pause; "Assemble a council of war."

His subordinate divisional and brigade Generals together with his Chief of Staff gathered beneath the lean-to. Roberts listened carefully. With the exception of Kitchener, all argued vehemently against further attacks, and pressed to continue the bombardment as the way to induce Cronje's surrender. Kitchener remained uncowed by the criticism of his tactics, and was adamant that direct action was the only solution. The tension between the formation Commanders and the Chief of Staff was palpable.

Roberts' first inclination was to support Kitchener. He admired him for his tenacity and perseverance, but could see that his tactics were crude, without brilliance or style - he found his cold insensitivity to casualties disturbing. He

35

pondered the available options before announcing quietly, authoritatively, "The mortality among the Boer horses and oxen must be severe," he argued. "Cronje has been deprived of mobility and is stuck in the drift. We will play the less costly waiting game."

Kitchener was more than a little irked when his battle-plan was discarded - he was convinced that he was right. With the meeting concluded, the participants began to disperse. As General Smith-Dorrien, a brigade commander, mounted his horse, Kitchener sidled up to him, "You could still seize the opportunity to make a final attack. With success you will be a made-man."

Smith-Dorrien was astounded at this suggested insubordination, "You know my views. I will only attack when ordered to do so by the Commander-in-Chief." With undisguised disgust, he turned his horse, brushed Kitchener aside, and cantered away.

Kitchener remained aloof amongst his peers. He absorbed their cold glances with a cultivated disregard. He was no longer in charge, and felt superfluous to requirements, so was quite relieved when Roberts dispatched him to Naaupoort Junction to supervise the opening of rail communications with Bloemfontein - so vital for the Army's onward advance.

He was left to reflect on Queen Victoria's observations in her letter to him on the eve of his departure for South Africa:

" ...It must be borne in mind that this is a very different kind of warfare to the Indian and Egyptian. Boers are a horrid brutal people, but are skilled in European fighting and well armed."

Begrudgingly, he acknowledged just how wise and perceptive was the little old lady.

He was not around when following several days of intense bombardment, Cronje, with four thousand men, emerged in defeat from their sodden trenches and battered laager.

CHAPTER 2

The Times 28 April 1900

" ... Hundreds of men ... were lying in the worst states of typhoid with only a blanket and a thin waterproof sheet (not even the latter for many of them) between their aching bodies and the ground with no milk and hardly any medicines, without beds, stretchers or mattresses, without pillows ... without a single nurse among them. In many tents there were ten typhoid cases lying closely packed together, the dying with the convalescent ... there was no room to step between them ... "

Extract from an article written by Mr W Burdett-Couttes, special correspondent for *The Times,* on the medical situation in Bloemfontein.

ENTERIC EPIDEMIC

It was a hard slog from Paardeberg to Bloemfontein. That day Rodger Borthwick's platoon marched eighteen miles over uneven, stony veld which caused feet to blister and skin to rub raw. Food was short. They had been issued with just two biscuits and a tin of bully-beef for the day – the salty meat exacerbated the constant thirst. No fresh water was available in this land devoid of natural springs and streams. Before starting out they had filled their water-bottles from the brown, muddy waters of the Modder River, consciously ignoring the bloated and putrefying corpses bobbing by – both human and animal alike.

As evening approached, thunder circled around, rain raged with terrific fury, and the heavens filled with great lurid flashes of flame which lit up the veld. Everyone was drenched to the skin. When the halt was called, Rodger wrapped himself up in a wet blanket and tried to sleep - a vain hope in the penetrating, sleep-depriving cold. He was almost glad to hear the bugle sing out reveille; at 4:30 am the march resumed. The cold autumn night soon gave way to a sweltering hot day.

Many horses had died on the march from poor food, the unfamiliar climate and just sheer hard work and neglect. It left officers compelled to march with their soldiers.

At first Rodger put the headaches and burning sensation down to the relentless sun – even the fainting attack. Then he developed an irritating cough and a bleeding nose. He began to sweat profusely, felt weak, drowsy, and despite the vigorous exertions had no appetite for his pitiful rations. He craved sleep. That was until he collapsed and lay prostrate, face down on the ground, his vista restricted to but a few feet in front of him. He spit the dust from his mouth and tried to stand; he couldn't. He felt consciousness and discomfort floating away - a blessed relief.

"Looks like yer not over clivvor Mr Borthwick. Yer've the fever. It's the wagon for ye."

Rugged but kindly hands lifted him into the ox-wagon; his mattress was dirty sacks strewn over rough boards. Others jostled for floor space; one soldier was thrashing about, agitated, shouting, occasionally screaming. The spring-less wagon jolted across the bumpy veld; was it one day, two, more …? He lost count as he drifted in and out of consciousness. When awake he felt the agonies of his sore and battered bones competing with the excruciating abdominal pains. Through the haze of fever he remembered arriving at the village of tents.

"God they keep coming! This is bloody ridiculous!" exclaimed the doctor. "Where are we supposed to put this lot? We're equipped for fifty and are holding almost three hundred."

"Sir, the tents are full. We've already six patients where there should be four," pointed out the nursing orderly.

"Then make it eight!"

Rodger lay on a waterproof sheet which offered no relief

from the hard, lumpy ground. A dirt-ingrained blanket was thrown over him. He physically touched the men on either side. One was calm, the other was delirious, rocking from side to side clutching at some imaginary object. Rodger felt tired; so tired. Totally spent.

The smell … it was awful … gagging. Momentarily he was lucid enough to realise that he was lying in his own excrement – how shaming: "Orderly! Orderly!" No one came. As the sun bore down on the canvass the heat inside the tent became overpowering, the stink from eight men sickening; he brushed the black cluster of flies from his face: "Orderly! Orderly!" No one came. He needed fresh air; he needed water: "Orderly! Orderly!" No one came.

He drifted in and out of consciousness; sometimes tormented and delirious; sometimes calm. He sensed the ghostly shadows of men flitting by; intangible; illusory. Was he being spoon-fed with condensed milk? He lost his grip on reality. He felt, rather than saw, the soldier next to him being rolled onto a stretcher and borne away – relief at last; now he could properly stretch his legs. Occasional voices penetrated his fiery, pained, hellish existence.

It was dark. The rain was drumming on the canvas; he felt secure against the outside storm – comforted. Instinctively, Rodger listened for the night noises: the bleating lambs; the eerie screech and hissing of the barn owl which lived in the rafters of the dilapidated building on the edge of Roman Wood. He could visualise the white-feathered predator circling above the hay field hunting for small mammals – he once saw one swoop down and snatch up an unsuspecting vole with its deadly, sharp talons. He enjoyed rough camping with his older brother. They never ventured too far from the family Hall; just far enough to feel free and independent, but close enough to scurry home should disaster overtake them. He wanted to be nowhere else: to the west the skyline was crowned by the Cheviot Hills; a few miles east were the long sandy beaches of the Northumberland coast. He felt inwardly content, serene, reassured in his familiar surroundings ...

But he felt cold; he was shivering. He could hear only the sound of agonising murmurs. He was wet; the rain was seeping under the canvas; he was lying in water and mud. The illusion was shattered: "Orderly! Orderly!"

"Wat's all the fuss then!" A soldier drew back the tent flap, "Woke up then 'ave we?"

Rodger rose painfully onto his elbow and spoke in faltering gasps as he mustered his reserves of strength, "Need water, food, clean clothes, a bed ... I'm lying in mud." He fell back into the sludgy, excremental mess.

The orderly sloshed to his side and squatted, "Got no bed-pans ne'er mind beds mate. Doctor says yer can't 'ave food, but we've got condensed milk, and sun 'll soon dry up the mess." He paused as a truth dawned, "Yer an officer?"

"Yes .... I'm an officer."

"Back in a jiffy." The orderly left soon to return with a medical officer, a young captain.

"I'm Captain John Renner, and you?"

"Lieutenant Rodger Borthwick ... Northumberland Fusiliers."

"Well Lieutenant Borthwick, you shouldn't be here. Afraid we've had plenty of mix-ups at reception ... your uniform's in tatters ... should really have been sent into town to an officers' hospital." He was apologetic. "Still, looks like your fever's broken." He took a thermometer from a top pocket and thrust it under Rodger's tongue. Following a short, silent pause he removed and read it, "One hundred and one - you should be on the mend from now on."

"How long have I been here?" enquired Rodger.

"Nearly three weeks." The young doctor half lifted his open hands in a gesture of despair, "Sorry about all this." His eyes cast about. "We do our best, but it makes one's heart sick to look at them. We're terribly overcrowded with a drastic shortage of everything. Most of our trained orderlies have been transferred up the line, instead we have a bunch of inexperienced convalescents who don't know what they are doing, and don't give a damn anyway. We are working thirty six hours in every forty eight, and still it's not enough."

Rodger looked at the doctor - probably no older than himself - his shoulders sagging under the weight of doomed patients; his eyes blood-shot with fatigue and moistened with tears.

"It's the best we can do ..," he sighed with weary self-condemnation. "Look, I'll send the orderly with condensed milk and we'll try to clean you up a bit whilst I arrange your transfer to a private hospital in town."

It was like a move from Dante's hell to heaven. He was received at the Bloemfontein Club, which served as a temporary hospital, by smiling nurses in crisp, clean uniforms. He was still ill enough not to be embarrassed as they cut his lousy rags from him, and washed his grimy body with warm, soapy cloths. He was dressed in a hospital gown and helped gently into a bed of clean, fresh-smelling sheets. Exhausted by his efforts, he was drifting off to sleep when he became aware of a visitor standing by his bed. A nurse stood reverently to one side and slightly to the rear of the figure.

"I'm Doctor Conan Doyle. I understand that you've just joined us from the Field Hospital. I think you'll find conditions here a little more conducive to recovery. Let me take your temperature ... one hundred and one ... mmm. I'm going to prescribe phenacetin to make sure the fever is broken. Don't worry ... no lasting damage. We'll have you back chasing "Johnny Boer" in no time."

The days passed pleasantly. He chatted amiably with the other patients, read out-of-date magazines, gradually increased his food intake, and slept soundly. His strength slowly but discernibly returned. He was issued with a new uniform, and finally felt fit enough to venture into the streets of Bloemfontein.

He left behind the Indian-looking balconies of the club-cum-

41

hospital, and wandered amongst the red-bricked, tin-topped, colonial-style bungalows with their neat front gardens crowded with chrysanthemums and tended by African servants. He admired the classical architecture of the Raadzaal, or Parliamentary Building, with its scroll-topped columns. No doubt, he pondered, it had been a small, quiet, rustic city, but now it was throbbing with a Khaki population ten times its norm. He wandered down narrow streets and emerged into the Market Square. He was met by a stillness. Civilians and military alike stood quietly as a sombre procession crossed the open space: soldiers slow-marched with arms reversed leading a creaking mule-wagon. In the back were piled shapeless figures sewn up in blankets. He saluted respectfully as the escorted dead passed him by.

"Shame! … Scandal!"

Rodger turned to the diminutive, black-suited man by his side. "Where are they heading?" he asked him.

"To the cemetery on the southern hill: thirty … forty … fifty a day. There must be a thousand unmarked graves there already. We are losing more men to enteric fever than we are to enemy action. Scandalous! The latrines outside the camps and hospitals are overflowing; contaminated water continues to be drunk. As a medical man, it is heart-rending to emerge from a hospital full of water-born pestilence to see a regimental water-cart being filled, without protest, at some polluted wayside pool. With discipline and proper precautions all those lives might have been saved. Scandalous!" He challenged Rodger, "Don't you smell it? The pall of death and disease hanging over this town is palpable. Scandalous! … and this is how the Boers chose to fight."

"The Boers?" enquired Rodger questioningly.

"Of course; the Boers! They deliberately exacerbate the tragedy by poisoning the water courses with dead animals. Commandant De Wet has captured the waterworks some four miles out of town and cut off the water supply. His men have cut the single railway line connecting Bloemfontein to the rest of the continent in a dozen places so that we can't bring in food, medicines and essential supplies. It's all part of the Boer plan to destroy Lord Roberts' Army."

The noise of the rumbling wagon, with its dignified escort and dismal cargo, gradually ceased as the sad cortège passed from view. For a moment those watching hesitated to stir, as if no-one wished to be the first to shatter the solemn mood.

"Be not deceived; God is not mocked; for whatsoever a man soweth, that shall he also reap," the doctor recited. "Young man, when you rejoin your regiment, remember the sight you have witnessed here today. Make sure the Boers reap what they have sown. I bid you goodbye". Having so said, the black-suited doctor melted away.

CHAPTER 3

If I was asked to answer the following question: "What is slavery?" and I should answer in one word, "Murder!" my meaning would be understood at once. No further argument would be required to show that the power to take from a man his thought, his will, his personality, is a power of life and death, and that to enslave a man is to kill him."

Pierre-Joseph Proudhon (1809-1865)

AMANITE/JOSIAH

The sharp blade of the iron plough cut through the fertile, moist soil which was then turned over by the mouldboard like a rolling wave, creating a deep straight furrow. Amanite tightly grasped the handles of the plough, ensuring that the angle of the blade cut correctly - neither too shallow nor too deep. In his right hand he also held the reins with which he guided the plodding pair of oxen. After four hours of labour he could sense their growing restlessness; their begrudging cooperation - he knew their moods. It was time to pause; to remove the burden of the heavy yoke; to allow them a couple of hours grazing.

As he out-spanned the oxen he noticed a figure against the skyline of the shallow ridge, perhaps a mile away. He watched as the indistinct figure advanced at a steady trot, taking on shape and form as the distance closed. It was Tsepe, his Chief's messenger. He was called after the antelope for he was of athletic build, lithe and fast of foot. With only a small sack of baked flour for sustenance, he could run bare-foot fifty miles in a day. He was gifted with an extra-ordinary memory and could transmit word for word the verbal despatches committed to him. As a messenger his person was inviolable; even in times of war he could pass unmolested through hostile territory. And now Amanite realised that Tsepe was moving purposefully towards him. He released the oxen to graze, and turned to meet his visitor.

Tsepe slowed to a walk: dusty, sweating, smiling, "Greetings my young friend. I hope I find you well."

"As well as I can be away from my home and people," replied Amanite. He was the son of an induna - a minor chief with authority over several villages. His father answered to the Paramount Chief of the Bakhananwa tribe, Malabokh.

Wesleyan missionaries had convinced Malabokh that the prominent sons of his tribe should be educated at their Mission Station near Pietersburg, about one hundred miles south of the Blauberg Mountains in which they lived. It would, the missionaries had reassured, provide a bridge between the African and Western world; an opportunity to understand the ways of the white tribes, their medicine, their writing, their Bible. So it was that after the ceremony of circumcision and the secret, separate period of teaching and initiation - when through painful rituals boys progress to manhood - Amanite and his cohort of young peers had been delivered to the missionaries. For the past eight years he had worked and studied under the tutelage of the Wesleyan ministers - by nature they were firm but kindly. Only occasionally had he been permitted to return home. He had been taught superior methods of agriculture, which he would soon teach to his own people to increase yields and prosperity. He had also studied English, as well as mathematics and geography. But central to his education had been the personage of Jesus of Nazareth, whom the missionaries claimed was the Son of the one God. He had learned to read the Bible and to aspire to Jesus' values of love, justice and peace. Disturbingly, he had been taught to question the legitimacy and powers of the witchdoctors, and to reject the veracity of ancestor worship. His mind and soul remained troubled by this conflicting teaching which was irreconcilable with traditional tribal beliefs and practices. He had allowed himself to be christened with a new name, Josiah, after a Jewish king. Apparently, this ancient king was close to God and a great reformer. The missionaries hoped that he too, on returning to his tribe, would be a catalyst for change; that he would influence the Bakhananwa and lead them to the one God, and peace and prosperity.

"Why do you seek me out?" asked Amanite.

"I seek you and the others of our blood who are here with the missionaries. The Afrikaners have visited our mountains to demand a census so that they can levy taxes against us. Chief Malabokh has refused them. Soon the whites will move against us. Your Chief says: "It is time to put your studies aside and to return home as warriors.""

That evening Amanite and his friends surreptitiously squirrelled away food into small sacks. They ensured that their water canteens were full and then, when all was dark and quiet, they crept out of the brick dormitory and began their long journey northwards, guided by the stars. They judged that the missionaries would not be sympathetic to their cause, and would refuse to issue passes so that they could travel legally. In the morning the local magistrate would be informed of their absence, and a hue and cry would erupt putting them at the mercy of every predatory Boer. They must take a circuitous route, and move as fast as possible.

Amanite arrived at his home village on the mountain-side just as dusk fell: foot-sore, exhausted, but elated. He was greeted by family and neighbours with great excitement and joy. He was expected. He was ushered by a noisy, doting throng to a stool by the fire in the circular court which surrounded his family hut. In anticipation of his coming a sheep had been slaughtered and a celebratory meal prepared. After three days of arduous travel he was famished. Without ceremony he led the way in devouring the feast of mutton, maize, vegetables and wild roots. Afterwards, he squatted around the fire embers with his father, uncles and male neighbours drinking beer from an earthenware jar, and vigorously discussing the possible outcome of tomorrow's deliberations. Custom and practice demanded that the Paramount Chief consult his subjects on occasions where the tribal interest and welfare required the adoption of important measures. What could be more important than a war with the whites? In the morning the *pitso* would be held outside the royal kraal.

Winter was approaching and the evening temperature dropped quickly on the mountain. Already the women and children had withdrawn into the huts, and the chill mountain air now prompted the men to follow. Amanite crawled down the tunnel into the dark depths of the conical hut. Inside, the dying glow of the dry-dung fuel gave off a yellow, flickering light. It was warm inside, and in the absence of any ventilation the smoke swirled about aimlessly, seeking unsuccessfully to escape, causing eyes to smart. Gradually, he became sufficiently accustomed to the gloom to be able to inspect the interior: on the walls hung the family war-shields, assegais, javelins and hatchets; at the far end of the hut was a slightly raised platform on which were placed vases containing wheat, several pots of beer in various states of fermentation, and bowls of milk slowly curdling. He felt comforted by the familiar odours. With the end of his punishing journey and the draining exhilaration of homecoming, he suddenly felt very tired. He selected his mattress of ox-skin and covered himself with furs. He heard his father following him into the interior, but he was beyond words. He slept soundly.

A tantalising glimmer of light crept down the tunnel-entrance to herald a new day. Outside in the court, Amanite could hear the sound of the women pounding wheat which would be mixed with the sour milk to provide the family breakfast.

He discarded his European clothes in favour of his traditional, scant battle-dress complete with short assegai and leather shield, for as a warrior he must attend the *pitso* dressed ready for war. Full of enthusiastic expectation, he joined the growing multitude of people snaking up the well-worn, rocky path to the broad plateau near the summit. Here was the main tribal settlement. It was in the form of a vast circle whose circumference was formed by circular huts made of the usual interlaced, pliable rods and reeds plastered on the outside with mud and cow-dung. The highest spot with the grandest residence was reserved for the Paramount Chief. In the centre of this royal kraal were a number of large enclosures, about six feet high, constructed from the branches of mimosa. In these the valuable cattle were secured at night.

The air reverberated to the rhythmic throb of the drums. A group of beautiful, bare-breasted, young women with shorn heads and dressed in long leather skirts decorated with coloured beads, danced zealously, their feet stamping in unison, their voices raised in lilting harmonies accompanied by the melodious tinkling of the numerous metal bangles adorning arms, ankles and necks. They were encouraged by an appreciative, vibrant crowd: clapping, shouting, whooping. There was a festive air as warriors and families assembled; their spirits and a sense of invincibility soared.

At a pre-determined signal the drumming and dancing stopped abruptly. An animal horn sounded and a respectful silence covered the crowd. All eyes turned to the royal hut. Malabokh appeared through a gap in the mimosa fence which surrounded his substantial residence. He was a descendant of families whose riches had entitled them to the most beautiful wives, and through selective breeding he possessed physical advantages over his subjects. He was taller than the average Basuto with great symmetry of limbs; he was bronze and statuesque and of noble and dignified bearing. He walked proudly, secure in his own physique and status. He was draped in a panther's skin; his head was encircled by a plume of feathers, and he carried a small club made of rhinoceros horn as a mark of his rank and authority. He was followed closely by his two principal counsellors – traditionally the eyes, ears and arms of the Chief. The three sat down on prepositioned stools. The one seated to the right of the Chief was called Goloane after a brave and venerated ancestor - he had command of the army.

Malabokh waved his club almost indiscernibly, but it was sufficient to summon the people to form an immense circle around their Sovereign – all sat cross-legged on the dusty ground. At the front were the indunas, behind them the village headmen, next hundreds of warriors, and finally, pushed to the periphery, came the women and children.

Goloane stood and addressed the crowd, "People of the Bakhananwa; today your Sovereign and great Chief, Malabokh, calls you to a *pitso*. Today we must determine matters of justice, matters of honour, matters of war and peace. As our custom demands, you have been called to give your counsel to your Sovereign at this time of crisis." He slowly traversed his head from left to right, his penetrating eyes intimidating his listeners. "You should know that the Afrikaner who calls himself the Native Commissioner, visited our Settlement and insisted of your Chief that he give permission for a counting of heads; a census of our tribe to enable a tax to be levied. What do we know of taxes?" he shouted rhetorically. "Which custom is this that we have forgotten that the white-man must remind us?" he challenged. "Your Sovereign refused. Are we prepared to fight for our freedoms?" Solemnly he took his seat.

A hushed anticipation covered the people. Now anyone was at liberty to speak, even to criticise his Chief.

A young warrior rose to his feet and addressed the elders, "But two generations ago the Afrikaner asked the permission of our grandfathers to share our lands. We allowed them to settle in peace. Then they laid claims to these lands calling them their own, and when we contested this theft they drove us into the mountains. They strive to contain us on sparse pastures; we must beg for pieces of paper in order to walk on the soil of our ancestors. Now we are to be counted like sheep so that they can steal what little is left to us." His voice rose to a shout, "We have our honour and our dignity and we must fight and die for our freedom!" With that he jumped high into the air, and on landing drove his javelin into the ground to signify his readiness to defend his opinions. The crowd hissed gently like a thousand snakes to signify unequivocal applause.

As the noise dissipated an elderly induna rose to his feet, and leaning on his stick began: "The young would seek battle for glory and fame, but such times are past. I am an old warrior. I have fought the Swazi and the Pedi and the Zulu, but our new enemy does not use the assegai and the javelin, but the rifle and the cannon. We can no longer outrun our enemy in clever manoeuvres, for the Afrikaner rides horses faster than our swiftest runner. As our wise ancestors said, "One should not lean over a gulf." It is wrong to expose oneself to unnecessary danger. We must think of our families." Once again he quoted a well-known proverb: "The trap catches the large bird as well as the small one." Wearily he sat down sensing that the crowd was not with him.

The discussion consumed the morning with most speakers exuding defiant confidence. As the sun reached its zenith a calm descended. Then twenty or more warriors picked their way through the seated crowd to stand in front of their Chief. As one, they struck their ox-hide shields with the flat blade of their assegais, showering their Sovereign with a white powder with which they had impregnated their shields.

Malabokh rewarded their act of support and approval with a gentle wave of his club and a thin smile. Now it was his turn to speak to his people. He stood tall surveying his subjects. His glance wandered slowly around the assembly in search of the heads of the principal families. He nodded knowingly, subtly commanding their obedience. He followed the time-honoured pattern required of these occasions. First he set forth the legitimacy of his claims to authority by tracing the genealogy of his family. Then he reviewed the historical background proving his lucid understanding of the events leading to the present situation. He noted wisely that: "One event is always the son of another." At this point he paused. Now was the time for the declaration of the royal opinion. He nurtured the engendered inactivity: the tense silence reinforced his majesty, magnifying the solemnity of the occasion. Finally he boomed out: "Tomorrow will give birth to the day after tomorrow!" The meaning of this ancient admonition was not lost on the people – this was not the time to defer the performance of duty.

At first the shrill screech was barely audible, but then it gradually grew louder and louder like a demented banshee, until it filled the air with ear-bursting intensity. Warriors jumped up and vigorously waved their shields in affirmation of their Chief's declaration of defiance. They screamed "Eee! Eee!..." to add to the mix of tumultuous sound.

That night Amanite did not linger by the fire, instead he escaped the descending, damp fog which embraced the mountain, and he crept into the hut soon after the evening meal. He snuggled beneath the furs in a reflective mood. It had been an exhilarating day - his first *pitso* as a warrior. The atmosphere had been invigorating; he had been swept up in the unbridled enthusiasm and boldness of his elders and peers. He had felt buoyed-up, invincible; and yet now, away from the reassuring bravado of his friends, he couldn't help but feel uneasy. Goloane had dispersed the warriors without announcing his plan to frustrate the Afrikaners.

Amanite awoke with a start. The external sounds were muffled and confusing; ragged and ominous. He scrambled out into the courtyard followed by the remainder of the family. The fog still hung thickly in the early dawn. Now from the plateau above shots could be distinguished and frantic screams heard. Quickly he retrieved his assegai and shield and groped his way up the path to the main Settlement; other warriors moved with him. Distraught women carrying or dragging bewildered children, hurried downwards colliding with ascending warriors; they screamed: "Afrikaner! Afrikaner! They are killing us! Run!" Amanite pushed upwards to be met with pandemonium: shocked, bewildered people running aimlessly; children lost or abandoned in the chaos crying for their mothers; desperate disembodied cries emerging from the fog; shooting … and as a haunting backdrop the greyness flickered with the flames of burning huts. As he moved forward cautiously, he almost tripped over a warrior's body; the face mashed, covered in blood, unrecognisable. Ghostly figures swept by; the shooting drifted away towards the Chief's residence and increased in intensity. His father appeared waving his arms and shouting, "To the caves! Everyone to the caves!"

Amanite hurried back down the path to his village, but already it was deserted. He climbed the nearby rocks and soon tumbled into a familiar gallery - he had spent many hours playing there as a child, now it was his refuge. It tunnelled into the mountain for about one hundred yards, but had no alternative entrance. About twenty villagers were already ensconced, others followed until they numbered close to fifty of all ages, but none from his family.

They waited. The furore outside eventually quietened. The sun gradually burnt off the fog. In the depths of the cave people talked in frightened, hushed whispers wondering what would happen next. There was no food, no water, and as time passed this began to have its effects, initially on the children who were bullied into silent acceptance of the thirst and hunger. Night came and with it near-freezing cold. There were no coverings; no-one slept. With the dawn Amanite and another young warrior decided to investigate the possibility of escaping from the cave. Perhaps the Afrikaner had deserted the mountain. But as they exposed themselves at the entrance a shot rang out and a nearby "splat" and "ping" announced the ricocheting bullet. They withdrew rapidly. They were trapped like animals in a pit. Another day; another shot and failed exit; increasing hunger and thirst; crying, inconsolable children; another freezing, sleepless night.

The inevitable was accepted. They would have to surrender. Amanite agreed to lead the way. He moved to the entrance careful not to expose himself, and then shouted to attract attention before tossing out his assegai followed by his shield. Nervously he emerged. There was no shot. A group of Afrikaners appeared from the cover of boulders and began to shout and wave their arms; the meaning was clear, and so all of them, men women and children, emerged to become prisoners. The women, children and old men were allowed to return to the charred ruins of their huts, whilst the warriors were imprisoned in the cattle enclosures.

As Amanite sat dispirited and forlorn, the air was periodically filled with the thunderous crash of cannon followed immediately by a loud muffled roar. The ground shook. Soon he was joined by traumatised, bloody young men. They recounted how their reluctance to leave their sanctuary had been met by impatient Boers who encouraged surrender by the simple expedient of firing a shell from a 9-pounder cannon into the mouth of the caves. But Amanite realised that many warriors had escaped, for when the battle ended barely two hundred of them had been imprisoned.

His hands were tied behind his back and his legs hobbled to restrict his movements. In this state he joined his compatriots on the long forced march to Pretoria. The mounted guards drove their prisoners before them on foot like animals; minimal food and water was provided, and any who struggled to keep up were encouraged by a stinging lash from the long, leather thong of a sjambok. On arrival the warriors were placed in a cattle-pen reinforced with barbed wire. They were to be indentured to Afrikaner farmers and forbidden ever to return to the Blauberg Mountains.

The days passed. Amanite watched as his friends were examined by visiting Boers, and either rejected or taken away as labourers. Finally:

"Stand up Boy! You ... Stand-up! ... Over here!"

Amanite was summoned out of the enclosure to be confronted by two Boers - he rightly assumed them to be father and son.

"What's your name?" the oldest asked in Afrikaans, not unkindly.

Although he understood, Amanite was not disposed to converse in his enemy's language. He said nothing.

"What's your name?" This time it was said falteringly in Sotho, Amanite's own tongue.

"My tribal name is Amanite, my adopted name is Josiah," he replied in English.

"Ah, an educated Kaffir!" exclaimed the younger of the two. "And which Mission Station did you attend?"

"Pietersburg."

"Did they instruct you on modern farming methods?"

"Yes."

The Boers moved out of earshot and discussed quietly: "He's strong and fit, and with his knowledge of farming we won't have to waste time teaching him what to do," suggested the father.

"Educated Kaffirs can spell trouble," pointed out the son, "particularly those influenced by the Wesleyans. They fill their heads with nonsense about being our equals and having rights. This one could stir up the other blacks."

"We'll keep a good watch on him. He's obviously intelligent and could make a good supervisor."

The son guardedly agreed and they returned to the sullen black who waited stoically. "You'll come with us." The father indicated a nearby cart, "Get on board."

Though his hands were free, Josiah was still hobbled. It was with considerable difficulty that he scrambled into the back of the cart. The father climbed onto the front seat and took the reins, whilst the son mounted his pony and assumed rear guard. With a shout of encouragement and a sharp tug of the reins, the cart lurched forward.

Boaz Van den Berg and his son, Jacobus, started for home with their new worker.

CHAPTER 4

For as long as but a hundred of us remain alive, we will in no way yield ourselves to the dominion of the English. For it is not for glory, nor riches, nor honour that we fight, but for Freedom only, which no good man lays down but with his life.

Declaration of Abroath 1302

THE LAST STAND - DALMANUTHA
(27 August 1900)

Louis Botha, Commandant–General of the Transvaal Forces, sat on his distinctive white stallion, and from his vantage point watched the battle below unfurl. In a citizen army where most men fought in their every-day clothes, he distinguished himself by wearing a simple uniform tunic. He had been born a British subject in Natal, and was descended from the earliest Dutch settlers who arrived in the Cape in the mid-seventeenth century. When he was aged five, his prosperous father moved his family to the Orange Free State and bought a farm near Vrede; that is where Louis grew up - the eighth child in a family of thirteen children. He was a physically big man, nearly six foot in height, and swarthy in complexion reflecting his mixed Dutch and Huguenot blood. He had deep-blue eyes and sported a distinctive, black goatee beard. Four years earlier he had been elected to the Volksraad where he had vigorously opposed and voted against hostilities with the British. But he unflinchingly accepted the will of his people, and was now a dedicated proponent of the war – a politician by nature, a general by necessity, but always a farmer at heart.

He had been thrust unexpectedly, but not unwillingly, into a position of supreme military authority when elderly and ineffectual patriarchs succumbed in quick succession to the rigours of war through illness, injury and fatigue. At thirty-seven years old, he represented a new ascending generation of Boer leaders.

His present antagonist was General Redvers Buller - the same man whom, at the beginning of that year, he had fought in the hills to the south of Ladysmith. Three times he had held and defeated attacks by a numerically superior British Army, only eventually yielding to crushing force. It was during these battles that he became revered by politicians, generals and his own men for his motivational leadership and tactical prowess.

Recent reverses had taught him that the rural Afrikaner Nation did not possess the material where-with-all and manpower to confront an industrial giant backed by a great empire. For months his forces had been swept before the British military juggernaut: Bloemfontein, Johannesburg, Pretoria, all lost. During this period of unmitigated disasters there had been black times of despair - he had even contemplated surrender - but now he had a clear vision. The British were pushing his commandos down the railway line towards Portuguese East Africa – the last remaining channel of communication with the outside world. But whilst the cities and the railways might belong to the invader, they did not control the expansive veld. He and his subordinate commanders had come to understand that they could only continue the fight in the countryside, and not by being drawn into costly set-piece battles which deprived them of their greatest advantage, freedom of manoeuvre.

He would hold Buller for a month and weaken his forces, before dispersing his commandos to fight in the countryside; each in its home territory. It was this knowledge which had kept the men in good heart during the blackest days. He would wear down the British until they despaired of victory and sued for peace. This would be the last set-piece battle.

He had carefully chosen the position for this final stand on the ultimate rim of the high-veld before it dropped dramatically to the malarial, sub-tropical forests which extended through the Portuguese Colony to the Indian Ocean. His position commanded a level, treeless plain stretching back to the west across which the attackers must advance, whilst a valley behind gave protection to his men and horses. To the north rose mountainous terrain, and to the south bogs and streams, both inhibiting cavalry movement and providing some flank protection. But he was only too conscious that his line of defence was very thin and without depth – a mere seven thousand men and twenty guns to defend along a front of fifty miles.

The day before, he had watched the usual screen of English cavalry tentatively probing forward. When the cavalry identified the Boer positions they withdrew and the field-guns trotted forward and unlimbered with impeccable discipline and precision. The bombardment began. All day the lyddite and shrapnel shells exploded over and around the defences, but thankfully the well prepared trenches and schanses provided good protection and casualties were slight. No attempt had been made to launch an assault, and with nightfall the attackers withdrew. Only the distant, flickering camp-fires had identified the location of the British soldiers as they cooked their meals and sought warmth on a cold, clear winter's night.

With the morning light it was apparent that the British guns had reorganised: no longer spread across the long line of defence, but instead concentrated opposite a kopje held by a small detachment of Johannesburg police. The position was at the apex of a small salient jutting out into the plain towards the British - the enemy had rightly identified this as a critical and vulnerable point in the defences. With growing concerns he watched hour after hour as the explosive shells tore up the ground, and others filled the air with a cloud of murderous shrapnel; the kopje was shrouded in the acrid, yellow lyddite smoke. There was nothing he could do but watch and wait. The British columns massing in front of this position was an ominous sign.

All day he watched the bombardment, and only with dusk did the Tommies rush forward with flashing bayonets and disappear into the swirling, shell-made cloud. He was relieved when moments later they fell back in disorder, dragging their wounded with them. But a short time later a new wave of infantry swarmed forward. The guns had lifted and were firing in depth, but between crashing shells he could still faintly hear the "pop" "pop" of the defenders' Mauser fire. Again the bloodied British reeled backwards. A further torrent of shells fell on the kopje, followed by a third desperate charge, and this time there was no withdrawal. The police had been annihilated. He watched gravely through his telescope as a sole survivor rushed down the rear slope only to fall under a volley of fire.

The line was broken. He could see the commandos adjacent to the breach abandoning their defences in fear of encirclement, and scrambling down into the valley in search of their horses. Reluctantly, he turned to his accompanying gallopers, "Tell the commandos to fall back to Machadodorp."

In the company of a couple of his staff officers, Botha trotted off despondently into the darkness. After a few miles, when it was clear that the British were not in pursuit, he hobbled his horse allowing it to graze lazily, whilst he enjoyed a mug of coffee and a piece of biltong – all that was on offer. He threw his blanket on the cold ground, and using his saddle as a pillow, slept fitfully. The next morning he road eastwards parallel with the railway line to Machadodorp; the small, nondescript village was deserted. He had half expected to find the President of the Transvaal, Paul Kruger, and his Executive Council in the train which now constituted the Republic's Capital, but learnt that they had moved east along the line out of harms way to Nelspruit.

There was only a single narrow road leading east which climbed over the remaining hill range. This single avenue of retreat was quickly choked with an assortment of fighters, wagons and fleeing civilians driving their sheep and cattle before them. He was full of pity and compassion as he gently manoeuvred through the pressing crowd. A babble of frenzied noise hung over this throbbing mass: the bleating of sheep; the strident shouts and cracking whips of the Basuto ox- wagon drivers; the rumbling of iron wheel-rims on uneven surface; the calling between families as they fought to keep contact in the surging bedlam. Then suddenly came a searing "whoosh" and terrific explosion barely one hundred yards to the right - soil and stones flew into the air. Women and children screamed, cattle and sheep stampeded, horses whinnied, frightened oxen struggled to shake off their heavy yokes. For a moment fear and panic swept through the column. Botha shouted through the melee, "Keep calm! Keep calm!" He dismounted and helped an alarmed mother gather in her terrorised children.

No further explosions followed. No-one seemed to be hurt. Once again the snaking column cohered and flowed slowly eastwards.

At the railway station in Nelspruit, now only a short distance from the Portuguese frontier, Botha found the Transvaal Government in the form of the Executive Council, most particularly the Vice-President, Shalk Burger and the State Secretary, F W Reitz. There was staggering news: President Kruger had been sent out of the Country via the Portuguese Colony and through the port of Lourenco Marques. His mission was to proceed to Europe and there promote the Boer cause, but the reality was that this old veteran of the iconic Voortrekk was too old and weak to survive the hardships of guerilla warfare, and too prestigious a person to fall into enemy hands. "He sat most of the day at the table in his railway carriage reading his Bible," confided one of the Executive Council to Botha. In the circumstances, the President had become a liability. He had been persuaded to leave temporarily, perhaps for six months, but few felt that they would ever see the venerable old lion again.

Botha's scouts reported that the British were encircling his forces from the west and south, and to the east lay the Portuguese frontier. Only the mountainous north still offered an escape route, and he feared that soon that too would be closed.

He gathered around him the more resolute burghers, and sent on the wounded, ill-equipped and the frail of heart to the frontier crossing at Komatipoort and inevitable internment. He ordered surplus guns to be disabled and tossed into the river, and all stores to be burnt. Then with his chosen two thousand burghers and the skeleton Transvaal Government, he struck off northwards for the remote high-veld, determined to pursue a different type of warfare – a type that with the Boers' inherent mobility, he was confident he could win.

CHAPTER 5

"There must be the beginning of any great matter, but the continuing until the end, until it be thoroughly finished, yields the true glory"

Sir Francis Drake: despatch to Sir Frances Walsingham 17 May 1587

GERRIT PRETORIOUS RETURNS
(October 1900)

Gerrit Pretorius had been in the saddle for over two weeks. He was bone-weary; spent. He halted his hardy pony on the low ridge which overlooked the white farmhouse nestling below in the slight depression – sited for protection from the cold, penetrating winds which could sweep across the open veld. He paused a moment, contemplating this oasis of peace. Ever since his wife and three children had died from cholera, it had been his place of refuge. Here he had found understanding, compassion, love. Its occupants, the Van den Berg family, had rescued him from the pit of despair and welcomed him as one of their own. In particular the old patriarch, Boaz, had patiently nurtured in him a renewed purpose in living.

It was almost twelve months to the day since his last visit. Then it had been very different. In his role as Field Cornet, or Magistrate, he had summoned the men to war. It had been a heady time: the prospect of a fight to secure freedom and independence; a time to rid the British from South Africa and to rightly claim the pre-eminence of the Afrikaner Nation. Boaz had been too old to respond, but his two sons with their sons had eagerly answered the call: Jacobus, with whom Boaz lived, and his son Jan; and Hendrick from the neighbouring farm and his twin sons Pieter and Hans. Together they had faced and defeated the might of the British Army under General Buller on the heights above the river Tugela which guarded the road to

Ladysmith. But victory had come at a price. He remembered with sadness the morning after the battle of Spion Kop, and how he had helped to carry down the bodies of Hendrick and Hans from the hillside, and place them reverently onto the ox-wagon. He vividly recalled the woeful scene of the ox-wagon with its wretched cargo and broken-hearted passengers as it lumbered away from the battlefield on its long homeward journey. That was the last occasion he had seen the Van den Bergs.

From his vantage point he surveyed the substantial homestead – the legacy of the Voortreck generation. They had arrived as frontier settlers escaping English tyranny, and from their first rudimentary buildings of daub and wattle and huts of reeds, had carved out homesteads, permanent centres around which their lives and those of their children revolved. With passing years the area of tilth expanded and cattle increased, orchards and gardens flourished; the early struggles became less a reminder of past bitterness, and more a measure of present content.

Outwardly nothing seemed to have changed. That was reassuring and comforting after the bloody tumult of the last year; after the chaos, death, destruction and deprivation which had been his lot for long months. He lingered, absorbing the tranquil scene: in the mature orchard, the warmth of late spring encouraged the flower buds of the apple trees to swell flushed with pink; the vegetable garden, adjacent to the house, was freshly dug – little greenery yet as the seeds would only just have been planted after the last frosts; by the puddled-clay dam, which provided the fresh water, stood two tall willow trees clothed in fresh green foliage, their rounded, drooping branches presenting a distinctive shape; a vast mound of kraal-dung stood like a neolithic obelisk providing the only reliable fuel in this tree-scarce land.

One hundred yards east of the farmhouse stood a clump of three poplar trees enclosed by a decorative wrought-iron fence - this was the family graveyard. On his last visit only Boaz's wife and Hendrick's young wife, who had died in childbirth, lay there, now two new crosses were clearly visible. Some things had changed.

As he lolled wearily in the saddle, he felt an unfamiliar mix of emotions: desperate to once again be embraced by the warmth and love which he knew awaited him; anxious of what he might find in this grief-stricken family. With a kick of his heels he nudged his pony down the gentle slope.

Boaz was sitting on the veranda reading his Bible and enjoying the lingering warmth of the failing sun. He looked up to see a lone horseman approaching at a gentle trot. He eased himself up from his chair, ignoring the pain in his left leg, and leaned heavily on his walking-stick. He squinted into the low dazzling rays and examined the dark silhouette as it assumed a recognisable form. At first he was a little puzzled by the gaunt, pale, grey figure, but how could he mistake that wide-face with its distinctive bulbous nose. "Gerrit! Gerrit!" Boaz struggled down the few steps, and as his visitor dismounted, he smothered him with a bear-like hug. "We've prayed so long for this moment; for your safety. Thank God you have returned to us unscathed!"

The noise brought the women and young children from the house.

"It's uncle Gerrit! Uncle Gerrit!" shouted Adrian who was eleven years old, and Hannie who was nine.

Gerrit stooped down and hugged each in turn, "Why, you've grown so much since I last saw you."

Jacobus' wife, Anna, and their oldest daughter, Ruth, hovered nearby whilst Gerrit fussed the children. As they waited, they noticed his haggard face grey with fatigue, his wild, grimy beard and his dirty, tattered clothes - he had lost weight. Finally, they too surged forward with tears of relief and hugged him. "So many have been killed; we worried for you and prayed for your safety daily," exploded Anna. With her apron she wiped her eyes wet with shiny tears.

"Well thank God! Thank God!" uttered Boaz excitedly. "He's

safe. Now, come in! Come in!" Boaz led the way into the broad sitting room with its heavy furniture and ancestral paintings. As Gerrit entered, his senses were assailed by the familiar smells of home; the composite odour: dung-smoke, tan & tallow, fresh roasted coffee, black tobacco, cooking. Uncharacteristically, his eyes filled with tears – an unbecoming indulgence. Ashamed and embarrassed by his momentary weakness, he rubbed the moisture from his eyes and drew a deep breath.

"Now woman," said Boaz gently to Anna, "why don't you bring us some of the best peach-brandy so that Gerrit can recover from his journey?" With that he motioned his guest towards sturdy rocking chairs by a newly-lit fire. "These days," he sighed apologetically, "I still feel the evening chills ... sign of age."

"Your leg?" Gerrit was concerned to see Boaz lame. Always he had been fit and strong as an ox, then he recalled that he must be almost eighty: a voortrekker, a founder of the Republic.

"An ox kicked my shin and broke it when I was inspanning him to the plough. It took a long time to heal, and in truth it's never been right since. Now I have swelling in the leg and it causes me considerable pain, but I still get about with my stick," Boaz explained phlegmatically.

Anna returned with an earthenware jug and two mugs and set them down on a small table. She poured each a drink of the home-made brew and handed it to them before retiring to the kitchen and leaving them alone.

Gerrit was anxious to understand the current family situation, "How is Jacobus recovering from his wounds?"

Boaz hesitated, considering his words, "It took several months for the bayonet wounds to heal. His right arm remains stiff; he can't raise it above shoulder height. He quickly gets short of breath and suffers from pains in the stomach, but he tries to hide it. Sometimes I see him in great pain, but he won't admit to it."

"And Ruth ... wasn't she troubled by the fighting?" Gerrit

had been disapproving of Ruth when she had joined them during the siege of Ladysmith under the guise of bringing fresh supplies - although secretly he admired her pluck.

"She sometimes wakes up screaming in the night, but not so much now. There are days when she is morose and melancholy. We just leave her alone and she comes around."

What about Pieter; with his father and brother dead, how does he managing the farm alone?"

"It's been very difficult. He lacks experience, and besides, for a long time he lost the will to do anything. "

Gerrit said nothing, but could empathise. When his family died he was distraught and aimless; life had no meaning. He knew that without Boaz's help he would never have got through the trauma.

"We help as best we can. Ruth is particularly good at organising the Kaffirs in their duties."

"And do you see anything of that American ... Barnham I think was his name?" explored Gerrit. This foreigner had joined the Commando as a volunteer. In truth, Gerrit had initially been suspicious of his motives and even his loyalty, but reluctantly acknowledged his bravery and commitment during a desperate assault on Spion Kop, where the American too had been lightly wounded.

"My family seems to have adopted him," replied Boaz with a slightly bewildered air. "They brought him back from the battlefield so that he could recover from his wound, and he's stayed ever since. I believe he and Ruth have developed feelings for each other. Who knows where it will lead? I remain unconvinced that an American lawyer can become a Boer." He paused to sip his brandy.

Their conversation was cut short as the door burst open and Jacobus, Jan and Henry Barnham swept noisily into the room.

"We saw the boy in the stable with your horse, so knew you were here!" exclaimed Jacobus. "Thank God for bringing you home safely to us."

There were unrestrained handshakes, man-hugs and pounding

back-slapping as Gerrit greeted Jacobus and Jan. Henry hesitated, before finally stepping forward and vigorously shaking hands.

Over the evening meal of bush-meat and vegetables, complemented with blackcurrant wine, they reminisced freely – careful only to recall the good times. Loitering over the celebration like a dark cloud was the continuing war. The Van den Bergs had been existing on rumour and nothing good had been heard for a long time. Eventually the inevitable question was asked of Gerrit: "How goes the fighting?"

Gerrit laid his cutlery on his plate. He paused, and then broke the anticipatory silence, "After Buller broke through the Tugela defences and relieved Ladysmith, Natal was relatively quiet. He was content to rest his army and sit on his hands. Because of the inactivity on this front, I was ordered to take our Commando, the Witbergers, to help stop Lord Robert's advance into the Orange Free State." He diverted for a moment, "You'll have heard of General Cronje's surrender to the English with four thousand men at Paardeberg? " There was suppressed anger in his voice at the thought of this humiliation and loss.

They had heard.

"Well, with the door wide open the English marched on to take Bloemfontein then Johannesburg and Pretoria. We were heavily outnumbered in men and guns and there was no way we could stop such a massive army. Botha's plan was to conduct a fighting withdrawal east to the Portuguese border, and then to disappear into the mountains and the veld to conduct guerilla warfare. Commandos have been ordered to return to their own districts so that they can operate in country they know well."

"The American rebels faced a similar situation during our war of independence," interrupted Henry. "George Washington's Army wintered at Valley Forge where they were depleted in numbers and without food, proper clothes, ammunition and supplies of all kinds. Their situation looked hopeless. But they went on to defeat the British. We can do the same."

"We! ... you are a Boer Mr Barnham?" Without pausing for a reply Gerrit continued, "I truly thank you for your encouragement and optimism." He was genuinely warming to this foreigner. He took up his cutlery and continued to eat.

"You may have wondered why we didn't return to the field of battle after Spion Kop?" asked Jacobus almost apologetically.

"Many burghers returned home after family tragedies ... with the prospect of our impending defeat, some even took the oath of neutrality so that they could return to their farms as if the war was over ... hands-uppers!" he said with disdain. "But I know that's not the case with you."

"We'll never be "hands-uppers!" reassured Jacobus. "I've been recovering from my wounds and we've been caring for Ruth and Pieter. We've been trying to run two farms ... only now is Pieter beginning to be active again."

"My dear friends, I don't say these things with any hint of condemnation. We must each cope with our own circumstances, but this war has entered a new phase bringing new opportunities to defeat the English. The enemy holds our cities and railways, and from the European perspective they think they have won the war. But what worth are towns and railways to farmers? The English control only as far as their artillery reaches. The countryside is ours. Botha has laid out his plans: we are to strangle the English Army by cutting its lines of communication, destroying its convoys and attacking wherever we identify weakness. No more set-battles; we shall operate like will-o'-the-wisp, drawing the English onto us, and then destroying them at times and in places of our choosing." With an uncharacteristic grin he added wisely, "It is the constant dripping of water which wears away the stone."

Little was said as everyone pondered on his words. Gerrit raised his laden fork, paused, looked around, "Are you with us?"

Everyone listening knew the import of this question. All able-bodied men between the ages of sixteen and sixty were duty bound to defend the Republic, and whilst the Transvaal Government continued to exist in the name of Acting President Shalk Burger, the British annexation was illegal and invalid.

"Of course we shall fight for our freedom and independence. Nothing has changed," asserted Jacobus. "We will fight to the bitter end."

"Good. That's what I'd expected to hear." Looking directly at Jacobus, Gerrit continued, "I would like you to be my Assistant Field-Cornet; I know you to be brave and reliable."

"Won't the others in the cornecy have to vote me in?"

"The days of voting for leaders is over. Now the best men are appointed. I've already cleared you with the Commandant."

"In which case, I'm honoured."

Gerrit leaned back in his chair, at last a smile stole across his creased face, "By day we are farmers, by night we are fighters. Like the chameleon, we change colours according to our environment."

This pronouncement brought murmurs of approval from the men who had secretly been feeling guilty at their inaction whilst great battles had been unfurling. Anna and Ruth suppressed their anxieties. The family graveyard with its two new graves served as a frightening reminder of the possible consequences.

Boaz interjected, sensing their concerns, "This evening we thank God for our dear friend's safe return amongst us. It's a time for rejoicing. Didn't the Lord say, *"Who of you by worrying can add a single hour to his life?"* Anna, the peach brandy! Ruth, play us a hymn of thanksgiving on the piano."

The spring sun was comfortably warm, and with the arrival of the rains, new shoots pushed through the dry stalks turning the veld into a sea of green.

Ruth and Henry sat together on a flat-topped boulder looking across the undulating plain towards a group of low kopjes. They watched the cattle grazing contentedly under the vigilant eyes of Native herdsmen. Ruth snuggled up to Henry; he placed his arm around her waist and drew her to himself. They both revelled in the warmth and intimacy of their bodily contact.

"Will you go tomorrow?" she asked - a raid was planned on the railway in the area of Middleburg.

"Yes," he answered tenderly, "I must."

"But you don't have to. You're not an Afrikaner, you're American. You could stay and help run the farms, particularly Pieter's. We all know he's not up to it. Some-one has to stay."

"Your father's going despite his wounds, and your brother Jan would expect me to be with him. Besides, after living with your family for so long I now regard myself as an honorary Boer. That means I have to go."

"You'll never be an honorary Boer!" she teased.

"Even if I stayed and married you?"

"Well then you'd be a real Boer." She stopped abruptly; the reality of what he had just said suddenly dawned. "Are you asking me to be your wife?" She drew out the words, questioningly, playfully.

He hesitated. Slowly, falteringly he spoke, "When this war is over ... when peace returns to this land ... if I survive."

She pulled away and looked at him longingly. Now he was tense, awkward. She realised that he was serious. "You know my father wouldn't allow it. We've barely known each other for a year, and you're a foreigner. You're not even a farmer and so hardly qualify. And you show no religious zeal." A tremor of excitement ran through her body; she shook involuntarily. Sensitively she asked, "Do you really want to marry me?"

"I really do." They gazed at each other in mutual love, her eager consent understood. He cautioned, "We must choose our moment carefully to announce our intentions ... I need to be totally accepted ... I need more time."

He gently pulled her back to his side; they hugged each other tightly and wallowed in the heat of rising sensuality. Their lips met as they became one, absorbed in a timeless, impassioned kiss.

Ruth stood on the veranda with her grandfather, mother and the two younger children. Earlier, Ruth and Henry had met briefly and surreptitiously by the sheering shed for a fervent and emotional goodbye. Now she watched as her father and Jan mounted their small, sure-footed Basuto ponies and Henry his Arab bay. With a guarded nod, the men turned and trotted off over the ridge heading for a rendezvous with their neighbours and the railway line.

CHAPTER 6

Life is mostly froth and bubble,
Two things stand like stone,
Kindness in another's trouble,
Courage in your own.

Adam Lindsay Gordon

RAILWAY ATTACK

Jacobus was in charge of this attack in his new role as Assistant Field Cornet. He had carefully chosen the place at which to derail the train - a gradient descending through a cutting. He worked furiously with Jan, Henry and others using spanners and crowbars to remove the bolts from the rails in order to dislodge the track.

"It's done," announced Jacobus. He put his ear to the metal rail, "And our timing is perfect!" He grinned.

The saboteurs clambered up the steep bank and joined the waiting burghers. They lay out of site, Mausers at the ready, poised to swoop on the crippled train and destroy or loot its contents.

The sharp puffing of the iron mammoth was audible long before its silhouette was discernible against the clear night sky. As Jan watched, it seemed to take an age to draw close as if the driver anticipated its imminent destruction; cautiously it chugged forward into the cutting and then involuntarily gathered speed with its descent.

With a screech of straining brakes the engine rocked crazily. Amidst a clamour of smashing, crashing, tearing metal it left the rails and buried itself into the far bank. The earth shuddered violently. The leading trucks telescoped. Gushing steam enveloped the engine and wafted over the carriages. The night was filled with a hellish noise of contorting metal.

The farmers surged forward like a crashing wave, yelling in uncontrollable euphoria.

Whoosh! Whoosh! Suddenly there was a blinding white light and a strong whistling sound followed by an explosion high in the sky. Instinctively everyone ducked.

"Distress rockets," exclaimed Jacobus.

Zip! Zip!

The man next to Henry toppled forward with a muffled groan; had he stumbled?

Zip! Zip!

Fears were confirmed: the military guard half way down the train was intact. Their forward flow halted: some took cover; some knelt: others stood still; all began to return fire in the direction of the hostile flashes. Instinctively, Jacobus, Henry, Jan and others began to work their way forward in measured bounds, whilst friends gave covering fire. The soldiers were firing high, blindly, unsure of their targets. Finally, Jacobus and his group were close enough to clearly identify half a dozen Khakis shooting from behind a wall of sandbags mounted on a flat-bed truck. He well knew that precise aiming at night was almost impossible – so difficult to align the front sight through the rear aperture. Suppressive fire and a quick assault were the solution.

"Fire! Fire!", he screamed. The defenders were hit by a wall of murderess steel which hurled them back from the sandbags.

"Forward! Forward!"

Jan ran at break-neck speed overtaking his lagging father and quickly reached the truck. A soldier raised himself above the parapet to better see his attackers below, but fell back with a shriek as several bullets smashed open his face.

Helping hands hoisted Jan and others onto the truck where they peered over the sandbags. Four soldiers sprawled on the floor in pools of blood; two others raised their hands. The train was theirs. But victory was short lived.

The sweeping beam of a searchlight heralded the approach of an armoured train. It was travelling fast in response to the distress flares. The Boers knew that with its maxim machine-guns and 9-pounder cannon, it was more than they could handle. Reluctantly, Jacobus gave the order to withdraw. As he and Jan climbed back over the bank they found Henry administering first-aid to a casualty, surrounded by an anxious group. Jacobus recognised him as Abram Janson, a blacksmith from Reedstreem, a small village north of Witberg.

Henry looked up at Jacobus, "We can't move him ... chest wound," he explained.

"We can't leave him," pleaded a relative.

"Look, if we move him he'll die. At least with the Khakis he has a chance," implored Henry.

"He's right," confirmed Jacobus. "Whatever we may think of the Khakis, we all know that they care for our wounded as their own. We must go quickly." He looked sympathetically at his wounded friend, "May God bless you and care for you." He cast around, "We must go!"

The first shell exploded harmlessly short of the rise as the Boers mounted their ponies and galloped off into the night, empty handed.

****

Rodger stared as the distant sky lit up with the colourful brilliance of bursting flares; the pyrotechnics lingered for a few minutes, hanging as if reluctant to expire. Soon the muffled sound of distant explosions rolled gently across the veld.

"Looks like the Boers have blown up a train," observed Sergeant Mellish to Rodger.

On his discharge from hospital Rodger had applied to join the newly forming Mounted Infantry Company from his Battalion. He was a good horseman – he had honed his skills over several years riding with the Percy Hunt. He had been relieved to be accepted – no more trekking over the endless veld. Rodger scrutinised his platoon sergeant, a chunky ex-miner from Shilbottle - a small Northumberland mining village not far from his family's modest estate. On first meeting this short, muscular man with his toothy grin and hardened expression, he had been a little unnerved by his rough manners and affected subservience - he demonstrated a natural assertiveness and sense of independence not readily found amongst the farm workers more familiar to Rodger. But he had grown to value Mellish's sound common sense, organisational skills and a selfless courage for which he had been decorated in the Sudan. The men admired and trusted him. He brought reassurance to the young soldiers although they feared his hot temper. He invariably acted in their best interests, at least when sober. For all their differences, Rodger liked to think that over the past months they had developed a sense of mutual respect and that they worked well together.

"Well, if they come our way we'll have a fight on our hands," responded Rodger.

"Be good to get those bastards," Mellish replied, eager for the fight.

They were riding at the head of their platoon, about five miles south of the railway line, moving parallel east to west as an outer cordon. Their task was to intercept hostile Boers, particularly those attacking the railway. Rodger did a quick assessment: if the Boers are travelling south then he could expect them to be somewhere on his line of march in about an hour's time. In this poachers' moon they should be visible over a considerable distance, particularly if he could gain a little height. He called his black Native scout, "Zebedee; are their any kopjes around here which will give us better observation?"

"Yes, sir, a couple of miles or so west."

"Take us there directly."

It was not long before Rodger had installed his men amongst a small group of low kopjes, the like of which rise periodically from the veld. He established two look-out posts and ordered the remaining soldiers to rest.

"You get some sleep; I'll take first watch," Rodger indicated to Mellish. And with that he awaited the Boers.

"Sir."

Rodger shook himself awake from his unscheduled doze.

"Sir, I thought I saw riders in the far distance heading south," reported the lookout.

"Are you sure?" enquired Rodger.

"Can't be sure, sir, but I think I saw movement."

Rodger looked at his watch. Nearly two hours had passed. He didn't want to lead his platoon on a wild-goose chase, but he must check this out. "Bring me Zebedee."

Rodger explained to his scout, "I want you to go where the sentry points and see if you can pick up the spoor of the Boer raiding party. "

Within the hour Zebedee returned and reported that he had found fresh hoof marks of about a dozen riders. Although his platoon numbered only thirty men, Rodger decided to give chase – it was too good an opportunity to miss.

****

Dawn broke with a beautiful, blood-red sky. Jacobus was conscious that after the destruction of the train, the Khakis would be searching for them, but his men and horses needed rest after a full night of activity. Ahead was a deep donga with only a trickle of water flowing along its rocky bottom. It would provide both concealment and a place from which to fight if necessary. On reaching it he established a two-man lookout, and gave instructions for horses to remain saddled and for men to rest. He hobbled his horse by threading a rope through the halter near the horse's muzzle and tying it close above the knee joint of the near fore-leg. By this means his horse could graze in comfort, but could not move away at any pace other than a slow walk and so could be caught in a hurry. He joined the others in a breakfast of traditional, thick, black coffee and biltong. Then he lay down on the grass, placed his hat over his face, and luxuriated in the warm sun. Soon all was quiet, bar the restless moans of sleeping men.

"Jacobus, they're here." The lookout prodded his still body, "There here!"

"How many?" questioned Jacobus as he fought to shake off a deep sleep.

"Can't say, but from the dust cloud, perhaps thirty ... maybe forty."

The word spread to stand to arms. Jacobus hurried to the lookout post. In the bright, cloudless morning visibility stretched for many miles. He saw a group of riders advancing in column; they were Khakis, and the formation suggested that they were moving for speed and control and were not expecting an imminent fight. A Kaffir scout was a little ahead diligently following their tracks. They would bring them directly to their location in the donga. The Khakis had no reason to suspect that the tracks would not emerge the other side and onwards, as long as they weren't seen.

Jacobus cautioned the lookout to remain concealed and then gathered the group together and explained the plan, "We'll line out in the donga, but stay just below the lip. When I give the word we'll all rise together and shoot." All nodded agreement, and grinning with confidence and resolve took up their places. Jacobus relieved the lookout, and ensuring that a bush was behind him to absorb his silhouette, he raised his head and observed the advancing Khakis.

He waited as his quarry cantered ever closer in total ignorance of the danger. When the black scout was less than one hundred yards from their position he shouted, "Fire! Fire!"

The narrow frontage of the column saved many from the murderous maelstrom which engulfed them. Horses reared and whinnied frantically, firstly frightened by the sudden deafening noise, and then from the hideous pain of ripping wounds as the bullets struck home. Several horses collapsed downing their riders, others fled wildly with soldiers clinging on for their lives. Within minutes the skirmish was over and the surviving Khakis galloped away in a cloud of dust.

77

Jacobus led the way out of the donga to inspect the killing-ground. Three horses lay still or writhing on the ground; two others were standing despite serious wounds. He counted five prostrate soldiers, a smaller number than he expected given the ferocity of their fire.

A shot rang out. Jacobus swung around. One of the burghers was standing over a body; "Kaffir," he explained with a dismissive shrug. No further explanation was offered or indeed thought necessary. The possibility of thousands of armed blacks challenging Afrikaner authority and supremacy after the war was anathema to all Boers. Besides, all Natives were subjects of the Republican Governments, and by working for the English they were traitors. Although Jacobus was troubled by the practice of summary executions, he said nothing.

Order quickly collapsed as the farmers raided saddlebags and stripped bodies of boots, watches and other items of worth. Jacobus knew that there was nothing he could do about the looting, it was the expected reward for fighting.

Jacobus summoned Jan and Henry as the two people he could still depend upon, "Jan, I want you to shoot the injured horses. Henry, check to see if any of the Tommies are alive … no one shoots any more wounded."

....

Ruth was in the vegetable garden earthing up the potatoes. Close by her younger siblings argued as they wielded their hoes, rudely ejecting weeds from between the rows of carrots and cabbages. Ruth was becoming increasingly annoyed with their constant bickering - was this an inevitable consequence of them growing up? She studiously ignored their childish squabbles and concentrated on the job in hand.

The sun idled overhead in a cloudless blue sky. It was on days like this that Ruth yearned for something more practical to wear other than her ankle-length skirt which swept the dusty ground and was uncomfortably hot. She refused to wear the large, white, traditional poke bonnet of the rural Boer women, and instead sought protection from the searching rays beneath a trim boater.

No matter how many times the men went, Ruth never ceased to be anxious whilst they were away on a raid. This was the second time this month that they had ridden north to cut the railway line between Pretoria and Balmoral. The men might deride the English and mock their incompetence on the veld, but could not deny their courage and tenacity, and there was always the possibility of a fight and casualties. She acknowledged her own internal contradictions and emotional ambivalence when it came to the fighting. Of course they must defend the Republic, but the fresh mounds and stark new crosses in the family graveyard were a constant reminder of the price already paid - hadn't the family suffered enough at Spion Kop?

Her mother called from the kitchen window that supper would soon be ready. Ruth shooed the children away, "Make sure you wash properly before the meal!" She lingered to scan the skyline.

"They're here! They're back!" It was Boaz who first spied them from his chair on the veranda. He rose unsteadily and leaned on the rail, "They're here! They're back!" He repeated loudly, unable to contain his relief and excitement.

Ruth instinctively counted the riders as they approached: one ... two ... three; but there was a fourth. How was that? Her father had left three days before with Jan and Henry; have they brought a guest? As they came closer she could clearly see the three men sitting upright talking and laughing freely, whilst the other rider was slumped over the neck of his horse - he was wearing khaki! She ran to greet them.

"Thank God your safe ... How was it?" She was shouting.

The riders dismounted; black servants spontaneously scrambled to grab the reins and led the ponies to the stables for food and water. Cutting through the tumult she hugged her father. After a few moments he gently prised her away.

"We got a supply train ... what destruction!" he explained.

"But before we could loot it an armoured train came along and we had to leave sharply. An English patrol picked up our spoor and gave chase. We hid in a donga and let them come onto us. They suffered badly and withdrew. When we inspected the field we found this wounded Khaki trapped under his dead horse. His friends had fled and we couldn't just leave him to die on the veld, so we'll have to look after him until we can give him back. We'll put him in the barn where you can take care of him."

Native workers eased the Englishman from his horse, carried him into the barn, and there laid him on a bunk with a maize-straw palliasse – there were eight bunks in all, used for family gatherings or community celebrations such as welcoming in the New Year, or commemorating Dingaansday; that time in 1838 when four hundred and seventy voortrekkers defeated more than fifteen thousand Zulus. Ruth followed. She stood over him listening to his unconscious moans. The sight of him brought back disturbing memories which lately had troubled her less frequently, but which always hovered menacingly at the back of her mind: the dark night; the charging, yelling soldiers; the glinting bayonets; the shooting and screams of the dying. She steeled herself against the resurging black thoughts and consciously focused on her Christian duty to tend to his injuries. She addressed her black maid, "Grace, go fetch scissors, hot water, soap, cloths and bandages." Grace scurried away.

In the temporary quiet and calm, Ruth studied the wounded Englishman; she could see that he was an officer. Beneath his obligatory moustache and untidy stubble she detected a handsome face – even kindly she thought. Grace returned. Together they gently removed his tunic and dirty, blue shirt. She examined his chest and back. The only visible wound was in the right shoulder: a neat pencil-like hole where a bullet had passed clean through missing the bone; bleeding was minimal. Not serious reflected Ruth. Together they cleaned up the entry and exit holes and tightly fixed a bandage. More worrying was the fact that he was unconscious. She ran her fingers through his dusty, unkempt hair thoroughly examining the scull, until at the back she found a lump of mixed dirt and coagulated blood. She cut off the hair around it and cleaned the area with carbolic soap exposing a nasty wound. Helped by Grace, she applied a bandage which they wrapped awkwardly around his head. They laid him back on the palliasse.

"His leg Missis." Grace pointed.

Ruth looked attentively. He was wearing long, laced, leather riding boots which partially obscured an abnormal alignment of his foot. The more intensely she examined his left leg, the more apparent was a deformity.

"We need to remove his boot, but be careful, I think the leg may be broken."

They unfastened the laces, and then with tremendous difficulty eased off the boot. I thank God that he's unconscious, thought Ruth, the pain would be excruciating. She cut his trouser leg up to the thigh and sure enough was revealed severe bruising and swelling just below the knee; cautious examination revealed that the tibia was broken – fortunately, the bone had not penetrated the skin. This was not the first fracture that Ruth had attended, and with practised expertise she set the bone and applied a crude wooden splint.

"There's nothing more to be done at the moment," said Ruth to Grace. "Go and fetch Josiah to sit by his side ... he speaks good English. He's to fetch me when the Khaki awakes."

Alone once again, Ruth found her gaze inexplicably drawn to her enemy. She couldn't deny that beneath that grime was an attractive, sun-tanned face. He was laid beneath a blanket, but she knew his body to be lean and muscular.

As if waking from a trance she gave a shrug of self-condemnation; how could she harbour such thoughts? She swept out of the barn.

"Would you like a sip of water?"

81

The words barely penetrated Rodger's consciousness.

Again, "Would you like some water?"

Crouching over him was a young, burly Native. His face was broad with tribal scars on both cheeks; his hair short and stubbly; his eyes wide and alert; his half-smile friendly.

"Where am I? Who are you?" Rodger felt disorientated. He sat up slightly and glanced around the shadowy barn. His head swam dizzily; his right shoulder throbbed with pain; his left leg ached; his chest felt tight – breathing excited stabbing pains.

"Here, drink."

Gratefully Rodger sipped the tepid, life-giving water. "Thanks." He slumped back.

"To answer your questions: you're in the farm belonging to the Van den Bergs ... Boers. Apparently they found you under your horse on the veld and decided to play the good Samaritan. Me, I'm Josiah. I belong to the Van den Bergs." He grimaced as he spoke.

As Rodger listened, his foggy mind began to clear. He remembered the chase; the sudden and unexpected volley from the unseen stream-bed; his horse being hit, stumbling and falling; then nothing.

"Are the Van den Bergs the ones who blew up the railway? The ones who ambushed us?"

"I wouldn't know that," replied Josiah evasively. "I'm going to fetch Miss Ruth."

It was not long before Ruth entered the barn. She looked down on her unwanted guest, "How do you feel?" she said curtly.

Rodger lifted his heavy eyes and examined the young lady towering over him. He had difficulty focusing properly, but even so he could see a slim, attractive woman of smooth, olive complexion. Her hair was pulled back into a bun, exposing a beautifully sculptured face.

"I seem full of aches and pains and rather light-headed." He paused, "Thank you for taking care of me."

"We do our Christian duty. Sit up and let me take a look at

you. I need to see if there's any infection." Tenderly, Ruth removed the bandage from around his head and examined the wound; it was healing nicely. She removed those covering his shoulder and declared herself satisfied with the progress.

"You say breathing is painful?"

"Yes."

"Probably cracked ribs ... not surprising. I'll bandage your chest." Without formality she began to bind him tightly with linen strips.

Rodger was bemused by what he judged to be her contrived severity; he was determined to ease relationships. "It's Ruth isn't it?"

"How do you know?"

"Josiah said so. Let me introduce myself, I'm Rodger Borthwick."

Ruth busied herself without replying.

"I come from a farming family like you."

"You're a British officer. An invader. My enemy."

"I'm not your enemy," he replied defensively. "I'm just doing my duty for my country."

"You would take our Republic, rob us of our freedom, and kill our menfolk to do so ... how is your leg?"

Rodger sensed that his attempt to nurture friendship was flagging, besides, he was feeling fuzzy- headed and tired. "My leg throbs, but otherwise seems fine."

"You're to rest until you regain some strength and your wounds begin to heal properly. Josiah will keep an eye you. I'll send over some coffee and broth." With that she turned abruptly and left.

In the days that followed Rodger drifted in and out of sleep, but gradually his strength and stamina began to return. The dizziness and headaches subsided. The tightness in his chest eased - he assumed that broken or bruised ribs were healing - and his shoulder became less sore. Thankfully, he escaped infection. At first Ruth would visit daily to inspect his injuries, but it was Josiah who tended to his routine needs: eating, drinking, washing. In those early days it was Josiah's smiling face which greeted him as he emerged from healing sleep. With returning health he felt able to concentrate and hold a conversation. They got to know each other better:

"How did you come to work for the Van den Bergs?" he asked.

"Not by choice," explained Josiah, "although they are not bad people. Like all whites they believe themselves to be superior to us blacks." He looked meaningfully at Rodger. No words were uttered, but the body language said: including you my friend. "I am Basuto from the tribe of Bakhananwa, my scars identify me as such." He pointed to three gashes on each cheek. "My tribal home is in the Blouberg mountains far to the north of here. My father is an induna, a chief, or he was."

"Was?" enquired Rodger curiously.

"Was. He is imprisoned in Pretoria; put there by the Boers together with all the other chiefs of my tribe after we defied their demand for taxes. We expect them to be freed soon by the English. Why does it take so long?" he asked rhetorically.

"And what about you?" asked Rodger. "Your excellent English tells me you were educated at a missionary school. Was it after that that you came to work for the Van den Bergs?"

"I am not here by choice!" Josiah reiterated sharply. A moment passed as he recovered his composure, "I left the mission to help defend my people against the oppression of the Boers. But all who defied them were indentured on farms around the country and are forbidden ever to return home. Without papers I can't leave this farm, if I do I place myself at the mercy of any white man who would use me for sport. We are not paid for our work, instead our wages are given to the government to cover my tribes unpaid taxes. You see, I was forceably indentured; really made a slave by the Boers, and the English, by their inaction, perpetuate the situation."

"And after the war?"

"We watch this war between the white tribes and hope that the English will win. The English Government is known for its sense of justice and fairness, and will release us from the bonds of oppression. When the war is won all the land will revert to the Great Queen, and she will redistribute it and right the many wrongs. Our ancestral lands will be returned to us once again. We will become full and equal citizens of this country with the end of repressive laws. Do not the blacks in the Cape Colony have the franchise? Are they not treated as equals with the whites?" Josiah paused; "For this, many of us are prepared to fight against the Boer."

"Does that include you?"

"But of course. I won't be a slave forever." Josiah was curious about this friendly white man from over the ocean and promptly changed the subject, "What is it like where you come from?"

"England ... Northumberland." It seemed so far away. "I live in a beautiful part of my Country with rugged hills ... not quite mountains, not like the Drakensberg or probably even the Bloubergs. There are green pastures and miles upon miles of sandy beaches."

"I don't know the sea, although I've heard stories of it."

Rodger reminisced in nostalgic mood, "The sea is a vast expanse of water far greater than the largest lake. Its mood changes daily with the shifting skies and unpredictable winds; sometimes it's glass-smooth, other times it's a boiling cauldron."

"And men catch fish in the sea as we do in the rivers?"

"Yes; where I come from they use a very small and ancient boat called a coble in order to catch sea-trout and crab. Sometimes larger boats trawl nets and catch thousands of herrings." In his minds eye he could visualise the hundreds of boats chasing the migrating shoals from the Isles of Shetland and Orkney south along the Northumberland coast. During July, or sometimes into August, he would head with friends to the small harbours of Seahouses, Beadnell and Craster to watch the gangs of hardy, weather-worn women laughing loudly, shouting crudities and sometimes singing as they gutted the catch in the open air oblivious to the elements. The women would stay only days, moving south with the fish from harbour to harbour.

"But you are a warrior ... a soldier."

"Yes; my father owns land which will pass to my elder brother, so I had to seek a different profession." His options had been rather limited. On leaving school he had been sent to work as a shipping clerk for his uncle's business in Calcutta. He had quickly come to loath the oppressive heat, the dirt and squalor, and the monotony of his work. He returned within a year to the alternative career options of Anglican Minister or Army Officer. He baulked at the prospect of the anaemic life of a rural pastor, so opted for the lure of excitement and glory. "Perhaps one day I will become a farmer," he added ruefully.

CHAPTER 7

Laws are silent in the time of war.

Cicero 106 - 43 BC

PIETER

Pieter lounged in the arm-chair with its threadbare fabric. He stooped forward to throw a shovel-full of dried dung onto the fading embers of the fire, and then sat back to tamp the tobacco into his clay pipe. He lit a taper from a flickering flame and patiently ignited the compacted tobacco; he puffed methodically to inject air into the pipe-bowl, and was soon rewarded with swirling smoke and the inhalation of sweet, calming nicotine.

Like his father, Pieter was tall and powerfully built. Aged only nineteen, with the death of his father and twin brother on the slopes of Spion Kop, he found himself the reluctant master of the family farm. The bodies of his father and brother had been laid to rest in the family graveyard at the side of a mother he never knew. He rarely visited; it was too difficult; too hurtful.

On return from the fighting, he had had little inclination to manage the farm. His spirit had been crushed; he existed in a shroud of emotional pain, barely aware of his own actions. Life had no purpose. Alcohol was his refuge. He would always be grateful to his grandfather and uncle for coming alongside him when he was sinking in a quagmire of despair. They had supported him compassionately, whilst firmly encouraging him to take control of his life and the farm. The road to recovery had been slow, but gradually the zest for life had returned. Little by little he had accepted   responsibility for organising the Native workers and assuming overall management.

But irreconcilable differences had developed between them. His uncle and cousin, Jan, had both, on several occasions, tried

87

to persuade him to join them in their attacks on the trains and Khaki supply columns. His uncle was prominent in the resistance and was embarrassed that his nephew would not join the fight. But what was the sense of that? The English had occupied Pretoria and pushed the commandos east across the Portuguese border. Only scattered remnants remained to harass the English. Surely, when the English annexed the Republic it was clear that all was lost; continuing resistance was futile. The Republic was no more. It was now an English colony. Further fighting would only bring about more death and destruction; the country would be laid bare. He had come to the conclusion that it was time for peace. They had fought the good fight, but had been overwhelmed by the might of the British Empire; there was no shame in that.

The break had come when he visited the new English-appointed magistrate in Witberg and took the oath of neutrality. He was intent on making it clear to both sides that he wanted nothing more to do with the fighting, that he was simply a farmer who wanted only to live and to work in peace.

He picked up his book to read it by the yellow glow of the bulbous oil-lamp. It was a book that had belonged to his mother - Great Expectations by Charles Dickens. She had been a lover of his books and had acquired a number of them: a glance at the bookshelf revealed copies of David Copperfield, Oliver Twist, A Tale of Two Cities and others. He had read all the books several times. Somehow they represented a palpable link with his mother; she had held the same books in her own hands; the very touch brought him comfort and reassurance, and, on occasions, tears.

He heard the muffled sound of horses' hooves despite the noise of the wind billowing around the farmhouse. He looked at the granddaughter clock: almost ten-thirty; who could it be at this time of night … marauding blacks? He had been required to surrender his Mauser rifle when taking the oath, but had not declared his shotgun. Should he take it from the cupboard? If the visitors were Khakis and he was armed, he would be in trouble. The horses stopped, agitated voices called out indistinguishably, someone pounded on the door. Anxiously, Pieter drew back the bolt and opened it cautiously. There were half a dozen riders, one or two were strangers, but most he knew as members of the local Witberg Commando. He had fought with them around Ladysmith and on the slopes of Spion Kop.

"We hear you've taken the oath. Is that right?"

Pieter looked up at the mounted inquisitor and recognised him as Gideon Gravett. There were no friendly preliminaries. "There's no sense in fighting any more," asserted Pieter. "The English have taken our cities and occupy the country with hundreds of thousands of troops; not just the English, but the Canadians and Australians too. It's hopeless to resist."

"We'll fight them all until there are so many dead their people will clamour to bring them home. We did it in eighty-one and we'll do it again," argued Gravett.

"This time is different. The English won't capitulate."

"We'll show the English. We'll fight on to the bitter end, and you'll join us!"

"I'm living in peace … caring after my own business," retorted Pieter.

"You know that under the laws of the Republic every able-bodied man from sixteen to sixty is required to defend our country," countered Gideon, "and you're no exception."

Others muttered in agreement; horses and riders fidgeted restlessly. Pieter sensed a rising tension.

"Our country is no more," he snapped defensively. "There's no obligation on me."

Without warning Gideon lashed out at him from his horse with his sjambok, the thong striking Pieter across his left upper-arm; he reeled back against the doorway shocked by the sudden pain.

"Botha has ordered every burgher to take up arms. And if you refuse, we're to confiscate everything moveable and to burn down your farm," screamed Gideon. "We'll return in a couple of days and you'd better join us or we'll burn you out."

With that the riders turned their horses and galloped into the night.

The following morning Pieter rode over to his uncle's farm. His cousins and aunt made their usual fuss of him, but his grandfather and uncle were more reserved. They had every sympathy for him wishing to be left alone to run the farm, but taking the oath was unforgivable; it verged on the treacherous. Pieter recounted what had happened the previous night.

"There are many small groups of burghers on the veld at the moment, remnants of commandos, many whose homes have been burned down. Botha doesn't have complete control over them all," explained Jacobus. "You say they were Witbergers?"

"Yes, Gideon Gravett was the leader, but I recognised Jan Bothma and Sarel Prinsloo amongst others.

Jacobus silently pondered, but before he could reply Boaz interjected, "Pieter, you have suffered much in your short life, but sometimes God tests us in the heat of the crucible. He allows the dross to sink and the purified metal to rise. This is a time of testing for us all. Perhaps God is calling you to throw off the aggressor as He did with Gideon of old. Like him, you may feel inadequate, but God will provide all the strength and courage you need. Renounce the English oath ... it's of our enemy and cannot bind you. Then your uncle can vouch for you with these others. When you are ready you can join him on his forays."

"Grandfather, these forays are attacks on the English. People are killed. I've had enough of death. The Republic is no more. Why can't you and the others see that? To continue to resist is to destroy our race and property and lands!"

Jacobus spoke gently to the tormented youth, "The English may say that they have annexed the Republic, but whilst our Government exists, the Republic lives. No burgher has the right to turn his back on his Government, by doing this they hold themselves guilty of desertion. As long as the President has not surrendered I cannot do so either, it is my duty. It is your duty. Renounce the oath and I can intercede on your behalf." He looked on this young man as his own son. He stared at him with a father-like passion, willing him to respond positively.

"I won't fight again!" With this Pieter stormed out of the house ignoring the entreaties of his aunt and Ruth. He stopped momentarily and glanced towards the family graveyard: inwardly, his aching heart clamoured for lost love; outwardly his body sagged, his eyes moistened. He mounted his pony and galloped away.

It was two days later when the English patrol called. The soldiers stayed outside on the verandah drinking milk which he had given to them, whilst the young Captain indicated for them both to go inside.

"You've taken the oath?" enquired the officer.

"Yes," confirmed Pieter.

"Then show me your protection pass," the officer demanded officiously.

Pieter produced the document issued to all Boers who took the oath of neutrality.

"I must remind you that having taken the oath you are now a citizen of the new colony of Transvaal. That brings with it responsibilities. Have you seen any rebels in the area? Perhaps they've called here for supplies: meat? maize?

"My oath was one of neutrality. If I report on the activities of either side, I'm no longer neutral."

"Don't play clever with me and answer the question," snarled the officer.

Pieter considered, then replied, "No … none."

"You're sure? We know that bands of rebels are active in this area. Perhaps some of your neighbours are sympathisers?"

"My neighbours are my family. They're not rebels."

"And if they were, how could you possible incriminate them?"

The Captain smiled contemptuously. He moved away walking slowly and deliberately into the main room, "A very nice farmhouse you have here," he said looking about. "Of course, you are aware that our policy is to burn down the farms of rebels and collaborators." He paused, "Perhaps the next time we come you'll have some useful information for us?"

....

Pieter had been raised to believe that manual labour was Kaffirs' work - the predestined purpose of a subservient race: the children of Ham. But today he eschewed convention and joined his black workers in the shearing shed. He grabbed a sheep from the catching pen and coaxed it firmly to his stand. He tipped the ewe over onto her back and propped her shoulders between his knees for support, so exposing her belly and thrusting her four legs into the air. With his blade-shears he skilfully applied long strokes from the top of the breast bone all the way down to the open flank area removing the dirty wool. Next he sheared around the inside hind legs and crotch. He adjusted his position to better remove the fleece from the inside legs, chest, neck, until the animal was fully shorn. Once completed, the sheep was ushered out into another pen and the fleece was collected by one of his black workers and thrown, wool uppermost, onto a slatted table for initial cleaning: faeces, dead skin, twigs, all foreign matter was hand-picked from the wool. Finally, the fleeces were folded, tied into bales and loaded onto wagons ready for transportation to the wool merchants in Heidelberg - fifty long miles away.

The work was dirty, sweaty and tiring, but Pieter welcomed the all-consuming physical and mental effort. He was modestly aware that he was not the best shearer - a couple of his workers were far quicker and more skilful - but the exertion temporarily blotted out life's worries.

He was just finishing his twentieth sheep and contemplating a break for coffee and a pipe-smoke, when the riders came into view. He stood still watching their approach and anticipating the worst. As they grew near he recognised Gravett at the head of a dozen or so burghers. He walked outside to meet them; to the inevitable confrontation. The black workers discreetly faded away.

"There's an English supply column moving south from Middleburg to Bethal. Botha is concentrating the commandos to attack it at the river crossing. Order your Kaffir to bring us coffee whilst we wait for you to get your things together." With that Gravett dismounted indicating that the others were to follow suit.

"I'm not coming. I told you last time that I just want to live in peace," reiterated Pieter. He studied his antagonist: only a few years older than himself, perhaps a couple of inches taller than his own six feet, broad shouldered, a dirt-engrained, angry face half- hidden behind unkempt, facial hair and a short, scruffy beard. Alone I could take him, assessed Pieter, but it would be madness to start a fight with so many of his friends around.

"I told you how we'd deal with cowardly hands-uppers. And don't think your uncle can save you … there are no exceptions".

Pieter stared unflinchingly into Gravett's eyes, "Who gives you authority? When we fought together at Ladysmith you were just a burgher like me."

"Ladysmith was another place in another time. Since then I've been appointed a corporal … that gives me authority, and if you don't join us now, I'll show you my authority."

Pieter was silent and unmoving.

"All right men, tie him to the wagon!"

Rough hands grabbed Pieter and dragged him to an ox-cart parked in the yard half filled with bales of wool. He was pushed face forwards against a wheel and his arms were stretched wide and tied to the outer rim. An unsuccessful attempt was made to rip the shirt from his back. "Here, let me do it!" shouted an impatient voice. Pieter sensed a knife cutting through the material and then his skin was exposed to the sun.

Gravett swung his sjambok with all his strength, the throng

of the hippopotamus-hide whip cut across Pieter's naked back. He screamed with the shock and pain. The onlookers laughed and taunted him: "Hands-Upper! Coward!" Gravett laid on again and again. Red weals criss-crossed the naked skin; blood oozed from the wounds. Pieter fought hard not to cry out, but couldn't avoid the involuntary gasps as each blow struck home and forced the air from his lungs.

It seemed an age before the flogging stopped.

"Shall we cut him down?" asked a burgher.

"No! Leave him for the Kaffirs," replied Gravett. He then bent forward and placed his mouth close to Pieter's left ear, "Next time we come a-calling," he snarled, "I expect you to join us, otherwise we'll burn the farm to the ground."

The burghers wandered into the farmhouse and helped themselves to provisions and anything else that caught their eye. They then rode off to round up fifty head of cattle and drive them away.

....

He glanced back over his shoulder at the farm as it disappeared in the distance. The low rays of the rising sun cast long shadows making it difficult to distinguish detail. Gradually the stead passed from view.

Pieter had heard that the Military Governor of the Transvaal had set up a camp on the outskirts of Pretoria for the protection of burghers who had voluntarily surrendered and their families. They could keep their livestock or sell it to the military at current market prices. When the war ended they could safely return to their farms.

It was almost a week since the flogging. He had been cut down by his black workers who gently lathered his wounds with honey. Very quickly the inflammation, swelling and pain subsided – he could once again bear to wear a shirt. The past couple of days he had spent supervising his workers in loading up the ox-cart with the bare necessities required to re-establish a home, and in boarding up the farmhouse. He distributed the fowl amongst his workers together with some sheep, and gave them permission to farm the land to support their families until his return. In the meantime, they were to safeguard the property. But first they must help him to herd the remaining cattle and sheep to the "burgher camp" which lay just a mile outside Pretoria.

••

Shortly after arriving in the capital, Pieter attended a public meeting held in the Rex Bar on Church Square. He was impressed when the meeting was addressed by influential Boers such as former Generals Andries Cronje and Piet De Wet - both brothers of famous rebel leaders - and astonished when even Lord Kitchener attended the event. The sentiments expressed were very much in line with his own thinking: the country was conquered and prolongation of the war was a futile tragedy which threatened the very existence of the Afrikaner nation.

He sold his livestock to the English Army for what he considered to be a fair price, but now being without responsibilities and work, he quickly became bored with camp existence. He thought a lot about what was said at the meeting, and gradually became convinced that he must do whatever he could to help bring about an end to this pointless war. At first he volunteered to become a cattle-ranger: to gather in livestock from farms and to protect the animals against recapture by the commandos. His zeal and trustworthiness were quickly noticed, and he was soon offered the opportunity to volunteer as a scout for the Army. This better suited his skills and temperament, and more actively furthered his aim of helping to end the war. That he would be operating against his own countrymen weighed heavily upon his heart, but those resisting were a minority, and how else might he save his people from ruin and extinction?

He was sent to join other volunteers in the town of Standerton - a mixed group of Afrikaners and English-speaking settlers. His task was to guide the English army columns across the expansive, confusing veld, and to locate the positions of the Boer commandos. He was issued with a blue band for recognition which he tied around his slouch-hat.

CHAPTER 8

A cat in gloves catches no mice

14th Century French Proverb

KITCHENER TAKES COMMAND

Kitchener stood on the platform of the Pretoria railway station. He was unimpressed by its stature - a paltry affair for a former capital city he thought. He watched the two trains disappear. The first was an armoured train providing protection for the second in which was ensconced Lord Roberts with his wife and daughter. The elderly Field Marshall was on his way home to England, where he rightly anticipated accolades, financial gifts and prestigious decorations for having beaten the Boers. But first he would undertake a pilgrimage to the grave of his only son, killed during the earlier battle at Colenso on the road to Ladysmith. Kitchener, newly promoted and now Commander-in-Chief, reflected on Roberts' words to him as he handed over responsibilities: "There is nothing now left of the Boer Army but a few marauding bands. A police action really. I would expect to see you back in England in three months ... four at the most."

Kitchener shared the Landau carriage for the short journey back to his residence with Sir Alfred Milner. The latter was the High Commissioner for Southern Africa and now also the newly appointed Governor of the two recently annexed Boer Republics renamed the Transvaal and the Orange River Colony. Milner was of German and English ancestry; a brilliant student and the winner of numerous scholarships at Oxford. He had first practised law before becoming a journalist, and then had dabbled in politics, but was defeated as a Liberal candidate in the elections of 1885. He went on to serve with distinction as an administrator in Egypt. He was tall with a high forehead and bright eyes; he sported the mandatory Victorian moustache, and with his steel-rimmed glasses, projected a dignified – some would say arrogant – countenance.

Both the Boers and the anti-war faction in England blamed his intransigence during the negotiations in Bloemfontein in June 1899 as the direct cause of the war. Milner was unperturbed by the criticism. He believed that the Empire was driven by a moral imperative, that there was a God-ordained responsibility to colonize those places unfortunate enough not to have been born under the Union Jack. In that vein, he remained convinced that the way to peace and prosperity in Southern Africa lay in a federation within the British Empire of the two Boer Republics and the Colonies of Natal and the Cape. He could barely comprehend that the Boers failed to share his vision.

Like Kitchener, he appeared to be a confirmed bachelor who spurned the distractions of marriage; a person for whom work and advancement were totally consuming – although he would later marry the officer's wife with whom he was pursuing a secret affair.

He and Kitchener had worked together in Egypt and the Sudan. There had been the inevitable friction between soldier and administrator, but this had been much healed when, following a party in a fashionable home in London, the two of them had talked far into the night, long after the other guests had gone to bed. Differences had been reconciled; a cautious friendship begun. However, Milner was under no illusions and confided in a friend: "It's fortunate that I admire him in many ways ... I am determined to get on with him. But shall I be able to manage this strong, self-willed man?"

The carriage passed through the gates of Melrose House and stopped in front of the main entrance. This had been Roberts' residence before Kitchener. It was a large Renaissance-style mansion recently built by a prominent and prosperous local business man. Its grand interior included beautiful, stained-glass windows and exquisitely ornate fire-places and ceilings. It was lavishly decorated with plush carpets in opulent colours, and filled with reproduction Chippendale and Sheraton furniture. It boasted an impressive collection of paintings by British artists. Kitchener, a lover of porcelain, adored the array of gorgeous porcelain ornaments. The mansion was large enough to house not only the Commander-in-Chief, but also his small, select group of staff officers. The grand billiard room, clay tennis courts and adequate gardens served most of their recreational needs.

Tea was served in the library by the Indian servants.

When alone, Milner opened the conversation, "Roberts has told the Government at home that the war is all but over, and that the Army in South Africa can be greatly reduced. We have an Army of two hundred and ten thousand against an enemy of six thousand. The Secretary of State for War, St John Broderick, is demanding savings; apparently this war has already cost eighty million pounds and the Chancellor wants to see an end to it."

"Despite what Lord Roberts may think and say, the fighting is far from over!" declared Kitchener. "Six thousand Boers? It's more like sixty thousand! And as for my Army, half are guarding railway lines, bridges and towns. Many of the yeomanry and colonials have finished their contracted year of service and are choosing to return home. Following Roberts' assurance about the war being over, the Army Remount Department is recalling its agents from abroad; we are running down our military capability. On the other hand, the Boers have sifted their ranks of the weak and disheartened leaving the seasoned and determined to carry on the fight. I am left with raw recruits, and too few of them! What I need is thirty thousand mounted troops who can ride long hours in the saddle, sleep rough, live off bully beef, and endure extremes of climate. I have ordered every infantry battalion to form a mounted company, but I need your support to mobilise the yeomanry at home if we are to win the war."

"Of course," reassured Milner, "I'll write promptly and represent your concerns and needs to the Government."

"Good." Kitchener paced the length of the room; stopped; turned to face Milner, "I believe there are only two courses of action open to us if we are to be successful. We can either enter into peace negotiations."

Milner looked alarmed.

"Or," continued Kitchener, "we can drive the guerillas into the open and destroy them."

Milner re-gathered his composure.

"I have been speaking to the leaders of the Burgher Peace Committee."

"Burgher Peace Committee? queried Milner.

"Yes, some of the more prominent and influential Boers whom we have captured or have surrendered and who are anxious to finish the war, have suggested tactics which could bring a fairly rapid conclusion." Kitchener was rarely the author of original thought and had been grateful for advice.

"How?" Milner's interest was excited.

"They strongly recommend that we attack the endurance of the guerillas. His towns and bases having been captured, the Boer looks to his own farms for resupply and shelter. They harbour commandos and even act as rallying points before an attack. Men and women left on farms, if disloyal to our cause, willingly supply burghers, if loyal, dare not refuse to do so." He looked directly at Milner with his steely blue eyes as if to emphasise his coming point, "The enemy's sources of supply are an essential and legitimate target in military operations."

"And your proposal?" Milner felt a sense of disquiet.

"Six months ago Lord Roberts initiated a policy of burning farms and houses in the vicinity of enemy attacks on our lines of communication, on the grounds that the inhabitants knowingly gave succour, and also as a punitive measure. This limited application hasn't worked. In the last month alone the railway system has been attacked and cut no less than seventeen times. Our tame Boers believe that an extension of the farm burning policy will not only deprive the commandos of shelter and supplies, but that the plight of their families will drive them to the negotiating table."

Milner's fears were confirmed; he was uneasy at the prospect of the wholesale destruction of property, "Pouring oil on the fire is not the way to quench it. Aren't there other ways of achieving our aims? What about capturing or shooting the Boers' horses? Commandos can't operate across the veld on foot."

"They would only steal horses from the Natives or towns, and food and other supplies would still be available to them," pointed out Kitchener. "No. The limited farm burning started by Roberts must be expanded into a full- scale scorched earth policy and applied ruthlessly."

"And what of the women and children displaced?" Milner felt uneasy. "If left abandoned on the veld they would starve to death or freeze in sub-zero temperatures. They would be at the mercy of the natives!"

"We already have refugee camps near some of our garrisons along the main railway lines for the protection of those surrendered Boers and their families who have been intimidated," reminded Kitchener. "These camps can be expanded and there we can concentrate all those non-combatants displaced by our tactics ..."

CHAPTER 9

*If thine enemy be hungry, give him bread to eat;
and if he be thirsty, give him water to drink:*

Proverbs Chapter 25 verse 21

INTERLUDE

With the passage of time, Rodger was no longer dependent on Josiah, and the latter returned to his normal work on the farm. However, occasionally in the evenings he dropped by to see how Rodger was progressing. One day he appeared, his face bursting in a smile; he held something behind his back taunting Rodger to enquire.

"All right, what is it?" asked Rodger.

"Something you really want."

"How do you know what I want?"

"I know. Guess."

"Er ..." Rodger caught sight of a stick or pole peeping above Josiah's shoulder blades. "A walking stick."

"Something better ... a crutch." With that he whipped it from behind his back and passed it to his friend.

Rodger examined it; it was perfect: strong with a soft pad made from a sheep's fleece. He was overcome with gratitude. Josiah was the first black man that he had really come to know. He now regarded him as more of a friend than a black worker or servant to be kept at arms length. Josiah was far from the stereotypical savage imprinted on his psyche by educational theories of racial superiority and prejudicial cultural norms. "Thank you; thank you for your thoughtfulness and kindness." He beamed, "Now I can get about ... no longer confined." That evening he hobbled around the cavernous barn perfecting his shuffle.

"And where are you going?"

Rodger squinted in the unaccustomed brightness, and as his eyes adjusted to the light he saw a young man in familiar Boer attire leaning against a fence, However, he wasn't broad-shouldered and heavy-boned like the Boer rustic, but slim, more like a town-dweller not hardened by manual labour. He looked at his questioner and smiled, "Just exploring my surroundings now that I can get about a little."

"Now that might just cause complications," proffered the man. He half turned his head towards the house and shouted, "Jan! Jan!" A youth appeared. "I think you should bring your father."

Rodger detected a distinct American accent. He hadn't expected his appearance outside the barn to stir up so much interest. Soon they were joined by a man of typical Boer proportions and the youth, apparently his son. The large Boer spoke: "Now that you're recovering well, we'll make arrangements for you to leave us. In the meantime you have two options: you can give me your word of honour that you will not attempt to escape, in which case you may have the freedom of the farm, or we can confiscate your crutch and tie you up in the barn."

"As an English officer I give you my word that I will not try to escape."

"Good. I accept the word of an English officer. But should you break it, then I feel free to shoot you."

Rodger searched his antagonist's tanned, be-whiskered face and hardened expression, and was under no illusions as to the veracity of the threat. "Will I be returned to Pretoria?" enquired Rodger.

"We'll have to see what's possible," replied Jacobus.

Rodger felt the days beginning to drag by slowly – the boredom was indicative of his improving health. He was delighted to find that his pocket-knife was still in its pouch on his belt. From a small pile of miscellaneous wood, which he discovered behind the barn, he carefully selected a piece of softwood about eight inches long with straight grain. He sat on a box, which he placed outside in the shade by the barn door, and passed the time whittling, relaxing and meditating. As a young boy he had loved to escape the bustle of the farm and sneak off to the towering dunes of Embleton Bay. He would sit for hours under the haunting ruins of Dunstanburgh castle - destroyed when besieged during the War of the Roses and a local source of building stone ever since - whittling whilst watching the changing character of the sea and skies. In the beginning he would carve knives, forks and spoons and give them to his mother, but there was a limit to how many she wanted, so he grew more adventurous and sculptured miniature animals: ducks, mice, sheep.

As the lazy days passed, from his vantage point he noted the daily pattern of life on the farm: before first light the buzz as the servants fed and readied the horses; the exodus of men into the fields; the sound and smell of cooking; the quiet of the later morning as the young children received their home schooling; the washing and hanging of clothes; the tending of the vegetable patch - a reassuring scene of untroubled domesticity.

"Can I help?" Rodger had moved quietly to the vegetable patch where Ruth was busy hoeing the weeds; he peered through a gap in the hedge of quince and peach.

She looked up slowly, not startled, as if anticipating his approach, "You're hardly in a position to help. You should be resting."

"All I do is rest and whittle. I'd like to do something a little more constructive ... help earn my keep."

Ruth scrutinised her unwanted guest. She had watched him over the weeks; he was courteous, thoughtful, kind. In different circumstances she might welcome him as a friend, but at this time ... "Perhaps you are confused by our kindness. We are enemies. Don't expect me to fraternise." She paused a moment before adding brusquely, "I suggest you return to your whittling until it's time for you to leave."

Rodger watched as Ruth turned away from him and resumed her hoeing. Inexplicably, he felt hurt by her rejection, by her strong rebuff, as if he had a right to expect more. Momentarily he lingered, attracted by her every movement.

The evenings were long. Rodger hit upon a plan to help relieve the boredom and monotony. In the barn he found the lid of a discarded packing case. With his knife he marked out a board of sixty-four equal squares, then using charcoal from a small fire, he shaded them alternately. Next he whittled twenty-four small regular counters and similarly shaded half of them. He was ready for Josiah.

"It's a board game called draughts," explained Rodger.

Josiah said nothing but listened attentively.

"You take twelve counters of one colour and place one on each of the black squares in the first three rows on your side. Your opponent does the same." Rodger demonstrated. "The object of the game is to capture all of your opponent's pieces or block them so they cannot be moved." He went on to describe the diagonal movement of pieces, the capturing of your opponent's counters, the making of kings and the general nuances of the game.

Josiah moved his counters hesitantly – at first Rodger gave guidance – but he quickly mastered the requirements of the game. His confidence grew and with it his skill and enjoyment.

Over the following evenings, Josiah visited regularly with an eagerness to play this new game. As they jousted with the counters they chatted freely and the bonds of friendship grew.

On occasions, Rodger would hear the sound of horses departing before sunrise. The men of the household, excepting Boaz, would be absent for several days at a time, always returning to a noisy, happy reunion. Rodger would stand discretely at the barn door and watch the unloading of sacks from pack-horses. He was alert to the guarded closeness of Ruth and the American as they warily trespassed into each others personal space with hesitant, secretive touchings.

Rodger sat in his usual place by the barn door, lazily whittling. He watched the venerated patriarch relaxing on the veranda, seemingly content in his autumn years. Cocooned in the warmth of a summer's day, it was not long before Rodger, lost in his own thoughts of home, felt drowsy. His head started to drop; the piece of wood and knife loose in his hands.

"Can you show me how to do that?"

Rodger was startled; he had not seen the young boy approach.

"Whittling?"

"Yes. I've been watching you for several days. I'd like to do that."

"You'll need a sharp knife. You'll have to ask your mother for one. If she says yes, then I'll teach you."

Whilst the young boy scampered into the house, Rodger searched through the wood pile for a suitable piece. The boy returned triumphantly, brandishing a multi-blade pocket-knife. "Mama said that this belonged to my nephew Hans. He's dead now, but I can borrow it."

Rodger patted the box for him to sit on, "Firstly," he said, "we need to exchange names."

"Oh I know your name."

"Do you?"

"Yes, my mama and papa call you Tommy."

"Of course, Tommy it is," smiled Rodger. "And your name?"

"Adrian."

"Right Adrian, first the wood. Choose softwood, it's easier to craft than hardwood. Check that the grain is straight and not going in all directions, and avoid wood with lots of knots. The first rule of whittling is to keep your knife sharp. Instead of cutting, dull blades have a tendency to glance off the wood and head towards your hand. The blade might not be sharp enough to cut wood, but it's usually sharp enough to cut human flesh." He looked at his student who was listening intently.

"Another thing; when you get in a hurry with your cuts, that's when accidents happen, so make every cut slow and controlled. I'm going to teach you several cuts, but this one is for rough cutting to carve your object into general shape. Hold the wood in your left hand and your knife in your right. Make a long, sweeping cut with the grain and away from your body. Don't cut too deep or you might split the wood. Make several thin slices to reduce the wood to the desired size and shape." He demonstrated. "Now you ... well done!"

And so the friendship was born. Most afternoons, when he had finished his home-lessons and chores, Adrian would join Rodger. Under his tutor's patient instruction and gentle encouragement, Adrian made a rough spoon for his mother, and then progressed to making a wooden knife for his grandpa. Sometimes the women and Boaz would sit on the veranda in such a position as to keep a discreet eye on proceedings, but they never intervened.

In the early days Ruth visited Rodger daily to check on his recovery and occasionally to change his dressings. Over time her appearances became rarer, although as he limped around the farm or sat whittling, he eagerly anticipated catching sight of her; and when he did, he felt an excited jolt of electricity pass through his body. They might pass the time of day, but she made it abundantly clear that she wanted to avoid any familiarity.

"You seem well."

It was early morning, and Rodger was surprised when he turned around to find Ruth standing in the doorway of the barn.

"Thank you. I'm much improved from when I arrived here five weeks ago. I'll always be grateful for your nursing and hospitality."

She ignored his thanks. "Sit down and let me finally remove your dressings," she commanded.

He removed his shirt, which had previously been returned to

him laundered, and sat on the edge of a sturdy wooden box. She sat by his side and gently wound up the bandages from his shoulder and chest. She carefully examined the wound and saw that it was healing well - no inflammation and the skin knitting. She stood behind him and inspected the gash on his head. He relaxed, soaking in her closeness, her femininity, her smell, her warmth, her softness. It was intoxicating.

"It's looking good, barely a scar. How's your chest?" she asked sympathetically.

"I can still experience sharp pains when breathing deeply, but it's getting better."

"And your shoulder?"

"Not so stiff."

"Just the leg then. Keep using the crutch and gradually take the weight on your foot until it feels all right. Don't rush it, but in another couple of weeks or so all should be perfect."

"When do I leave?" asked Rodger, encouraged by the prognosis.

"Father said that it would be soon, very soon. But remember, you have given your word not to escape. Please understand that should you try to do so, my father will track you down and shoot you." She looked at him sternly, "And that would be a waste of all my nursing ... I'd be so annoyed."

Rodger glimpsed a guarded, sardonic smile. At last, he thought, a little humour; is she softening? "You have my word," emphasised Rodger with a grin.

"Good. Then this evening you are invited to supper. My family are curious to meet a Khaki before you leave us."

"And you?"

"Me? I've met you already ... nothing special," she commented dismissively.

He watched her as she departed: so assured, attractive, sensuous ... beautiful.

"Tell me Lieutenant Borthwick ... I'm pronouncing that correctly? Good ... what do you make of our home-made peach-brandy?"

Rodger looked directly and respectfully at the old patriarch with his leathery, scorched skin and long, white beard, grateful for his efforts to put him at ease by engaging in rather innocuous conversation. Boaz sat in his usual rocking-chair, the other men sat on a varied collection of wooden chairs and a bench on the farmhouse veranda; the sun was dropping below the horizon. Previously, the others had been sparing in their conversation and contact with Rodger as they had gone about their business on the farm; none had felt obliged to introduce themselves or engage him in conversation. This evening was different; they were extending the hand of hospitality. Each introduced himself in turn: the grandfather Boaz, his son Jacobus and his son Jan. There was another Boer present who introduced himself as the local Field Cornet, Gerrit Pretorius - cold and hostile thought Rodger. Also present was the American who seemed to be in permanent residence with the Van den Bergs - he was civil and wary as if intuitively sensing and resenting Rodger's attraction towards Ruth. The women were absent - he assumed busy preparing dinner - and the two youngest children apparently early to bed.

"The brandy? ... a little fiery, but otherwise very good."

"No doubt you prefer a scotch?" interjected Henry.

"And you a bourbon?" responded Rodger.

"And did you come to South Africa just to steal our Republics?" Gerrit cut through the polite irrelevancies.

Rodger was taken aback by the abruptness of the question, as apparently were the others given the awkward silence which followed.

"Sir, I came at the behest of my country. I am a soldier ... I do my duty."

"And in doing your duty you are prepared to kill those who would defend their lands and culture and families from unwarranted occupation. This family which has saved your life by practising those Christian values which demand that we love our enemies, has suffered greatly at the hands of the

English Army. Outside in the family graveyard we laid to rest two loved ones killed during the battle for Spion Kop. Jacobus, here, bravely bears injuries which would cripple a lesser man, and our American friend too, carries scars. Even Ruth bears the mental wounds of battle. For you, no doubt, it's a foreign adventure. For us it is about our very existence as an independent, peace-loving people."

Unable to stem a rush of indignation Rodger blurted out, "Sir, may I remind you that it was the Boers who started this war by invading the British Colonies of Natal and the Cape. Having driven the invaders back across their borders, it would be foolish not to secure regional peace and prosperity by ending destructive rivalries. We believe unification of the Colonies and the Republics under British hegemony to be the solution. That, sir, is what brings me to South Africa!" Rodger was surprised at the vehemence of his own statement. He paused: tense, uncomfortable, embarrassed.

"Well Lieutenant," interrupted Henry, speaking slowly and deliberately, "you're most certainly a convinced apologist for rampant British imperialism, but there are those who have no wish to accede to British narcissism and threats. My countrymen rejected your oppression over a hundred years ago, and the Afrikaners do the same now."

"Besides, you can never win!" added Gerrit sharply. "You English think like the Europeans you almost are. You seize and occupy our towns and capital cities and believe that the war is won. But we are a rural people. The countryside is where we live and work, and as long as that remains in our hands we are unbeaten. The English Army skulks in the towns dependant upon vulnerable railways for all its sustenance. We will destroy the railways, and with them the English Army."

Rodger was ill at ease. This was not how it was supposed to be. On leaving the barn he had consciously resolved not to be drawn into contentious arguments. His worst fears were being realised. Why had he allowed himself to be provoked into a confrontation by that malicious magistrate? Damn!

"Supper is ready."

All eyes turned towards Ruth who, in the intensity of the discussion, had entered unnoticed. She turned and led the way into the main room with its large wooden table which was laid for the meal. "Perhaps you would sit there Lieutenant." She indicated a chair. The men took their seats; Jacobus helped Boaz who moved with increasing pain and difficulty, whilst Anna and Ruth stood at the end of the table ready to serve steaming food from large dishes. A silence descended. Rodger cast about surreptitiously and saw that heads were bowed; everyone waited upon Boaz to offer thanks:

"O Lord, in whom is the source and inexhaustible fountain of all good things, pour out thy blessings upon us, and sanctify to our use the meat and drink which are the gifts of thy kindness towards us, that we, using them soberly and frugally as thou enjoinest, may eat with a pure conscience ... Amen."

Wooden plates laden with mutton and fresh vegetables were passed around the table. Conversation erupted. Rodger's young neighbour, Jan, turned to him, "I understand that when you're not a soldier, you too are a farmer."

"Yes, my family has a small estate in Northumberland close to the Scottish Border. The land is divided into a number of farms. We have tenants, but we farm a couple of hundred acres ourselves."

"Hundreds!" exclaimed Jan. "Our farms cover thousands of acres."

"The quality of land is much different. Here one acre might support a single cow, in England one acre can support ten or more."

The conversation drew in others and embraced varied subjects from agriculture to literature. The heaviness and antagonism of the early evening evaporated, and with the help of the lubricating wine an atmosphere of conviviality gradually emerged.

As people were finishing their meal, Jacobus shouted across the table to Rodger, "On my last visit to Pretoria I heard some of your soldiers singing an amusing song; something about a young lady called Dolly Gray, I think. Do you know it?"

"Only the chorus."

"Will you sing it for us?" He did not pause for an answer, "Ruth, you can accompany him on the piano!"

Hesitantly, Ruth looked across to Henry. His affirming nod was barely discernible; he smiled gently. Reassured, she took up her place at the grand piano. Rodger joined her. He discarded his newly crafted walking stick and leaned against the piano for support. Boaz sank into an arm chair whilst the other men gathered around - less Gerrit, who hovered awkwardly at the rear; detached, stern, disapproving. Inwardly, Rodger was pleased for this opportunity to be so close to Ruth. For a moment they consciously held each others gaze. "I'll sing and you follow me as best you can," he prompted softly. With that he launched into song:

"Goodbye Dolly I must leave you, though it breaks my heart to go,
Something tells me I am needed at the front to fight the foe.
See, the soldier boys are marching and I can no longer stay,
Hark, I hear the bugle sounding, Goodbye Dolly Gray."

"Again!" urged Jacobus. "This time we'll join you."

The stentorian voices of the increasingly inebriated men filled the room and drifted through open windows into the dark surrounding veld. They sang the chorus over and over again. For a brief moment the war was forgotten; the pain smothered; the mutual enmity suppressed.

....

Grace deposited the mug of hot coffee and the plate of rusks on a box and scurried out of the barn without a word. Rodger threw back his blanket and sat on the edge of his bed. He sipped from the mug savouring the strong, compelling taste - the first coffee of the day was always the best. He drank gratefully and ate his breakfast. Perching on the end of the bed, he pulled on his riding boots and began the tedious job of lacing them up. Suddenly, he was plunged into shadow as the bright morning sunlight bursting through the doorway was blocked; he looked up; he stared at a dark silhouette surrounded by a halo of sunlight and at first could not recognise the figure. He shaded his eyes; "Oh, it's you! Morning Henry."

"Hope you've finished your breakfast, Mr Borthwick. The time has come for you to leave," he responded tersely.

"Where to?"

"To join your own."

Rodger was struck by the caustic tone of the reply; last night's geniality had quickly dissipated. With no more information forthcoming, Rodger returned to his laces.

"You won't beat the Boers."

Rodger looked up.

"You won't beat them. You Limeys are so arrogant. You believe you're superior to the rest of the world. We kicked you out of America and so on the rebound you takeover India, Australia … wherever you can; and now your attention has shifted to South Africa. But you don't know your enemy."

Rodger was bemused at this tirade; he examined his visitor.

Henry continued, "These are the descendants of Dutchmen who fought for fifty years against the power of Spain, intermarried with irrepressible French Huguenots who gave up home and fortune to escape persecution. What you have is one of the most rugged, unconquerable races the world has ever known. For generations they fought against savages and wild animals in an unforgiving land. They have the skills of the huntsman: shooting and riding; and are fired by the Old Testament religion and an unquenchable patriotism. The Boer is the most formidable opponent who ever confronted British imperialism."

Rodger bent down without comment and finished the tying of his laces; it seemed that the earlier truce was over. He looked up again at his foe and rival, "And where do you fit into all of this?"

"Me? I just hate bullies; particularly British ones."

Rodger grabbed his stick and brushed past the American into the yard. His senses were dulled by the after affects of generous amounts of peach brandy, and he was in no mood to verbally wrestle with his antagonist.

"Climb up by me." It was Jan sitting in a Cape cart waiting for him.

"Where am I going?"

Jan shrugged non-committally.

Anxiously, Rodger looked about, his gaze searched the veranda, the vegetable garden, the farm yard; there was no sign of Ruth. All was quiet as if deserted. He knew it was unreasonable to expect her to say goodbye; why would she? But it did not prevent his sense of deflation and disappointment.

Then the house door burst open. Adrian emerged and ran towards the cart with a small sack; Ruth, Anna and Hannie followed onto the veranda and stood impassively, watching.

"For you!" Adrian held up the sack for Rodger to take. "Mama has put food in it for your journey."

"Say thank you to your mother ... wait." He fumbled in his belt, produced his pocket-knife and handed it to Adrian, "Goodbye my little friend."

Adrian was unsure about accepting the gift. Finally, he took it hesitantly before withdrawing a little and halting. He fought back the tears, "Goodbye Tommy."

"I'm sorry about this," it was Jan, "but we don't want you bringing your Khaki friends to visit us." he explained jokingly. With that he tightly fastened a blindfold around Rodger's eyes.

The cart lurched forward throwing Rodger back against the

hard, wooden seat. He was rather unnerved by this sudden departure, but as he gathered his composure, he resolved to return. With Henry as out-rider they passed over the gentle ridge and struck out across the featureless veld. It was a hot summer's day. Conversation was sparse and inconsequential.

After about four hours Jan removed the blindfold and pointed towards a convoy in the far distance; they altered course to intercept it. As they drew near, Rodger's spirits sank as he realised that this was the remnant of a captured British supply column. Leading the way was a Boer advance guard, followed by a dozen or so ox-carts piled high with loot. Then came weary prisoners stumbling forward, being driven at a fast, unsustainable rate, encouraged by sjambok-wielding guards; then more ox-carts and further prisoners. At the rear was a large wagon drawn by eighteen oxen on which were loaded the wounded - about twenty of them. They were suffering intensely from medical neglect, dirt, heat and flies. About one hundred yards behind this last wagon rode half a dozen Boer guards in extended line, while along the flanks horsemen were spaced about twenty yards apart. It transpired that they had orders to shoot any escaping prisoner without challenge.

Gerrit Pretorius broke away from the convoy to meet the new arrivals. He greeted Jan and Henry with a relaxed bonhomie, but smiled coldly between narrow lips when addressing Rodger, "Welcome Mr Borthwick. Now you are my prisoner. Your holiday is over."

A guard shoved Rodger unceremoniously onto an ox-cart, which halted just long enough for him to board. He was wedged between boxes of biscuits and sacks of flour. He grasped his walking-stick and watched his escort depart. He returned Jan's friendly wave; Henry ignored him. Only now did he fully appreciate the relative comfort, safety and compassion in which he had been recovering. For a time he had escaped the grime and brutality of war; the returning reality hit him like a body blow.

After their successful destruction of the supply column, the

115

Boers anticipated a British force in pursuit. They therefore planned to move by day and night - beasts permitting - until they were safely in the bowels of the Eastern Transvaal. Rodger calculated that with every passing mile his chances of returning to British lines lessened. He resolved to escape.

That first night he watched the pattern of the Boer guards. Like the prisoners, they had been on the go for days; they too were struggling against the debilitating fatigue. He noted, silhouetted against the starlit sky, the hunched figures of the out-riders as they slept in their saddles. He decided that at the hour of lowest alertness he would drop from the cart and allow the convoy to pass on. But he needed to be in the last wagon, otherwise he would likely be stood on by marching troops or crushed under wheels. Of course, there was always the chance that he would be trampled by the Boer rear guard or shot.

At about 4 p.m. the following day the convoy halted. The oxen were outspanned and put to graze in the care of the black wagon drivers. The exhausted prisoners collapsed to the ground; many were asleep in minutes. Rodger inched cautiously to the rear wagon where he found a cavalry officer with a bullet wound through the calf of his leg. He discussed his plans and enlisted his help. It was agreed that they would swap places. Rodger would travel on the wagon with the other wounded, whilst the cavalry officer would replace him on his cart and huddle under a blanket; hopefully the watchful Gerrit would believe that Rodger was still in his allocated place. Rodger gathered up what he could from the meagre supper rations - helped by his co-conspirator he accumulated two ears of boiled corn and four hard biscuits which he stuffed into the small sack given to him by Adrian.

Ten o'clock at night found the worn out, cursing prisoners on the move again. The hours passed. The guards nodded in their saddles. Quietly, Rodger slipped off the back of the wagon and rolled several times before lying still. He waited tensely as the sound of the rear guard came closer. Would the guards see him? Would the horses stand on him? Would they shy at an unfamiliar bundle on the ground? But even these iron men and tough horses were like everyone else: weary and hollow-eyed. The hoof beats swept around him and gradually grew faint. He rose and hobbled away from the noise of creaking wagons and cracking whips.

With the aid of his walking-stick, he headed north guided by the stars. He was aiming for the railway line which ran due east from Pretoria; but how far?

The morning light was breaking. Ahead was the grey of a kopje dimly outlined against the sky; he might hide there during the day. However, on nearing it a Boer farm loomed at its base; dogs began barking in a kraal. A short distance away was a small maize field, the stalks rising about four feet high. He carefully picked his way through the plants trying not to cause any damage or leave tell-tale marks. He sank down out of sight and was quickly overtaken by sleep.

He was woken by the heat of the sun, and soon became aware of the commotion in and around the farm just a hundred and fifty yards from his hiding place. Groups of Boers came and went. Others were re-sighting and familiarising themselves with newly captured British rifles by firing at tin-cans set on ant-hills. He lay still, desperate for water. Carefully he removed an ear of corn from his sack and slowly sucked out its moisture, then he ate the kernels. He waited hardly daring to move, warily stretching cramped limbs. It was a long day.

As soon as darkness fell he headed north once again. After about two miles he came upon a spruit where he paused to drink and splash refreshing water over his face. Reinvigorated, he pressed on - his leg was aching, but holding up well. He picked up a cattle track, and sacrificing caution for speed, hurried along. He trudged up an embankment alert to the rising sun and the need to find refuge for the coming day.

"Halt!"

Rodger shuddered to a stop.

"Come over here before I shoot you."

Rodger had blundered into a Boer who levelled his shotgun

at him - he was out hunting. This mountain of a man resembled a rough-hewn monolith: well over six foot tall; his massive thighs were sheathed in trousers of bark-tanned sheepskin held up by a draw-string. He wore a check-shirt and waistcoat of dappled calfskin open at the neck, and was topped with a broad-rimmed hat with a tapering crown which gave him a slightly ludicrous appearance.

"You're English?" he asked rhetorically. "You must have escaped from the convoy we destroyed or the prisoner column."

Rodger said nothing.

"I should shoot you and be done with it ... why should I bother to take you to the Field Cornet ... such a bloody nuisance."

Rodger watched anxiously whilst his captor debated with himself as to his course of action.

The Boer inspected his dirty, red-eyed, wretched, hungry prisoner; he wasn't armed; he couldn't put up a fight. "Walk over there." He indicated the direction with a jerk of his gun.

Rodger was fearful; he tensed in anticipation of the fatal shot. They walked a couple of hundred yards to a wire fence where was tied a small pony and a Cape cart.

"Jump up!"

Rodger visibly sighed with relief.

The Boer climbed up beside him and placed his shotgun between them. He took up the reins and they started off at a brisk trot towards a farmhouse on the skyline.

Rodger relaxed with the assurance that he was not to be summarily killed, but he knew that once at the farmhouse there would be little chance of escape again. He eyed the shotgun and wondered if he might grab it and jump from the cart, but he had already observed that this bear of a man was extremely agile and could easily grab him with his bony paw. He racked his brains for an alternative idea ...

Rodger lent forward with his head in his hands as if asleep; then suddenly he caught the Boer by the bottom of his trouser leg and threw him heels over head into the dust. The reins dragged on the ground and the pony broke into a startled gallop. However, within a mile the animal conquered its fear and settled down to a gentle trot. Rodger scooped up the reins, glanced back at the still figure lying on the ground, and with a grin of self-satisfaction urged the pony forward at a steady canter. He drove on relentlessly, stopping only at the occasional spruit to allow the pony to drink. He frequently looked behind expecting the enraged Boer with neighbours to be in hot pursuit. Sometimes he saw groups of horsemen in the distance, but hoping that they would detect nothing suspicious in a single cart, he avoided them, waved disarmingly and pressed on. He was relieved when at last darkness descended and he could rest for a few hours.

He decided to travel only at night, and so shortly after midnight he was on the move again. He made good progress, and with the breaking dawn sought refuge in a donga. He relished the refreshing rains of a short-lived storm and ate the last of his meagre food – a rusk from the Van den Bergs - and was famished.

At dusk, he once again renewed his weary journey. It was about 4 a.m. when he crested a slight rise and saw the glow of camp-fires ahead. The light breeze carried the familiar odours of a military camp: burning wood, cooking, horses. He dismounted and gingerly led his pony forward. He detected the sound of voices.

"Halt! Who goes there?"

"Lieutenant Borthwick, Northumberland Fusiliers"

"Advance and be recognised!"

He was with friends. His ordeal was over.

CHAPTER 10

To every man upon this earth
Death cometh soon or late.
And how can man die better
Than facing fearful odds,
For the ashes of his fathers,
And the temples of his Gods?

Lord Macauley ("Lays of Ancient Rome" 1842)

BATTLE OF NOOITGEDACHT
(13 December 1900)

The march from Pretoria was hot, dry and tedious. Rodger was reminded of home - the verdant, fertile strip lying between the North Sea and Cheviot Hills - as he led his company westwards through the Moot; this luscious, green valley about five miles wide, which runs approximately east to west between the hills of the Witwatersberg and the more mountainous Magaliesberg. The region was renowned for its picturesque farms and lush, patch-work of fields in which grew wheat, maize and tobacco, and for its grazing herds of dairy and beef cattle. Now it was the scene of devastated crops and smouldering homesteads, as the British column ravaged this rich, agricultural land like a swarm of devouring locusts.

A week earlier, to the north of the mountains, a convoy of one hundred and twenty six fully laden wagons en route to Brigadier-General R G Broadwood's garrison in Rustenberg, had been captured by De la Rey and his Commando - British casualties had been heavy. Major-General Clements, with his mixed force of horse, artillery and infantry - including four companies of Northumberland Fusiliers - was ordered by Kitchener to cooperate with Broadwood in order to cleanse the area of predatory Boers, and to wreak retribution on those who would provide intelligence and succour to a callous and brutal enemy.

The order to make camp came late in the afternoon as the column reached the farm at Nooitgedacht - a point where the Magaliesberg rises precipitously almost one thousand feet above the valley floor. Behind the white-walled, mud-brick and thatched farmhouse, lay the entrance to a wooded gorge in which a footpath climbed to the summit between towering cliffs, and down which a stream of pure water trickled onto the plain.

Clements called his officers together: "This will be a good base from which to conduct operations hereabouts. We have a guaranteed source of clean water, and by situating the heliograph on the mountain behind us, we can communicate directly with General Broadwood. I believe him to be with his Cavalry Brigade about eight miles north-west from here. Together we will clear this area of the Boer."

"We will need to picket the mountain top in some strength," observed Lieutenant Colonel Legge of the Mounted Infantry." He was concerned that it totally dominated the camp.

"Quite so," confirmed Clements. "Captain Yarman, I want you to take your Fusiliers up the gorge to the summit and to establish a strong picket on either shoulder. You will also provide close protection for the heliograph post. Colonel Legge, you are to place a picket line across the western approaches of the valley. Colonel Jackson, you are to do the same on the eastern approaches. De la Rey only has about eight hundred men; we outnumber him two to one. I don't imagine that he will attack, but we must take all necessary precautions."

Sickness and casualties had reduced numbers of officers and men alike, and Rodger had had little opportunity to recuperate before he was thrust into temporary command of a depleted company consisting of about one hundred men. He led them up the steep footpath bending under the weight of his forty-pound pack. His leg was still troublesome and ached following excessive or arduous usage. He paused occasionally, ostensibly to allow stragglers to catch up, but in reality it was to rest his leg in order to ease the throbbing pain. It was a slow, sweaty ordeal with little protection from the blistering summer sun. The saving grace was the cold refreshing water of the babbling stream which, periodically, they splashed on their faces and drank from cupped hands. Once on top he moved his company to the designated position, and supervised his men in their preparation of the defences. It was too rocky to dig down so they built upwards, piling rocks to create sangars. They worked late into the night against the backdrop of a sky reddened with the flickering of burning homesteads, cruel witness to their trail of wanton destruction. After an initial spasm of fevered activity, the days that followed were relaxed as they settled down to a routine of eating, sleeping and sentry duty. The sun shone fiercely, but the rocks provided welcome shade. The view across the valley and beyond to the hills was breath-taking. The days passed peacefully enough.

Rodger sat resting against a boulder with a half-written letter to his parents on his knees. He placed it on the ground; his heart was not in his writing. Instead his mind wandered. Ruth's image consumed him: her elegance, her beauty, her blue eyes, the marbled contours of her smooth face, her feminine tenderness as she dressed his wounds, her natural fragrance ...

His warm reflections in the lazy stillness were broken by a bird's rapid call: "klooee-klooee-klooee". He gazed upwards to see an eagle soaring on the thermals: dark head, white lightly-spotted breast with very dark under-wings; he marvelled at its majestic, effortless flight. The only other occasional sound was the annoying clatter as the shutters of the heliograph winked its morse-code messages to Broadway's cavalry.

With dusk his men routinely stood-to, waiting in their defensive positions for the Boer attack which never came.

When the darkness had descended, Rodger passed the order: "Stand down." He checked that the sentries were in place before lying on his mattress of cut grass and pulling his coarse blanket around his shoulders. He fell asleep to the reassuring sounds of men quietly chatting and joking as they played cards by the muted light of a storm-lamp, and the occasional raucous burst of laughter.

****

It was impossible to ride along the boulder-strewn crest, and soon everyone was leading their horses on foot, picking their way in the darkness over the uneven surface. Progress was difficult and slow. The order came to halt to allow the guides to undertake the final reconnaissance of the enemy's positions.

Jan slumped to the ground close to Henry whilst his father left to attend the kriegsraad. They, like everyone else in their commando, were close to exhaustion. For two days and two nights they had trekked without sleep almost one hundred miles across difficult terrain, avoiding contact with Khaki columns which seemingly littered the veld. They had been sent by Botha under a newly appointed young leader, General Beyers – former attorney and Transvaal rugby forward – to join forces with De la Rey and strike a decisive blow against the English. Together their forces would outnumber the enemy's column. Clements' camp offered an ideal opportunity. The plan, as explained to them, was simple enough. Beyers' force was to split into two: half to take up a blocking position to prevent Broadwood coming to Clements' aid, and half to attack the Khakis on the mountain summit – this was their task. Simultaneously, De la Rey would sweep down the valley and fall upon the enemy camp. The enemy's retreat would be thwarted by another force under General Smuts, which would capture the dominating kopjes to the south-east.

Jan felt his shoulder being gently but firmly shaken; he had fallen into a heavy sleep. "It's time," his father had returned. "The guides have returned. They report that the main enemy camp is at the foot of the mountain, and that a strong picket of Tommies are about a mile down this ridge. We're to leave our horses with appointed men and advance in extended line on foot. We are to destroy the picket."

Shaking himself awake, Jan took up a position with his father and Henry. He cocked his Mauser forcing a bullet into the breech, then he removed the magazine and replaced the bullet before returning it to the rifle - this gave him an extra shot before needing to reload.

The advance began. The night and rock-strewn ground made coordinated movement extremely difficult; slowly they groped forward.

Jan was on the extreme right of the line by the cliff edge; he sensed, rather than saw, the steep drop into the valley. He had only been moving forward for about ten minutes when heavy and sustained firing broke out below. He was later to learn that De la Rey's commandos had advanced too quickly along the valley, and in the dark had blundered into the picket of the Mounted Infantry. For a moment it had seemed as if the Boer momentum, amidst the chaos and confusion, would enable a break through, but half-dressed soldiers rallied, and following vicious close-quarter fighting, gradually repulsed the attack.

As they picked their way amongst the rocks, the realisation grew that with the commotion below surprise had been lost. Sure enough, a torrent of rifle fire burst from the *schanses* ahead. In the half-light, Jan saw several friends collapse - dead or wounded? Instinctively, he followed the others in seeking cover amongst the rocks. Only Beyers stood tall, with revolver in one hand and riding-switch in the other. "Voorwaarts! Voorwaarts!" he yelled. The enemy fire slackened. The cry was taken up, "Voorwaarts! Voorwaarts!" The cowering Boers rose and surged forward. "Come on son!" His father stood, fired an aimed shot and dashed forward. Jan was carried by the energy of the sudden rush, and cautiously left the safety of his cover. He hurried onwards to catch up with his father and Henry. Spontaneously, a pattern of movement emerged: Jan, Henry and his father would dash forward about twenty yards whilst neighbours provided covering fire. Then they would fire to allow the other group to draw level. In this way they moved ever closer to the Khakis' defences. Some dashed forward recklessly shouting and cheering only to be shot down – casualties were high. As they reached the schanses, group cohesion collapsed – it was everyone for himself. They swarmed over the rocks shooting point blank, parrying bayonet thrusts, clubbing with rifles. Jan jumped adroitly to one side to escape a stabbing bayonet and then fired directly into the grim, frightened face of his attacker; he was splattered with the blood and brains of the disintegrating flesh and skull – the short high-pitched scream of his dying assailant was to haunt him for months afterwards.

The burgher in front of him mounted a schanse, only to fall backwards clutching his groin with two bloodied hands; Jan was felled by his writhing hulk. There was no time for pity. With hands and threshing feet he roughly rolled the wounded man to one side and scrambled to his feet. Momentarily, he paused to gather his breath, and then with rifle at the ready clawed his way up the pile of stones to tackle the Tommies. He took aim; his quarry swung around to face him; Jan hesitated ...

****

Broadwood was withdrawing back to Rustenberg having learnt that the town was under imminent attack – false intelligence fed to him by Beyers through a gullible, collaborating Native chief. He stopped on hearing the sound of battle wafting through the still morning air. His heliograph winked to Clements: "Do you need help?"

The canny Boers on the heights above Nooitgedacht farm intercepted the message and reassured him: "Everything all right. No assistance required."

With a sense of relief, Broadwood resumed his dash to Rustenberg and away from the fight.

****

The early morning calm was shattered by a volley of rifle fire in the valley below. Intermittent firing followed. The ragged sound of musketry, mixed with indiscernible shouts, spiralled upwards like hot air rising. The intensity of noise increased.

"Stand to! Stand to!" shouted the sentry.

Rodger flung off his blanket and scrambled to his appointed position. "Stay here!" he ordered his Company Sergeant Major and set off to check the defensive line. It was still dark, but the first streaks of light heralded the coming day. It was with difficulty that he covered his perimeter, but was heartened to find that the men were all in place. He grinned at them reassuringly and offered encouraging words: "Are you ready Knox? Good." He looked at the young man's anxious, determined face: "Shoot straight, hold your post, and the Boer will never break through our position."

"Yes, sir."

As the fighting below subsided, Rodger stared into the grey gloom searching for the enemy. Surely, he reasoned, they wouldn't attack in the valley without first securing the heights. Perhaps their manoeuvres are out of sync, in which case we could be attacked at any moment. He thought he saw movement; a fleeting shadow; then another; possibly another. This was it.

"Fusiliers, present … fire!"

To his front yells and shouts filled the air. The ghostly figures disappeared.

"Fusiliers, select your targets independently. Fire at will!"

At first only occasional shots were returned, but gradually the intensity of incoming fire increased. Then, without warning or preliminaries, the shadows poured forward in the breaking dawn. Bullets hissed past him or ricocheted off the rocks with a haunting whine. He peered over his cover and fired a quick unaimed shot, but drew back under the weight of the enemy fire. Next to him his Sergeant-Major adjusted his position and raised his rifle to take aim, then crumbled, falling backwards with a neat bullet wound to the forehead. It seemed that within seconds the Boers were amongst them. He fired at a huge chunk of a man who mounted the parapet of his sangar; he toppled backwards into the arms of a following attacker. Rodger swung to his left to confront another intruder cocking his rifle as he did so. He fired carelessly from the hip, striking his opponent in the stomach who reeled backwards with the shock and collapsed clutching his wound. Rodger had a sense of being drowned under an unstoppable tidal surge - there were so many of them. He turned again to face a new enemy ... and froze. He recognised his young assailant.

Rodger never saw the rifle butt as it crashed into the side of his face.

* *

After a stiff fight, the collapse of the Fusiliers' defence came suddenly. Jan was detailed to stand guard over the soldiers as they collected their wounded and established a first-aid post - the dead remained where they had fallen. He summoned a Khaki stretcher-party and indicated the place where Rodger had fallen. He watched with ambivalent feelings as they gently lifted his inert body onto the canvass and carried it away. Seriously wounded Boers who could not ride, were also gathered by their friends and laid with the Tommies, for they had neither doctors nor drugs and were dependent upon the compassion and honour of the English – a trust rarely broken.

Looking down into the valley Jan could see that the English had abandoned their camp and were withdrawing towards Pretoria. Apparently the plan for Smuts to block any retreat must have failed. He noticed that the field guns had been saved, and watched as occasionally a battery would unlimber and fire a few shells to discourage pursuit.

He found his father and Henry, and together they descended the path in the gorge. They reverently stepped over and around dead Khakis who had been killed mercilessly by plunging fire from the cliff top as they climbed to the assistance of the Fusiliers. Jan was thirsty, but the blood from bodies sprawled in the trickling mountain stream coloured the waters pink making it undrinkable.

The English camp was full of all kinds of supplies which were becoming increasingly scarce: tea, coffee, salt, sugar, tinned food, clothing, boots and even champagne! They each liberated a horse from the English lines where many stood picketed, and used them as pack-horses; they loaded all they could.

Jan paused for a moment from the clammy work and looked around; the scene had degenerated into one of indescribable mayhem. A disorderly swarm of Boers was ransacking the tents looking for prizes particularly in the officers' kits; some were searching saddlebags or looting the wagons before setting them on fire. One burgher sat on an officer's canvass stool drinking from a bottle of rum - spilt liquid washed his dirt-encrusted beard. A venerable, elderly predikant led a small pious group in thanksgiving and the singing of psalms - exploding ammunition from a wagon unwisely set on fire by the looters provided a hellish accompaniment. There was no longer any thought of continuing the fight; control and discipline in this citizen army had dissipated in a frenzy of looting.

Into this anarchical free-for-all rode Beyers, his fury evident: "This is not the time for looting. Follow the enemy! Destroy them in their retreat!"

Men stopped their manic activity and stared at him dumbly.

"Are you not ashamed of doing nothing?" accused Beyers.

A thickset farmer with torn and bloodied clothes stepped forward. Jan knew him as a neighbour, a corporal in the Witberg Commando, and a person who had fought fearlessly on the cliff-top. He stopped close to Beyers' horse and looked up at the General, "We understood that the purpose of this attack was to capture much needed supplies, and not to capture soldiers who we are required to release as there's nowhere to keep them. Let De la Rey's men harass Clements. We've done our part in today's work, let them do the rest."

From the vantage point of his horse, Beyers looked down on his battle-weary men. He saw in their strained faces a determined, rebellious mood. He knew his compatriots to be stubborn, tenacious and ultra-individualistic. For the moment they would not respond to his or to anyone's' orders. Over the past few days he had driven them hard with little food and sleep; they had just won a desperate and fearsome battle. They would have their deserved reward whether he condoned it or not.

Without further comment he turned his mount and trotted off down the valley.

"They're here!" announced Jacobus as a neighbour approached with their ponies which he had brought down the gorge from the mountain top. "Let's find a place to rest".

They trotted a mile or so down the valley and found a clump of trees which would offer protection from the sun. They examined their booty. They had sufficient food for several weeks, and clothing – albeit khaki – to refit them from head to heel. They discarded their Mausers as ammunition was no longer available, and instead each carried an English Lee-Metford rifle. That night they had a feast washed down with more than a little champagne. They slept the sleep of the exhausted, undisturbed for twelve hours.

The following day began the grim, depressing task of burying the dead. Jan helped to dig a mass grave near the farmhouse, whilst Jacobus and Henry joined the group which retrieved the bodies from the mountain top and carried them down the gorge. When all the dead had been laid to rest and the soil replaced, De la Rey gave an eloquent, affirming address which moved Jan and the others to tears.

A period of welcome rest followed.

On 16 December, Jan and his father joined a religious gathering on a nearby kopje to commemorate Dingaansday.

Henry had no intention of intruding upon what he saw as essentially a Boer celebration, and decided to seize the opportunity to see how Rodger was progressing. He felt little affinity towards him, but was driven by an inexplicable pull of conscience. He found him still in the first-aid post on the mountain top, together with fifty or more casualties. "I've come to visit Lieutenant Borthwick", he explained to an enquiring orderly, who then indicated a figure lying beneath a canopy slung between two rocks to shade the sun.

"I thought I'd come and see how you are."

Rodger was lying on his back staring at the tarpaulin with a blank expression. The left side of his face was swollen like a balloon, and badly bruised; he was almost beyond recognition. He didn't respond.

"Rodger, Rodger; it's Henry from the Van den Berg's farm."

Slowly, tortuously, Rodger turned his head to look at his visitor. He stared at him and paused as if searching a faded memory. At last he spoke, "I know you … the farm ... Ruth … Adrian." He fell silent as if exhausted.

"Yes, that's right. You're not having a lucky war. How are you feeling?"

In reply Rodger turned away sharply and vomited into a strategically placed helmet already half-filled with his stomach waste. His breathing raced, only gradually returning to a normal rate. He again faced Henry. "I have a roaring headache, dizziness and recurring nausea. But looking around, I think I got off pretty lightly ... don't you?"

Henry cast his eyes over the many prostrate Tommies and a few Boers: some perfectly still and silent, others writhing, some moaning gently. Orderlies moved amongst them offering water, encouragement and changing bloody dressings. It was a pitiful and harrowing sight.

"You might have a point there," conceded Henry.

"Who's here with you?" enquired Rodger. "I thought I saw Jan. Was I right?"

"Yes; and Jacobus."

"All well?"

"Yes."

"I'm pleased. Give them my regards … they fought well … you all fought well." Rodger closed his eyes, "My bloody head!" He rolled it from side to side. "When I open my eyes I get dizzy. Sorry … I need rest … thanks for coming," he stuttered between laboured breaths.

"I hope we next meet in better circumstances," added Henry. There was no reply. Rodger once again lay on his back holding his head between his hands, his eyes clenched tightly.

The following day, Boer scouts brought the news that General French had left Pretoria with two thousand cavalry and was heading for the Moot. It was time for the loot-laden commandos to leave.

****

The wagons carrying the wounded lurched and pitched on their journey to the General Hospital in Pretoria. For two days and one night they travelled under scorching sun and through torrential rain, rolling thunder and vicious lightening. Rodger was classified as "walking wounded", albeit during his recurring bouts of dizziness, he could only remain upright with the support of willing hands.

The stay in Pretoria was short. Dressings were expertly replaced, and the wounded hurriedly despatched to the hospital train waiting in a siding.

Rodger was helped down from the wagon and given into the care of the train orderlies. Gently, he was ushered into a carriage.

"Head injury," announced the orderly to the waiting nursing Sister.

"Over there," she indicated a bottom bunk.

As each patient came aboard, their injury was announced and the Sister allocated appropriate bunks:

"Fractured thigh."

131

"Which? Left or right?"

"Right."

"Over there."

The soldier was slipped on his back accordingly, injured leg on the outside so that it could be readily accessed.

The cries rang out as the train filled to its capacity: "Fractured shoulder; neck; shot to right thigh; lung; shattered forearm ..."

Rodger was surprised, but delighted, to find on his bed a "Good Hope" bag. In it was a pair of pyjamas, towel, brush, sponge, soap and toothbrush. Encouraged and helped by the orderlies, he removed his dusty, blood-stained khaki, and revelled in the luxury of clean body-clothes between fresh sheets. Food was served: hot, thick, tasty broth. He relished the strong tea, but watched with a little jealousy as the stomach and lung cases received milk and brandy. But he was out of it. Not for weeks the sun and dust, the foul water and weary marching, the booted sleep and rancid bully-beef.

A young, enthusiastic doctor, fresh from an English county-hospital, passed between the bunks generously administering morphine. The prick of the needle was the precursor to blessed relief. Rodger was already sleeping when the train steamed south along the single three-foot-six gauge line.

CHAPTER 11

"What men they were, these Boers! ... Thousands of independent riflemen, thinking for themselves, possessed of beautiful weapons, led with skill, living as they rode without commissariat or transport or ammunition column, moving like the wind ..."

Winston Churchill

GUERILLA OFFENSIVE
(January 1901)

The burghers lay formless, sleeping within the copse of poplar trees and beneath the shade of the willows by the cooling waters of the puddled dam. With dusk the heat of the day dissipated and men stirred in anticipation of leaving. But first they could enjoy the traditional baked rusks and hot coffee brought to them by the farmer's wife and children. The waking Boers chatted easily with their kindly hosts, and fussed affectionately over their offspring.

At the recent kriegsraad, Botha had made his intentions clear: outright victory against the British was impossible, but they were sustained over stretched lines of communication. British policy would weaken in the face of their inability to achieve a lasting victory, and the European powers would eventually intervene. His immediate plan was for the commandos to launch coordinated attacks against English garrisons along forty miles of railway in order to sever lines of supply and so paralyse the Army. The Witberg Commando was ordered to attack between Balmoral and Middleburg.

The raiders collected their ponies which were grazing on the green veld, hobbled by foreleg and halter. Soon they were on the move leaving the secluded farmstead behind: bobbing heads under slouch hats, rifles in left hands, reins in right, bandoliers slung across their chests. They travelled light and fast.

Black clouds rolled towards them; crashing thunder half stunned them with its roisterous din. Rain raged with terrifying fury, and as if from all parts of the heavens great lurid flashes of flame lit up the veld, momentarily turning night into day. The riders were drenched, but undeterred as they rode purposely towards their objective.

The method of train wrecking had greatly evolved. Earlier that day Jacobus had prepared the initiating device. He had taken an old Martini-Henry rifle and sawn off the butt behind the breech, and the barrel a few inches in front of it. He had removed the trigger guard. Now, with the help of Jan and Henry, he scraped away the stones under the rail to make a hole which they packed with dynamite. He opened the breech and inserted a cartridge from which the bullet-head had been removed; carefully, he closed the breech. He placed a dynamite cartridge in the shortened barrel and then put the mutilated rifle upside down on top of the dynamite with the trigger just touching the underside of the rail. When the train passed its weight would make the rail sag and so press the trigger. Lately, the English had taken to pushing an empty carriage in front of the engine to initiate and absorb any explosion. The skill was to so place the improvised device that the full weight of the engine was required to fire it.

****

Kitchener was not unaware of Botha's plans - a hands-upper had been only too happy to swap information for financial reward and preferential treatment. He intended to disrupt Botha by mounting a sizeable offensive to clear the Eastern Transvaal of all guerillas and was on his way to discuss his plans with General Smith-Dorrien in Middlesburg. He was surprised when his train made an unscheduled stop at Balmoral.

"Go and find out what the matter is?" he tasked Maxwell, a

trusted ADC.

He poured over the map laid out on the table of his first-class carriage with its mahogany panelling, brass fittings, hissing gas lamps, and comfortable, lavish furniture. The map lacked detail; whole swathes simply indicated unsurveyed veld with a few villages scattered about. He was full of admiration for the Boers who roamed this featureless plain and could find their destination with pin-point accuracy never needing to consult a map.

Recent experience had made him realize that the conventional army structure of divisions was too ponderous and clumsy for this new type of warfare. He had already issued orders for his Army to reorganise into thirty-eight columns of mixed arms: cavalry, mounted infantry, artillery and foot soldiers. This would give him more flexibility, but he lamented the fact that the preponderance of foot soldiers would restrict the speed of his columns to marching pace.

As he repeatedly studied the map, his plan crystallized. He would deploy as many columns as possible sweeping south-east between the Natal and the Delagoa Bay railway lines. By this tactic he would drive the guerillas before him killing or capturing as many as possible, and push any remnants into the mountains of Swaziland. To ensure that the guerillas could no longer operate in liberated areas, he would destroy all means of sustenance. His knowledge of military campaigns offered him a precedent for a scorched earth policy. During the American Civil War, General Sheridan had devastated the Shenandoah Valley and thereby effectively denied the Confederacy of the means of feeding its army. He was anxious to explain his new tactics to his Generals.

Maxwell flung open the door and stood in the frame distracting Kitchener from his studies; the latter looked up in expectation.

"The Garrison Commander has received intelligence from some Kaffirs that there is a raiding party in the area. He recommends that you remain here over night until he can sweep the line with a patrol in the morning."

"I haven't the time to sit here all night!" grumbled Kitchener. "What about the pilot-engine? Can't it clear ahead?"

"Too risky, sir. The guerillas' methods are much more sophisticated now. It's not just a matter of breaking up the rails which is detectable, but of invisible explosive devices."

"Has the pilot got a truck up front?" asked Kitchener.

"Yes, sir."

"Is it full ... for the weight?"

"I don't know, sir."

"Then check that it's full ... make it as heavy as possible," instructed Kitchener.

Maxwell turned to leave again.

"No; put two laden trucks at the front."

Kitchener rested, oblivious to the hurried activity outside his carriage as the pilot-engine shunted to lock-on to two trucks full of flour sacks. Maxwell rejoined Kitchener and stretched out along a seat.

A gentle shudder indicated that the train was moving forward; it chugged along cautiously at a relatively slow speed.

****

"It's coming!" Henry shook his friends awake; quickly men began to stir, ready to attack the coming train, eager for booty.

The pilot-engine nudged forward gently, feeling its way, anticipating an explosion at every yard.

"There's two of them!" exclaimed Jan.

Everyone knew that this was unusual. The first train was protecting the second. What is it carrying that is so important? Then gradually, through the gloom of the night, they could see that the lead train was pushing two trucks. That confirms it, thought Jacobus, our target is the second train. He felt frustrated at being unable to react to the changed circumstances.

The explosion filled the night. The two trucks disintegrated showering metal, wood and flour into the air – the last hung like a white shroud. Tightening brakes screeched as the driver fought for control; the engine left the track tottering crazily from left to right, before finally coming to rest, spewing steam, but still upright.

Jacobus and the others stood up and watched helplessly as the second train backed down the line. "I wonder who's in that train?" uttered Jacobus aloud, reflecting everyone's thoughts.

****

The outpost had been established for several weeks without attracting any enemy interest. The main position was on ground rising gently from the undulating. It was manned by two companies of Liverpudlians and was protected by two detached posts, each of a half company: one facing west towards Machadodorp, which also sported an obsolete 4.7 gun - lovingly named by its crew, "Lady Roberts" - and one facing east towards Waterval Boven. Each location was protected by shallow trenches built up with stones and sandbags. The task of this outpost was to safely escort convoys laden with stores and provisions en route to Lyndenburg through their area of responsibility, and hand them over to the next secure outpost at Zwartkopjes.

Botha was known to be in the area! Troops slept with boots on, loaded rifles by their side, and accoutrements laid ready immediately outside their tents.

The night was so black it was almost palpable. Suddenly, the moon broke through the clouds with an unusual brightness; there was no sound; no living thing stirred. The sentries were nervous, anxious. They strained to catch the slightest noise: the scraping of boots on stones; the click of a rifle bolt; an unguarded cough. The clouds cast shifting shadows over the veld, turning every bush or boulder into a potential enemy.

Then the moon disappeared and once more the darkness became impenetrable.

****

They left their horses in the care of the young boys; the final approach was on foot. Jacobus and his men were to attack the position which housed the gun. They reached the foot of the incline and silently picked their way upwards. They stopped just short of the summit, pressing their chests to the ground to minimise their silhouette, and waited for the signal to attack. All three positions were to be assaulted simultaneously.

Jan was between his father and Henry. As he lay on the stony ground he could physically feel his heart beating; the sound grew louder and more intense; surely, he thought, the enemy can hear me. He was tensed ready for the fight; coiled like a spring under pressure waiting to be released.

Crack! Crack!

Hearing the prearranged shots they scrambled to their feet and dashed forward. The heads of two sentries were visible behind the wall of sandbags immediately to their front; Jan stopped and fired; a bloody face fell backwards. The other disappeared. They clambered over the meagre defences and sprinted into the camp. Soldiers rolled out of their tents - some half-dressed. Jan moved forward firing as he advanced; he shot a sergeant who was shouting encouragement to his men – the Khaki clasped his stomach and doubled up like a pen-knife. The retort of Henry's rifle by his side confirmed his friend's close proximity. Simultaneously, they ran out of ammunition. They dropped behind a wagon, and prompted by sheer exhilaration and rushing adrenalin, smiled knowingly at each other. Jan snatched a clip of five rounds from his bandolier and rammed it home into the magazine. He cocked the weapon driving a bullet into the breech. It had taken only seconds. A mutual nod and Jan and Henry threw themselves once more into the maelstrom. Together they rushed towards the gun - it stood about fifty yards in depth of the position. The gun-crew had been sleeping around it. They were confused, half asleep, stunned by the suddenness of the attack. They couldn't fire their weapon at such close range into an intermingled mass, and hesitated. Jan fired, a gunner pitched backwards. Henry shot a second; the remaining two gunners quickly raised their hands. Henry pushed passed them ignoring their surrender. Jan followed. They reached the horse lines. One man had mounted bareback and was about to ride off.

"Stop! Stop!" screamed Henry, but the soldier clung onto the horse's mane and violently kicked its flanks. Henry aimed steadily and fired. The rider lurched forward before tumbling heavily to the ground.

Jan looked around; a tense calm was descending. Soldiers milled around, shocked and dazed by the sheer momentum and ferocity of the attack; hands were raised as they awaited orders; some attended to wounded scattered on the ground. The fight was over. The whole affair had taken little more than ten minutes. Jan looked across to the main position, there too the tumult was dying down, but at the other detached post, the fight continued viciously.

Jacobus told-off an escort for those prisoners able to walk: "Round them up and get them to our horse-line. Any of our men too seriously wounded to be moved, are to be placed in the lee of the rise, out of danger's way and left for the Khakis." He noticed questioning stares. "Leaving them here is the only chance that some of our friends have got." He quickly changed the subject, "Now we must get the gun away: Jan, Henry, Noah ..." he detailed a dozen men.

They manhandled the gun off the height and dragged it across the open ground towards their horse-line. Jacobus directed others to remove the two ammunition wagons, but the breaking dawn brought with it a problem. The Liverpudlians in the unsubdued post had direct line of sight to the ammunition, and they were not allowing anyone near it. Every approach invited a tremendous volley - two burghers were killed and several more wounded in the attempt.

It was time to go; delay would bring down English columns. "Leave the ammunition! Back to the horses!" shouted Jacobus.

The Commando coalesced with all three attacking groups combining for the withdrawal. Burghers scouted ahead, whilst others guarded the flanks. In the middle, the main body rode in column as sombre escort to the five dead burghers draped over their horses: they would be returned to their loved ones. Jan, with his father and Henry, formed part of the rearguard in readiness to block a pursing enemy; but they never came.

As the hours went by Jan took pity on the Khaki prisoners - more than two hundred of them. They struggled on under the fierce sun, many without head covering, some helping wounded comrades. The Boer guards were unsympathetic even callous, cracking their whips and shouting abuse in order to drive them along. There was no question of stopping until a safe distance had been placed between the Commando and the Khaki bases. There was no water and food to spare. The soldiers stumbled on: tired, footsore, parched with thirst, ravenous, dispirited. The strong helped the weak; those suffering from the sun and dehydration were slung between the shoulders of comrades. Their pace slackened, slowing down the whole column.

After several hours with the sun now at its zenith, a halt was called and Jacobus joined the other Boer leaders to confer.

"What do we do with the prisoners?" asked one. "We have to move quicker."

"We've no way of feeding them and they're becoming a liability," said another.

"We'll have to let them go," asserted a third.

"Yes, but not until we've had the opportunity to relieve them of their belongings."

Harsh orders to strip were given to the soldiers, who reluctantly complied. Spitting anger and contempt, they piled their clothes and belongings on the ground. "Go! "Go!" they were ordered and released naked and humiliated to walk back to their base amidst a laughing chorus of ridicule, cruel jibes and crudities. As they slowly and painfully dragged themselves towards the distant skyline – some in great distress - the burghers fell on the abandoned clothes like vultures on a carcase. Good boots were in great demand, and Jan soon located a pair which fitted him perfectly.

A good job done. It was time to go home.

CHAPTER 12

No free man (woman) shall be taken or imprisoned or dispossessed, or outlawed or exiled or in any way destroyed.

Magna Carta 1215

EMILY HOBHOUSE
(January – May 1901)

The bare, wooden seat of the second-class railway carriage was hard and uncomfortable, but her heart went out to the soldiers in the open trucks behind who were crammed so tightly that they could not lie down, and who were exposed to the pitiless sun and torrential downpours of a South African summer. As the chugging, military train left the conurbation of Cape Town, Emily Hobhouse gazed out of the window to see the trees full with their leafy garb, and the hilly countryside covered with lush grass and exquisite wild flowers which blossomed in a profusion of colour: fields of white daisies, pink chrysanthemum-like flowers, distinctive but varied proteas. The whole, a natural garden of absorbing beauty. Over all hung a deceptive, restful calm – ominously, every bridge, every culvert, every point at which the line might be cut or blown up, was guarded by a small detachment of bored, bristle-faced soldiers.

After several hours the train struggled up the Hex River pass onto the Great Karoo - a brown, dusty semi-desert which stretched away on each side as far as the eye could see. Only the clusters of small, dusty hills capped with jagged rocks broke the monotonous landscape.

Eventually, the train pulled into a siding and rested by a water tank from which the engine sucked thirstily. During this operation, she alighted from the soporific carriage into the arid air beneath a cloudless sky. There was a smattering of tin buildings. A sign above one of them announced its designation as the refreshment room, but she did not enter. Instead, she stood beneath her parasol on the primitive platform, together with a small gaggle of army officers and officious civilians. All avoided embarrassment by studiously ignoring the rude soldiery who had clambered from their confining trucks to stretch their legs and publicly urinate with bladder-relieving sighs.

Her attention was drawn by noise and movement. She peered down the single track which lifted and danced in the hazy heat. A hospital train approached slowly and slid by, its red cross sun-faded, the side panels of its wooden carriages warped, its paintwork blistered. The soldiers shouted encouragement and comradely obscenities to the passing wounded; at the windows were smiling faces and bandaged waves – men content to be out of the fighting.

• •

On the face of it Emily Hobhouse was a most improbable person to be travelling alone in a theatre of war. In 1860 she had been born in the rectory of St Ives, Cornwall, and lived there for thirty-five years. Her mother died when she was nineteen, and her dominating father's health steadily deteriorated until he became a chronic invalid. Her days and years were spent nursing him, and at his bidding attending to parish affairs. She fell in love with a local farmer's son, but her father disapproved of this demeaning match. The young man abandoned this hopeless relationship and emigrated to America.

When her father died, Emily left the village never to return. She too went to America, to Virginia, Minnesota, at the behest of the Archbishop of Canterbury in order to care for the welfare of Cornish miners working and living there. She met and became engaged to the handsome mayor, John Carr Jackson, who ran a general store. Together they moved to Mexico where they bought a ranch, but the enterprise failed. Her fiancée sank into financial difficulties and then spent all her money, at which point he disappeared. That heralded the end of romantic attachments.

She returned home and found work with the Women's Industrial Council which promoted the interests of women at work.

It was late summer 1900 before Emily read of the hundreds of Boer women and children made homeless by British military operations. She was shocked to read how these families had been deported from the towns were they had collected to seek shelter and sustenance, instead being driven back onto the veld and into the Boer lines. With like-minded friends and supporters she formed The South African Women and Children's Distress Fund: *"To feed, clothe, shelter and rescue women and children, Boer, British or others, who had been rendered destitute and homeless by the destruction of property, deportation, or other incidents of military operations."*

She had been stung by the criticism of her philanthropic initiative from some quarters – there were those who sought to politicise her actions. One prominent clergyman thought that to keep Boer women and children alive might "prolong the war."

She determined to travel to South Africa to see conditions for herself, and to personally distribute the aid. She sailed on 7 December 1900 and arrived in Cape Town on Saint Stephen's Day.

•••

At Norval's Pont, the train rattled slowly and cautiously across the trestle bridge which spanned the Orange River and separated Cape Colony from the recently annexed Boer Republic. The skeleton of the earlier bridge poked out of the brown waters, a monument to the destructive power of dynamite and the audacity of the Boer guerillas. Now having entered the Orange River Colony, evidence of the fighting was widespread. As they approached the station in the small town of Priors, the train slowed to walking pace. Hesitantly, it crept forward on tracks newly laid by the Railway Pioneer Corps. They passed a gang of Native labourers toiling under the sun and singing in melodic unison as they heaved wreckage aside. The old railway line was torn and twisted, coiled up like some huge serpent. Smoking piles marked the place where once stood the railway buildings, while iron frameworks and heaps of smouldering woodwork showed that a passenger train had been totally destroyed in the recent violent cataclysm.

"De Wet," indicated a fellow passenger to Emily.

Emily looked quizzically at the slight woman in her flowery, cotton dress. By her accent she was English; probably a colonist, she thought.

"Yes," volunteered the woman, "the Boer General. He's in charge of all the commandos in what was the Orange Free State. He's forever attacking the railways and capturing wagon convoys. Lord Roberts couldn't catch him, and neither can Lord Kitchener."

Emily smiled politely, and without comment turned away to glance out of the window where the brown desert had given way to the summer-green of the high-veld. She searched the landscape and noticed that not a single farmhouse was intact, only roofless, blackened walls indicated the location of once prosperous farmsteads. Her distressed looks drew further explanation from her new acquaintance:

"They were burnt down because of the attacks on the railway."

"I had heard; but so many?"

"Yes," continued the woman, now enthused at the thought of informing her ignorant companion, "Lord Roberts issued a proclamation stating that all farms within a ten mile radius of an attack are to be destroyed and the families expelled ... a punishment to discourage the others."

"And does it?"

"Does it what?"

"Does it discourage the others?" prodded Emily.

There was a pause; then, "It doesn't seem to."

Emily sank into a disturbed silence and resumed her outwards gaze, making it clear to her would-be friend that the conversation was over.

As they approached the Colony's capital and her destination, Bloemfontein, she reassuringly took from her bag a letter of introduction given to her by the High Commissioner, Sir Alfred Milner. On arrival in Cape Town she had been granted a meeting with him; he had greeted her kindly and proved to be sympathetic with her cause. She sensed that he was very uncomfortable with the policy of farm burning and the dislocation of families, and she had asked for his help to reach the destitute women.

"Martial law has been declared over much of Cape Colony and the ex-Republics, freedom of movement is impossible," explained Milner. "However, I am not averse to you visiting the camps. Also, I am very conscious of the feelings amongst the Dutch Cape Colonists, and I believe it would be appropriate for you to be accompanied by a lady from the Dutch Relief Committee. Of course, Lord Kitchener must agree to your movements. I'll telegram for permission."

The Commander-in-Chief had not sought fit to authorise a Dutch companion, and had limited Emily's movements.

She removed the letter from its envelope, unfolded it, and re-read it for the umpteenth time:

"Dear Miss Hobhouse – I have written to General Pretyman, the Military Governor of the Orange River Colony, asking him to give you any assistance in his power. ... as you are aware Lord Kitchener is not prepared at present to approve of your going farther than Bloemfontein. I do not think that there can be any difficulty about your visiting the camps either there or at any place on the railway south of it. In any case, you can show this letter as evidence that as far as I am concerned such visits are authorised and approved of – Yours very truly."

Lord Milner had kindly provided a truck in which Emily had packed several hundred pounds worth of groceries, clothes and hospital items. With this she reached Bloemfontein on the afternoon of 24 January 1901.

She secured her goods in a station shed and booked into a modest hotel. Without delay she strolled through the town to the Government Buildings – a sprawling, single-storey edifice with a high clock tower – and introduced herself to the Military Governor.

"I received a telegram from Sir Alfred to say that you were on your way," explained Pretyman. "I'm very pleased to meet you. I do hope that your journey was not too tiresome." He discreetly examined this trim, attractive, strong featured woman.

"I believe that two days and two nights on a slow moving train in the summer heat is a necessary discomfort if I am to fulfil my task to the destitute."

"Yes, quite," affirmed Pretyman.

There was a second man hovering in the oak-panelled anti-room who was now introduced, "I would like you to meet Mr Randle. He is the Superintendent of the refugee camp here in Bloemfontein."

A small, bespectacled man in a neat brown suit stepped forward and courteously shook hands, "You are very welcome to visit the camp, and I'm sure that you will find that all is in order. I have here for you a permanent pass to ease your comings and goings."

Emily thanked him.

"And please, Miss Hobhouse," added Pretyman, "should you have any recommendations for improvements, I would be happy to receive them."

The next morning Emily was up early, and after a quick breakfast she strode resolutely to the camp which was a thirty minutes' walk on the outskirts of the town. It had taken so much in effort and time to reach this point, and now, as she neared the tented settlement, she felt apprehensive, anxious,

147

excited; she was about to discover the truth.

She had considered at length what her appropriate response might be. She reflected on the situation and reminded herself that she must not set her standards too high, after all, it was a time of war. There was tremendous pressure on the lines of communication as she had witnessed on her journey. Clearly, there was pressure on supplies, pressure on transports, pressure on the exchequer; in fact pressure everywhere. She must accept the lowest standard of comfort compatible with health, and would spend her funds only on what would nourish, cleanse or give warmth – there could be no unjustifiable luxuries.

She showed her pass to the guard on the gate and entered the barbed-wire enclosure. Unhurriedly, she strolled between the rows of white bell-tents smiling, nodding, politely passing the time of day. Some women eyed her suspiciously – perhaps they did not speak English – others returned her greetings. As she walked, observed and spoke to the inmates, some things were quickly apparent, and others were to emerge in the following weeks spent with the women and their children.

The shelter was totally inadequate: eight, ten, even twelve people were crammed into a single bell-tent. When fully occupied there was no escape from the fierceness of the sun or dust or rain storms. There was no room to move and the atmosphere inside was indescribable.

The water supply was inadequate with insufficient to meet basic needs. There were few mattresses. Fuel was scanty, and she learnt that it had to be cut by the women from the green scrub on the kopjes, and this was only possible when passes were issued which sometimes was problematic.

The food rations were slight; daily: flour or meal (maize) one pound, meat three quarters of a pound, coffee and sugar one ounce, salt half ounce. Children, and families with male members on commando, received half rations. No vegetables or fruit. Her observations revealed that frequently the actual food distributed did not come up to the official amount, making them starvation scales. The quality of the food was poor, and she was shocked to find that on occasions the meat was putrid with serious health implications.

Most disturbing of all was the sanitation. Routinely, unemptied pails stood for long hours in the boiling sun spawning an unpleasant and harmful odour which, on hot still days, hung over the whole camp like an obnoxious shroud.

Despite the atrocious conditions, Emily was surprised by the stoicism of most of the women: "We know it is wartime and we cannot expect much," they said. But she was determined to confront the authorities and bring about improvements.

Mr Randle listened with unconcealed irritation as Emily listed the camp deficiencies and argued for swift changes.

"Soap!" exclaimed Randle, "That's a luxury. Brick boilers for the water … they might be built. The price is prohibitive to lay on a water supply. The food scales are those directed by Lord Kitchener and I have no means to supplement them. Sanitation; some of the women have filthy habits and do nothing to alleviate the situation, but I will seek improvements."

"There are very few refugees who have mattresses," pointed out Emily. "I have funds to purchase covers if you would allow the women to forage for stuffing."

"That won't be possible," asserted the Superintendent. "The veld around the camp is heavily grazed due to insecurity farther afield. The immediate vicinity is bare of grass. I fear there is no other substitute."

Emily decided that she would visit other camps to ascertain conditions there, and for the next two months moved backwards and forwards between Norval's Pont, Aliwal North, Springfontein, Kimberley and Mafeking. Broadly, she found that the same needs prevailed in each. But the situation was to change dramatically for the worse.

Emily sat patiently in the railway carriage grateful to be out of the broiling sun. Summer was on the wane and she eagerly anticipated the cooler autumn weather, but today it was as hot as ever. Her train was delayed whilst another crept into the station; she watched as very slowly it pulled into a parallel siding and stopped. She saw that the occupants were Boer women and children in open trucks and under military guard. They were covered in black dust, witness to the fact that the trucks had previously been used for hauling coal. They were so crowded that not all could sit, never mind lie down to sleep. The women stood or sat impassively, some nursed babies or comforted young children; through her open windows she could hear the cries of the young demanding food and drink - pleas which went unheeded.

Emily sprang from her seat and hurriedly, carefully, picked her way over the tracks to the trucks. She spoke to a dishevelled, dirt-encrusted, middle-aged woman pressed against the side, "What's happening here?"

"Happening?" she replied scornfully. "Our farms have been destroyed and we're to be imprisoned in a camp."

Emily saw her utter exhaustion, "How long have you been travelling?"

"We travelled in ox-wagons for a week, and now two days in these filthy trucks. We're not allowed to leave them for *any* reason; they're foul. We are all soiled. There's not enough water and some have passed out in the heat. We've not been given food since we were herded into these trucks. Sickness is rife, particularly amongst the children. I'm told a baby has died in the following truck."

Emily was shocked into a stunned silence at what she was seeing and hearing. Such callousness was incomprehensible. She burned with anger at those who could so casually inflict such misery and pain.

"Miss Hobhouse! Miss Hobhouse! We're leaving for De Aar with or without you!" It was the conductor from her train.

"Coming! … Coming!"

She looked through tearful eyes at the anguished woman and spluttered, "I'll do all I can to help."

150

Reluctantly, she tore herself away from the desperate scene and re-boarded her train. As it pulled out of the station she looked back at the wretched women and children; the cries of the children haunted her as she collapsed back in her seat. She could do nothing immediately for these families, but perhaps she could plead to the authorities on their behalf.

On her return to Bloemfontein, she found that it was no longer designated a refugee camp, but was now a concentration camp. Its population had doubled in a matter of weeks to nearly four thousand, and was growing daily with the unannounced and unplanned arrival by train and ox-wagon of destitute families. Sickness in the camp was widespread. Those she had left hale and hearty and in reasonable physical condition, were now changed almost beyond recognition. Surely, she reasoned, the authorities must realise that doctors, nurses, above all extra food, clothes and bedding must be poured in to prevent a disaster.

"I estimate that in the deteriorating conditions, the death rate in the camp has risen to twenty percent. Can nothing be done to stop this influx?" she demanded of the newly appointed Deputy Administrator of camps, Major Goold-Adams.

"I believe that all the people in the entire country are to be brought in, with the exception of those in towns on the railway lines." His exasperation was evident. "Since Lord Kitchener began his sweeps and scorched earth policy, we are overwhelmed. We just don't have the resources to cope."

She could see that although he was sympathetic to the plight of the Boer women and children, his humanity was crippled by a lack of means. But then, unpredictably, his mood changed, his warmth chilled.

"You telegraphed to Sir Alfred to request permission to visit the camps in the north?" he questioned forcefully." He did not wait for her confirmation, "He has asked that I pass on his regrets, but your request is refused."

"Did he say why?"

"It is reported that you are showing personal sympathy to the inmates," he explained. "This could be construed as being unpatriotic."

Emily was astonished by the assertion, "Showing sympathy and to help people in trouble; isn't that just what I came to do?"

"It is how you do it. Gifts can be given out without expressing sympathy."

"You mean in a machine-like way? I can't work like that. I treat the people like fellow creatures and share their troubles."

"I still maintain that that is unnecessary." He turned and picked up a letter from his desk, "I have here correspondence from the Military Headquarters in Pretoria. I understand that letters from you criticising our work with the refugees have been read out at a meeting in London. This does not reflect well on our cooperation and undermines our working relationship. In fact, many regard your actions as pro-Boer and by virtue of that fact, anti-British."

"I'm well aware of the meeting to which you allude," defended Emily. "It was a private meeting in my uncle's house of subscribers to the Distress Fund. Naturally, these people require some account of what is being done with their money. It was not a political meeting."

"Yet opposition MPs such as Lloyd George are quoting your letters in attacks on the Government."

"That is not of my doing," she protested.

She had recently had sight of The Times dated 2 March 1901, in which the Secretary of State for War, St John Broderick, had quoted Lord Kitchener in assuring the House of Commons that all the people in the camps had "a sufficient allowance, and were all comfortable and happy." Furthermore, that "the people came to the camps for protection, and those who came might go." It was lies!

She was further infuriated to read the comments of Dr Conan Doyle who had long left South Africa, but asserted that: "No *money was spared,"* and that: *"Every child under six had a bottle of milk a day."*

She knew the inmates were miserable, under-fed, sick and dying, but to show sympathy was to invite disapproval and condemnation. This sympathy, so needed by a sick and bereaved womanhood, was to be denied them. Disease and death were already loose in their midst. If adequate help was to come in money, kind and working staff, if an immense death-toll was to be averted, it could only be done by a strong warning to the government of the serious state of affairs, and a mandate from England to enforce a more humane and compassionate system.

She reasoned with herself that adequate expenditure would never be forthcoming in South Africa, and so that left her with two options: to stay on and dole out meagre gifts which would only begin to scratch the surface; or to return home and alert the Government and the public to the urgent and massive needs to save the lives of at least the children. She determined to return home.

"Now, We Are Good Friends"

CHAPTER 13

"Lord Roberts burns our houses down;
The women out he drives,
He cannot overcome the men,
So he persecutes the wives."

FW Reitz, State Secretary Transvaal 1899 - 1902

SCORCHED EARTH

The Witbergers answered the call to concentrate at Olifansfontein. Together with the other commandos - several thousand men in total - they awaited Botha's arrival. It was the following day before he rode amongst the assembled burghers, together with his small escort. The Commandant-General remained mounted on his distinctive white stallion, whilst his men gathered around him on foot: expectant, excited. Pretorious, who knew Botha quite well, remarked that he was looking thin, but it was soon evident that he had lost none of his energy and confidence.

From his elevated position, Botha looked across the sea of hardened, tough, unkempt farmers united in their love of country and freedom. He addressed them, not with loud, rousing oratory, but in a firm, calm, assured manner, projecting his voice to the far corners of his audience:

"I have intelligence which tells me that Lord Kitchener has decided to bring the Boers to their knees." There was a swell of angry defiance. He raised his hand for silence. "At this moment around fifty thousand troops are moving along the Johannesburg – Natal railway line, preparing to sweep over the high-veld on a front of over sixty miles. Kitchener's intention is to clear the Eastern Transvaal and then repeat the process elsewhere until we are all dead or captured. We cannot fight the English over open ground when they have such numerical

154

superiority and guns. Instead we will keep just ahead of them, drawing them onto us, but then give way and let them punch into thin air. In this way we will wear them down until we choose to fight them on our terms."

He spoke encouragingly of the righteousness of their cause, and called on God's protection for the Afrikaner Nation, before riding away amidst the vibrant cheers of the farmers.

It was another two days before the Khakis came.

The eastern sky gradually brightened with the rising sun, proclaiming another beautiful day. Jan, with his father and Henry, mounted their horses and anxiously scanned the plain in front of them. There was movement, but only with the intensifying sunlight could they clearly discern the threat. First came a screen of cavalry stretching as far as the eye could see from east to west; behind was a dense mass of marching infantry; then, throwing up huge clouds of dust, came the artillery and supply wagons. Slowly, inexorably, the juggernaut advanced.

Burghers fired cautionary shots at the cavalry who then dropped back to the safety of their regiments. Field guns sprang forward and unlimbered, and soon the air above them was thick with hissing shrapnel.

The explosion tore the world apart; rushing hot air almost unseated Jan. Then all was quiet. He was left with muffled sounds: remote, faint, disembodied. Gradually, through ringing ears the world returned. The curdling shriek of a nearby neighbour penetrated his misty consciousness. Jan watched, horrified, as the man slid from his frantic horse, his body virtually sliced in half by a red-hot sliver of metal.

"Let's go!" shouted Jacobus. He noticed Jan's shaky posture, "Jan, let's go! Let's go!"

They turned their ponies and galloped to the rear with shrapnel raining down - two more men were wounded. They rode hard and away from the immediate danger, before pausing by a spruit to allow their ponies to drink. Jacobus gathered in his neighbours and encouraged them to form another ragged line of resistance. They waited. It was two hours before the pursuing hordes came in sight once more. All along the line, the Boers fired ineffectively on the cavalry screen, which again, with practised drills, parted to allow the artillery to deploy forward. Soon speculative shells tore up the ground around them. Whoosh! The shock-wave of a passing missile lifted the hairs on Jan's neck.

Behind this barrage the weary infantry plodded forward under the hot sun, intent on closing with their illusive enemy. They grew closer.

"Pull back! Pull back!" Jacobus shepherded his men to safety.

This pattern repeated itself until darkness brought respite to both sides.

Flickering camp fires denoted the English lines, but behind them the night sky was aglow with ominous tongues of flame. From their vantage points the Boers peered silently at the spectacle, dreading the worst. What could this mean? With daylight would come the appalling truth.

Jan and the others rose whilst it was still dark and hurriedly made coffee. They stood shivering before their horses anticipating the new day, and waiting for the English to appear. As dawn broke they could see columns of black smoke swirling upwards behind the English line of advance.

A Cape cart came racing towards them. Jacobus intercepted and brought it to a halt. It was driven by a distraught, dishevelled, elderly woman; she could barely speak: "They're burning the farms!" she screamed.

"Who are?" asked Jacobus.

"The Khakis! The English!"

"Why?" quizzed Jacobus in disbelieve.

"Because they say we feed and house the guerillas ... you and the others!"

"And the women and children; what's happening to them?" Jan, Henry and several burghers had gathered around and were anxious for their families.

"They're taking them away?"

"Where to?"

"I don't know. They're putting them onto wagons and taking them away ... and they're killing all the animals and destroying the crops!"

"Are you sure?"

"Of course! I've just seen it! Why would I flee?"

"Where are you going now?" Jacobus asked, genuinely concerned for her welfare.

"To Ermelo; I have family there." With that she tugged the horse's reins and started off at a gallop.

The burghers stood in shocked anger watching the plain before them erupt into a simmering sea of fear and panic. Word was spreading quickly that the English were scorching the country, and the civilian population was on the move. The veld was soon full of ox-wagons and carts of every description carrying women and children, and hastily laden with bedding, pans, food, clothes – whatever was quickly to hand. Herds of cattle and flocks of sheep were driven on by Native servants. Fear distorted the faces of those who were fleeing. The burghers watched helplessly, grieved by the sight of so many distressed women and children: mothers with babes in arms, little ones clinging to their skirts. Eventually, word filtered down from Botha that all displaced persons were to be directed towards the Swaziland border.

"They hope to discourage us," said Jacobus to Jan and Henry. "They want to deny us food and shelter and to make us fearful for our loved ones. They think we'll throw down our arms. But if they think they can intimidate us they're wrong. It'll only make us more determined to fight on to the bitter end." The others strongly concurred, but all hearts were heavy with worry. What of Boaz, Anna and the children?

****

Rodger was feeling much better after a month's recuperation, but was still plagued with occasional debilitating attacks of migraine. He had been classified as unfit for mounted operations, but nonetheless, he was pleased to be back with his old platoon - albeit there were many new faces, replacements for earlier casualties.

He was unhappy and deeply unsettled by his current orders. As the main forces drove eastwards rolling up the enemy, he was tasked to follow in their wake and to destroy the Boer farms. He worried that rather than forcing the enemy into surrendering, it would instead increase hatred and resentment, and fuel a stubborn resistance. He knew that some of his men shared his distaste for the work, but others seemed to delight in the legitimised vandalism of smashing furniture and burning homes.

Yesterday he had come upon the site of the skirmish where he had been wounded - he had identified his old saddle on the vulture-stripped skeleton of his horse. He had been unconscious when taken to the Van den Berg's farm, and blind-folded on leaving, but he sensed he must be close. Already today his platoon had torched three farms; now he felt unease and trepidation as they followed a cattle track towards a gentle crest – his stomach knotted uncontrollably in dread anticipation of what he might find. He stopped. It was the sight he had feared.

Below was a familiar, tranquil rural scene: a white farmhouse nestling in a gentle depression; sprawling outbuildings – including the barn which for six weeks had been his home - a small orchard and neat vegetable garden. There were people moving about. He took out his binoculars: black workers in a crowded sheep pen; a black – was it Josiah?- apparently repairing a plough by the barn door; a young boy feeding hens in the yard; a slim woman wearing a straw boater hanging out washing ... Ruth.

Sergeant Mellish, who had been bringing up the rear,

disturbed his reflections, "Shall I stay and picket the hill whilst yer attend to the farm?"

"No ... not on this occasion. Leave me a section and take the rest. Do what you must." Sergeant Mellish turned to leave. "And sergeant; I don't doubt the menfolk are on commando, but you'll treat the women with all respect."

"Naturally, sir." The sarcasm was lost on Rodger as he renewed his observation.

Rodger watched as the larger part of his platoon trundled down the slope the short distance to the farm. Soon he saw that Mellish was in a vigorous argument with Ruth. The buzz of words carried on the gentle breeze, but were indiscernible. A second woman appeared on the verandah wearing the traditional large, white poke bonnet, Anna. The body language was angry.

"Where are yer men?" demanded Mellish of the women.

"On commando defending our country!" snapped back Ruth.

"Then we'll burn yer farm so the rebels have nowhere to rest and find food. You have ten minutes to pack up yer things and get ready to go. A wagon 'll be along directly."

"You can't do this!" protested Anna. "What of Lord Roberts' proclamation? Only farms within ten miles of an attack are to be destroyed. He stated specifically that a burgher being absent on commando was no justification for burning his house!"

"It's Lord Kitchener who's in command now, and he says we're to burn yer farm ... yer ten minutes is running out!"

"But my grandfather is sick in his bed ... he's almost eighty and can't be moved. You can't burn the house!" pleaded Ruth. She looked fiercely into the Sergeant's eyes; she saw an uncompromising hatred. "For God's sake have pity on an old man who's done you no harm," she implored.

"If yer need help to lift him out, then I'll detail a couple of men," replied Mellish coldly. With that he turned to his soldiers and shouted orders for the systematic destruction of the farm and its livestock.

"Quickly," said Anna to Ruth. The two women rushed inside to find Boaz half out of bed, alarmed by the arrival of the soldiers and the heated commotion. They hurriedly stripped off his night-shirt and dressed him with clothes from his wardrobe. They each held an arm and helped him to walk; he was dizzy, light-headed and almost fainted. On reaching the veranda he slumped heavily into his favourite rocking chair.

"Howway hinny." With that, two soldiers brusquely, but kindly, picked up the chair with Boaz still seated, and set him down fifty yards from the house.

"Adrian, Hannie, go and stay by your grandfather!" shouted Anna.

Anna and Ruth ran back into the house; what to take? It wasn't as if they hadn't previously discussed this scenario, but they just couldn't imagine that the English would be so cruel and heartless to a virtually bed-ridden, old man. They had an implicit trust in God, and a naïve belief in English fairness. Surely, they wouldn't be evicted?

Soldiers followed them into the house: "Time's up hinny." A corporal pushed passed them and with undisguised glee brought his rifle-butt down onto the ivory keys of the grand piano. Other soldiers laughed at the mangled noise and splintering wood. Another opened the piano lid and forced it backwards until it drooped awkwardly on its strained hinges; he then seized a dining chair and drove it into the interior, wrecking the hammers and strings. Some had armed themselves with sledge-hammers and tree-axes from the barn, and with euphoric cries and shouts swung wildly, destroying furniture, smashing crockery, and ripping portraits of stern-looking ancestors from the walls. For them it was great fun.

Ruth stood frozen in shock, unable to grasp the brutal reality of what was happening. She stared unmoving at this malicious destruction. How could it be that the farm, carved out of the wilderness in the face of hostile savages over three generations, was to be obliterated by another civilised nation; by whites who purported to follow the same God? With a jolt she snapped out of her coma-like trance; illusions disappeared. She rushed into the master bedroom and opening a drawer, scooped up a wad of pound notes and pushed them down her blouse.

"I'll take those."

She swung around; it was the odious Sergeant standing in the doorway. "Then you'll have to put your hands into my blouse," challenged Ruth. "Will you add my violation to your other crimes?"

The two antagonists eyed each other angrily. Mellish remembered Lieutenant Borthwick's parting admonition. He hesitated.

"Get out!" he shouted.

Ruth brushed passed him scooping up bedding as she left. She found her mother and two younger siblings standing by her grandfather. They were surrounded by an assorted collection of clothes and food – all that they had been able to gather up in the little time available. Together they watched as soldiers carried hay into the house from the barn, which they stuffed under stacks of furniture piled up in each room. The distinctive smell of paraffin wafted from the house as it was poured generously over the floors and pyres. The fire quickly took hold and flames burst out of the windows and doors with a loud roar; black volumes of smoke billowed upwards. The heat was tremendous, forcing them further back for safety.

Ruth struggled unsuccessfully to fight back the tears of despair which coursed down her cheeks streaking her sooty face. Anna tightly clutched the hands of the two small children, her body visibly shaking as she sobbed quietly. Boaz watched his enemies with no attempt to hide his contempt and disgust. Several times he had beaten the Khakis in battle, but now in his old age and infirmity, he was helpless to defend his family. Inside he boiled with fury.

Ruth wiped away the tears with the sleeve of her blouse. She wouldn't give the Tommies the satisfaction of seeing her beaten. Unconsciously, she stood straight and proud amid the mayhem unfolding around her.

The yard was soon littered with the corpses of chickens and ducks. Ruth watched in disgust as one soldier put his boot on the neck of a goose and hacked at it with his entrenching tool. Others were having sport chasing and bayoneting the pigs which squealed hysterically, almost human-like. The sheep in the pen had already been clubbed to death. She noticed that every fruit tree had been hacked down, and that the vegetable garden was wrecked – the culprit stood nearby boasting a flour-sack filled with booty, smiling, pleased with his handiwork.

She watched incredulously as sacks of flour were hauled from the barn and slit open, the contents spilled onto the earth. Boots ground the maize-flour into the dust. What she couldn't see were her black labourers, under the direction of several soldiers, rounding up the cattle and driving them off to feed a rapacious army - but not before they were driven backwards and forwards over the ripening crops.

She winced visibly when she saw the Sergeant leading Henry's Arab bay from the stable. On his last visit he had left it to recover from a leg wound after it became entangled in barbed wire.

Mellish was thrilled with his find. He had long wanted something better than the hags issued by the army, and here was a prize indeed – a horse as good as any ridden by an officer. The breed was world famous for its speed, endurance and good nature; smaller than most horses, but muscular and physically strong. Boastfully, he paraded it through the yard inviting his subordinates to admire its gleaming, reddish-brown coat and black main. But then he noticed: the animal was limping.

"Damn! It's no bloody good if it can't walk right ne'er mind run … 'ere!" In his angry disappointment he summoned a soldier, "Take it away and shoot it!"

Methodically the soldiers burnt the outbuildings and even the nearby kraals of the Native workers. They waded into the dam and destroyed the puddled-clay walls with axes, and to make sure it was unusable, they threw the bodies of dead sheep into the muddy bottom.

Even as the destruction was underway, a small convoy of ox-wagons lumbered into sight and stopped close to the conflagration. The wagons were full of distressed and miserable victims of earlier farm burnings: women, children, and men too old to fight.

"Climb up you lot!" A soldier indicated a space in the back of one of the vehicles.

Outstretched hands helped Boaz climb up; he slumped onto the dirty wooden floor, the exertion leaving him short of breath and racked with chest pains. Anna wrapped him in a blanket. Hannie and Adrian clambered aboard and snuggled into the reassuring warmth and failing strength of their grandfather. Ruth wrapped the food in a blanket and lifted it up to her mother.

"You won't need that," said Mellish snatching it from her. "Wer yer goin' everything is provided: plenty of food, good accommodation, new clothes. Yer don't need nowt. You'll live the life of Riley."

Ruth hesitated unbelievingly. She stared at him feeling vulnerable and intimidated by his malicious grin.

"Where's your officer?" she demanded. "Why are you allowed to treat us like this?"

"Mr Borthwick's watching to make sure yer rebels don't interfere with us. It's no use appealing to 'im. I'm in charge 'ere. Now get on hinny," he said threateningly. "Don't cross me twice."

As the wagons pulled away swaying tortuously, Ruth looked at the silhouette on the skyline. Throughout their ordeal he had remained there a spectator, statue-like, callous and impervious to their suffering. A coward who sent others to do his dirty work.

As dusk approached it began to rain. Soon everyone was

soaked. Even those in wagons fortunate enough to have buck-sails fared no better, for every one of them leaked. With darkness the convoy halted. The Native drivers and leaders were inexperienced and knew little about the care of oxen. The animals were not released to graze, but instead remained tied to the yoke standing unhappily in the mud.

Ruth quickly realised that the escorting soldiers were colonials – Australians – who were bored by their demeaning task and cared little for their charges. No food or water was issued. Indeed, the black wagon driver insisted that it was his passengers' role to feed him. From the scraps secreted away someone gave him a piece of bread and some cheese, for which he agreed to walk almost a mile to fetch water from a spruit which they had passed earlier. It rained on and off throughout the night; children cried or whimpered incessantly and could not be consoled by their mothers. Everyone was cold, hungry, miserable and heart-broken.

With dawn the trek continued. The land was desolate, littered with scorched ruins and the sweet- sickly smell of thousands of rotting corpses of slaughtered sheep and cattle. No halt was made. No food distributed. It continued to rain.

At 9 pm on the second day a halt was called. A leg of mutton was rudely tossed into the back of the wagon by a mounted guard as he trotted past. How to cook it? A pan was procured and the driver was again persuaded to find water. A number of planks were prised from the wagon to supplement gathered brush-wood and a fire made. Eventually the meat was boiled and shared as fairly as circumstances permitted. The cooking water made a weak soup and was fed to the most vulnerable. Anna took some in a tin and gently poured it between Boaz's lips. He was shivering, pale, and most worrying of all, coughing up blood.

The wagon's occupants became particularly concerned for a young woman of perhaps eighteen years of age, who tightly clasped a baby wrapped in a thick shawl. She was struggling to breast-feed; her milk had dried up. There was a desperate appeal around the wagons which produced a single tin of condensed milk. The young mother, aided by two female relatives, tried with little success to dribble the liquid down the baby's throat.

The ground was too wet and muddy to lie on, but not everyone could stretch out in the back of the wagon; some sat leaning against the side. Exhaustion encouraged patchy sleep.

With the first streaks of light Anna, Ruth and the other women and girls briefly wandered away from the wagons, for no arrangements for their privacy and convenience were made during the day.

The sun shone and with it spirits rose slightly. In the afternoon the column halted at a small mission station, and there the women had the opportunity to buy a few vegetables - two tins of condensed milk were procured for the baby. Ruth managed to pick up a cooking pot and several utensils.

The trek resumed. The oxen were weak and distressed from lack of grazing, rest and proper care. One collapsed. The wagon shuddered to a halt. The driver wielded his thirty foot whip and lashed the back and flanks of the stricken animal, but nothing could make it stir. He was joined by other drivers, and together they dragged the ox to the side of the track; a soldier put his carbine behind its ear and shot it dead.

"Let's get moving! And close up!" ordered the officer in charge.

They suffered two more days of trekking which were punctuated more and more by halts as worn-out and abused oxen collapsed in their yokes and had to be disposed of. It was the wettest summer for many years. All were soaked, soiled, without a change of clothes and fed only occasionally. Infrequently, tins of bully beef were tossed into the wagons together with packets of hard biscuits – saltless things made of coarse meal and hard as a stone. Illness was now rife. Several children developed diarrhoea which drained them of strength and exacerbated the hygiene problems. Anna and Ruth were increasingly concerned about Boaz's deteriorating health. He

165

was growing weaker, shivering almost constantly, short of breath, coughing and spitting blood. They knew that he desperately needed warmth, rest and strong, nutritious broths. They tucked his damp blanket around him, hopelessly trying to keep him warm; they prayed for their arrival and the end of this nightmarish journey.

At last they approached the small railway town of Middleburg. They stopped about a mile short of the settlement outside the gate to a temporary camp. It was delineated by two parallel barbed wire fences in-filled with coiled wire. Military guards patrolled the perimeter with rifles slung over their shoulders. It was a depressing scene.

"Get down and take all your things with you!" shouted the colonials. They were clearly eager to be away with their wagons. The passengers descended stiffly, and could only watch with dismay as the wagon drivers threw their meagre belongings into the mud. The surviving sick and weary oxen trudged away.

They were left waiting outside the gates under the silent watch of the sentries. The leaden and gloomy skies discharged a fine, cold, persistent drizzle. Anna held on to Hannie and Adrian, whilst Ruth comforted Boaz who sat listlessly on the wet ground. Close by, the young, traumatised mother clung tenaciously to her silent, motionless bundle, aggressively rejecting all help and unable to contemplate the sad, unbearable truth.

They waited. They shivered. Time passed.

At last the gates swung open and disgruntled Boer orderlies emerged: "No one told us you were coming ... this way," they commanded, indifferent to the sufferings of the new arrivals. Ruth was to learn that these were hands-uppers, burghers who had surrendered to the British and taken an oath of neutrality; they were despised by the other inmates.

The sorry party shuffled through the gate carrying their few belongings. Boaz, by now unable to walk unaided, was assisted by two orderlies.

They entered a sea of white, military bell-tents laid out in untidy rows. As they walked between them, grey, gaunt faces stared out at the newcomers through half-raised flaps.

"This is your tent," indicated the orderly.

Ruth pulled back the flap to expose an emptiness: the sides had no lining for warmth and rain dripped through the soaked canvas; the floor was bare and muddy; there was not a stick of furniture, not even a bed for her grandfather.

"This can't be right!" she exclaimed in horror. "We've been driven from our beautiful house with every comfort to this wretched tent! We must have beds ... my grandfather is sick ... we need waterproof covering for the floor ..." She paused, consumed with disbelief.

"You gets the same as everyone else," stated the guide flatly.

"And food?" enquired Anna.

"Well, today's Saturday. Rations are issued on Mondays."

"And what are we to eat in the meantime?"

The guide shrugged disinterestedly.

"The doctor? When will the doctor see my grandfather?" pleaded Ruth.

"Tomorrow if you can find him, but he doesn't normally visit the camp on Sundays."

Anna spread their only blanket on the wet floor, and the orderlies lowered Boaz onto it, and then quickly disappeared. Hannie and Adrian tucked into their mother's skirt seeking comfort. They were cold, pale, hungry and sickly.

"Can I have something to eat?" appealed Hannie.

Anna wept.

CHAPTER 14

He who wills the end, wills the means.

R South "Twelve Sermons" 1692

BLOCKHOUSES

The bell on the mahogany, long-case, grandfather clock struck five, echoing through the quiet calm of the house. Dawn was still an hour away.

Kitchener and Major Jimmy Watson, his senior ADC, emerged from their bedrooms wearing dressing gowns, unshaven and with tousled hair. Captain Maxwell had been busy for a couple of hours deciphering and arranging the telegrams received during the night from the many column commanders and elsewhere. He put aside those unconnected with operations – they could be attended to later.

"Good morning, Brat," said Kitchener curtly. "I take it all is prepared?"

"Yes, sir, as normal." Captain Frank Maxwell was another ADC personally selected by Kitchener. This twenty-nine year old cavalry officer had recently won the Victoria Cross. He was full of charm and of perfect manners, with a great sense of humour. He looked deceivingly young, and within days of his appointment, Kitchener had nicknamed him "the Brat".

Kitchener grabbed a handful of telegrams and crawled over the maps laid on the dining-room floor. Careful he plotted the location of each column and marked it with a little red flag. Soon the pattern of deployment was apparent. He had been thinking through the next moves during the night, and retained all the details in his head. He was loath to discuss his plans with his subordinates, and was cautious about allowing them too much discretion – everything must be tightly controlled. He began to tersely dictate explicit orders to Maxwell for conveyance to his field commanders: "Gough is to make for Heidelberg and entrain for Volksrust. Lawson is to halt where he is. Haig is to march to Carletonville ..."

After dealing with the operational telegrams he disappeared to shave and dress. At 6:30 a.m. prompt, he re-entered the dining room - now re-arranged for breakfast by the servants. As he strode towards the table he glanced at a vase of freshly-cut flowers standing on a chest of drawers: a colourful array of lilies nestling among gerberas and roses. He paused, then approached the flowers; gently he removed two lilies and repositioned them within the display. He then took a pace backwards and studied his handiwork. "Much more balanced," he commented to no-one in particular. Satisfied with his floral artistry, he joined his small personal staff who sat patiently, respectfully, familiar with their boss' foibles.

Kitchener was exasperated by the illusiveness of the Boers who dissipated before his sweeps; he was anxious at the apparent ineffectiveness of his current tactics. As he ate, he voiced his concerns, "The Boers have divided into small parties of three to four hundred men and are scattered all over the veld without apparent plans and without hope. On the approach of our troops they disperse to reassemble in the same neighbourhood when our men pass on. In this way they continue an obstinate resistance without retaining anything, or defending the smallest portion of this vast country."

"It appears that they fight where and when they wish, so retaining the initiative," concurred Maxwell.

"The problem," observed Watson, "is that there are no natural boundaries such as mountains or rivers against which they can be driven. What's needed is to be able to divide the country into better defined areas within which we can destroy the commandos."

"Lord Roberts instigated the building of blockhouses at vulnerable points along the railway line between Cape Town and Bloemfontein, and between them he constructed sangars," Major Birdwood reminded them all - a Bengal Lancer and now

Kitchener's Deputy Assistant Adjutant-General (DAAG). "Not only has this protected the railway line, but reports indicate that it is prohibitive to Boer movement. Now if we were to expand this idea to include all railway lines, and even across the veld, we could build our own barriers and divide the country into manageable segments."

Quickly Kitchener's mind raced with possibilities. He could visualise lines of fortified blockhouses dividing the country into small areas within which he could concentrate columns swiftly by train, and drive the Boers against these artificial obstacles. He aired his vision excitedly, "We could use the blockhouses as stoppers, and rather as beaters in a grouse shoot, drive the birds against the butts."

"Exactly!" exclaimed Birdwood.

"I'm sorry to pour cold water over this idea," interrupted Maxwell, "but it takes about three months to build a stone blockhouse at a cost of around one thousand pounds. We would need thousands of blockhouses."

This injection of reality brought the rising enthusiasm to a sharp halt. Kitchener pondered for a few moments before eyeing Maxwell, "Brat, give the problem of designing a cheap blockhouse which can be quickly constructed to the Royal Engineers. They should consider the possibility of prefabrication ... it's an operational priority."

Breakfast over, Kitchener retired to his office for his daily meetings with his department heads.

It was almost two weeks later as Kitchener was dismounting after his routine afternoon ride, that he was met by an exuberant Maxwell, "Sir, there is a Major Rice of the 23rd Field Company Royal Engineers waiting to brief you on his idea for blockhouses. I think you'll approve!"

"Bring him to my office." With that Kitchener marched into the house.

Rice was shown into an office which smacked of administrative chaos: papers and files littered every available surface. He saluted and nervously awaited permission to speak, overawed by the presence of the revered but much feared Commander-in-Chief.

"You have something of interest for me?" Kitchener peered from behind his desk.

"Yes, sir, I have designed a blockhouse which I believe will fit your requirements."

"Please explain," encouraged Kitchener.

"Well, sir; the principle is quite simple. The blockhouse comprises two cylinders of corrugated iron about six feet high, one being two feet smaller in diameter than the other. The smaller is placed inside the larger, and the gap between them is filled with gravel and stones. There is a four foot door, and we punch a dozen loopholes around the sides. Finally, we add an overhanging pitch roof."

"I see." Kitchener was attentive; his interest aroused. He had a couple of questions: "How long does it take to construct and at what cost?"

"Once the foundations are in place it takes one day to build. The cost is less than twenty pounds."

"Excellent! Excellent! Well done Major! One final point: can these blockhouses withstand artillery fire?"

"No sir, but I understand that the Boers have few guns and little ammunition."

Kitchener dismissed Rice with his thanks and summoned his staff; he briefed them on the proposed blockhouses. "How many of them will we need?" he asked.

"We must first determine the precise routes of these fortified lines," advised Watson, "but our preliminary estimate suggests we will need to cover between three and four thousand miles. At first we might place the blockhouses a mile apart, but then we would need to fill in the gaps to only a few hundred yards. That will mean that every blockhouse will be protected by those on its flanks, and that no blockhouse can be attacked in isolation."

"Numbers?" probed Kitchener.

"At least eight thousand."

"To truly be a fortified line we must connect the blockhouses with barbed wire and trenches," added Maxwell.

All agreed.

"Already I am desperate for sufficient troops to fill the attacking columns. How will we find more to man the blockhouses?" quizzed Kitchener.

"Firstly, we could use some of the infantry who are pretty ineffectual at chasing mounted Boers, but there is another source of man-power," suggested Birdwood. "As we clear the veld of farms and kraals, we have an increasing number of Kaffirs stagnating in the concentration camps. We could use those."

"But we would have to arm them!" cautioned Maxwell

"Yes, of course," affirmed Birdwood.

"Such a move would cause outrage amongst the Boers, reminded Maxwell. "Nothing incenses them more than the idea of armed blacks. This would drive a coach and horses through our tacit agreement to make this a white man's war."

Kitchener studiously ignored the protestation. With brimming confidence he declared, "Gentlemen, the way forward is clear at last: scorched earth, internment, containment, destruction. We will defeat Johnny Boer."

CHAPTER 15

The concessions of the weak are the concessions of fear.

Edmund Burke (On conciliation with America 1775)

MIDDLEBURG PEACE TALKS
(28 February 1901)

The Indian servant showed her into the drawing room, "His Excellency will be a few moments. Please take a seat. Can I get you tea?"

"Thank you."

The servant withdrew leaving her alone. She was familiar with the room's overt opulence, and wandered around browsing idly. The walls, decorated with flower wall-paper, were cluttered with contemporary English art mounted in bold, ornate, gold frames. She stood and admired an oil painting depicting a trout fisherman in an idyllic country scene; she peered at the signature: H. J. Boddington. She was attracted by a set of porcelain figures standing on a mahogany drum-table in the curve of a bay window, and sauntered over to them.

The door opened and the servant returned carrying a silver tray with china cups and tea pot. He placed it on a low table, "Shall I pour, madam?"

"Thank you, but I will await Lord Kitchener."

"Certainly madam." He withdrew leaving her alone.

Moments later another door opened on the far side of the room, and in strode Kitchener, "Good morning Mrs Botha. It's always a pleasure to see you." He noticed that she was standing by the porcelain figures, "They are very attractive pieces don't you think? - the stocking mender and the hairdresser." Clearly animated by the subject he explained, "The artist was French, Etienne-Maurice. The pieces were initially made in the 1770s in the Derby Porcelain Factory, and then reissued between 1830 and 1835. Those pieces are of the later manufacture ...

173

unfortunately, not mine; as you know I'm only a temporary resident here, but my landlord, Mr George Heys, has very good taste."

"I didn't know that you were such an expert in porcelain, your Excellency."

"Not an expert, but I do have a keen interest." He smiled uncharacteristically, "My sister, Emilie, used to joke that it was the feminine side of me. Please sit down and take tea."

They both moved towards settees around a low table; instinctively, Mrs Botha took up the teapot and poured, handing him the cup.

"Thank you," said Kitchener. "I must be careful not to relate your kindness or your people may accuse you of fraternising with the enemy."

Mrs Botha detected an embryonic smile which she returned more openly. Annie Botha was South African born, but of Irish blood. Her descendent, Robert Emmet, was an Irish Protestant and nationalist, who led an abortive rebellion against British rule in 1803. He was captured and executed for high treason. From her early years, Mrs Botha had showed daring and independence, running away from a loveless, planned marriage to become a pupil-teacher at a well-known school in Bloemfontein. She married her brother's friend and thrived as a pioneer on the wildest frontier of an infant Republic. She was brave and tough, but despite being a mother of four and in her mid-thirties, she remained attractive, graceful, charming, full of sparkling wit and humour.

"I once had an attractive house, not lavish like this of course ... but regrettably, your soldiers burnt it down." She said this without malice, but could not prevent her thoughts momentarily wandering to the once capacious house which stood by a river with its planted lines of trees laid out along the avenues of approach. It had rung with the laughter of growing children and the boisterous noise of visiting friends and neighbours. Inside it had been full of old family treasures and portraits, and all those things which make for a warm and beautiful home. Now it was a heap of ashes. "Today I must live in cramped rooms in a rented house." She looked pointedly at her host.

"The exigencies of war, madam." The atmosphere noticeably cooled. "So tell me, how can I be of assistance?"

"I wish to visit my husband on the veld, and once again I must request a letter from you granting safe passage."

"And how is your husband?" enquired Kitchener.

"Surely, your Excellency, you don't expect me to give away secrets?"

"Madam, you and your lady friends give away my secrets every day. You go out of your way to befriend my staff and hang on their unguarded talk. You watch the comings and goings of my troops and relay this information to your husband. Perhaps I was seeking a little quid pro quo?"

"Then I must respond. General Botha is in rude health; and I thank you for your kind enquiry."

"I understand that your son has joined his father. At nine years old isn't he a little young to be on commando? I would much regret should he be injured in any way by my soldiers' actions."

"There are those who believe that you are never too young to fight for freedom."

"But need we fight?" countered Kitchener. He had quickly come to realise that this messy war would bring him no honour and was sick of it. There would be no clear victories and accolades, just the wearing down of a stubborn, brave enemy by the ruining of a country and the mass displacement of women and children. He wanted to end this war as quickly as possible and move on to his next chosen advancement. He had already agreed with Broderick at the War Office that he would take up the post of Commander-in-Chief India, but not whilst he was embroiled in this distasteful fight. He looked at this strong woman and continued, "This war will leave the country desolate, the Afrikaner Nation decimated. Already we have tens of thousands of burghers incarcerated on St Helena and in

Ceylon ... they may never be allowed to return. I believe the time is opportune to talk of peace."

"And this is what you want me to convey to my husband? Do you have a proposal for me to deliver?"

"No proposals, madam; just a willingness to talk of peace, but *not*," he emphasised, "of independence."

"And what if peace is not enough?"

"Then the war will continue."

....

Botha was accompanied by the Acting-President's Secretary, Mr Van Veldon and his own Military Secretary, Mr De Wet. Despite the difficult circumstances in which they were living, they had made a concerted effort to ensure a good appearance. Botha wore a clean tunic, riding breeches, shining boots and a slouch hat turned up on one side - he had even used scarce soap to wash his white stallion. Now he waited as the English escort rode out to meet them at the agreed rendezvous three miles south-east of Middleburg.

Kitchener's drive in the Eastern Transvaal had disrupted his plans to invade Natal and placed his commandos under great pressure. They had been forced onto the defensive by the predatory columns which were sweeping all before them and denuding the veld. A great slab of the country had been subjected to the terror of war. His casualties had been high with nearly four hundred burghers killed, and almost one thousand captured. In the Orange Free State, De Wet had been neutralized and was desperately trying to avoid encirclement and capture. It was in times like this that he could be plagued by bouts of doubt, depression and lack of self-belief. But he found solace in the knowledge that despite their temporary advantage, the English were despairing of ever winning this war, and were anxious to coax him into surrender. If the terms on offer were favourable then he had nothing to lose; and if not, then he would hold out for more.

The military escort halted fifty yards short; Major Watson

trotted forward alone. He saluted, "Sir, I presume I have the honour of addressing General Botha?"

"Yes, Major, you have."

"Sir, I have orders to escort you to Lord Kitchener."

"Then lead on."

A trot became a canter, then Botha mischievously broke into a gallop leaving the bewildered soldiers to follow. As they approached the small town, he slowed down once again, allowing the escort to draw alongside and so permit a more dignified entry. The escort stopped outside a modest house with Dutch gables, the residence of General Lyttleton who was away on business in the Cape, and which had been temporarily commandeered by Kitchener. As they all dismounted, the Boers' horses were taken by waiting grooms, and Kitchener strode out to meet them.

"Welcome General." Kitchener took Botha by the arm and detached him from the others. He led him firmly into the house, through an inner door and into a lounge of heavy oak furniture; odours of tobacco and charcoal permeated the atmosphere. "Your staff will be well cared for ... we'll meet them again during lunch, but I thought we should talk freely without inhibition. Do you agree?"

"Yes, of course."

The two men discreetly took stock of each other, like boxers in the ring weighing up their opponent. Kitchener was favourably impressed by a pleasing expression and the quiet authoritative manner of this Boer General. Botha knew of Kitchener's reputation as a hard, cold, calculating officer, but saw before him a man trying earnestly to be respectful, relaxed, even convivial. He noted the black arm-band worn on the right arm of Kitchener's khaki uniform, and remembered that the old lady, Queen Victoria, had recently died.

"Tea General?"

"Where would you English be without your tea - even on the hottest day?"

"The very foundations of the Empire are built on tea,"

quipped Kitchener.

They both paused whilst a servant, who had been hovering discreetly in the shadows, served them. "You can go now," ordered Kitchener. The door closed behind the servant leaving the two Generals alone.

The preliminaries over, Botha lost no time in opening the negotiations, "You will understand your Excellency, that the independence of the two Republics is the primary and essential condition for any compromise."

Kitchener was a little taken aback at this opening gambit, after all he had made it clear through Mrs Botha that independence was not on the table, "His Majesty's Government never could or would assent to a restoration of Boer independence, but would be prepared to make a number of recommendations. Sir Alfred Milner has been appointed Governor of the Transvaal, it would be as well for you to meet him."

"I have no wish to see that man!" retorted Botha sharply.

"Why not, he's such a nice person?"

"That may be, but I decline to have anything to do with him."

"Surely, General Botha, you are strongly prejudiced against him, probably because you don't know him. Once you get to know him you will certainly alter your opinion."

"No, sir! I am too familiar with recent South African history, and probably know considerably more than even your Excellency of Sir Alfred's acts and opinions. The fact is that I, and every other of my Afrikaner compatriots, have lost faith in Milner, whom we regard as the man of all men who has done most to bring about this present trouble." He continued in quiet exasperation, "I am astonished that the British Government should be so singularly tactless as to install at the head of affairs this man who has done nothing but sow hatred and create race rancour among the two white peoples of South Africa, when it was obviously the intention and aim of British policy to conciliate the two races."

Kitchener well knew that the Boers blamed Milner for the

collapse of the negotiations in Bloemfontein which immediately preceded the war. He was not going to penetrate this wall of hatred and decided to move swiftly on, "Tell me General, what if we were to agree proposals which are acceptable to my Government, but not agreeable to President Steyn and General De Wet of the Orange River Colony. Would the Transvaalers stop fighting?"

"No," declared Botha emphatically. "We commenced this war together, and we will continue and end it together."

They both sipped their tea in uncomfortable silence.

Eventually, "Would you like some more?" offered Kitchener.

"No thank you." Botha hesitated for a moment, then looked his opponent in the eyes, "I must protest at the maltreatment of the women and children of those burghers still fighting, and the burning of farms, and the thousand and one other useless acts of vandalism and cruelty."

"But every Boer farmhouse appears to be a Boer commissariat. Under the circumstances I have no choice but to deport the families, who, I believe, are very fairly treated."

"Is it fair to forceably deport the old, the weak, the infirm. And I must protest at the ill-treatment of our women by Kaffirs who accompany the English troops."

"No reports of ill-treatment have reached my headquarters, but I will investigate any incidents where my soldiers may have been over-zealous in carrying out their duties."

Botha was not convinced by this half-hearted promise. He drove home his fears, "The treatment of our women and children in the concentration camps is inhuman; the mortality rate amongst children is worrying. I would plead for more food and better medical care."

"We afford all possible care to the Boer families that the exigencies of the situation permit. You will appreciate that the frequent disruption of our lines of communication by your commandos restricts the supplies available. We must lay down strict priorities for the conduct of the war. But I too must protest," countered Kitchener, "of the Boer practice of putting pressure on burghers who have surrendered and taken the oath of neutrality, to rejoin commandos."

"I am entitled by law to force every man to join," stressed Botha, "and if they do not do so, to confiscate their property and leave their families on the veld."

"Then as long as you continue to force unwilling and peaceful inhabitants to join your commandos - a proceeding totally unauthorized by the recognised customs of war - I have no other course open to me, and am forced to take the very unpleasant and repugnant steps of bringing in the women and children."

Kitchener was anxious to move away from this exchange of grievances and to cover matters more pertinent to a possible peace. He deliberately changed the thrust of the conversation, "Let me explain the nature of any future administration. In the first instance there would be a period of military Government until all was settled and peaceful. This would be replaced by Crown Colony Government. In the course of time there would be full representative government ... a self-governing colony."

"And how long would the process take?"

"Perhaps three to five years."

"And the Native franchise? Don't forget, we have long experience of the barbarism of the blacks. The two white races must be the sole arbiters of the country's future."

Kitchener was fully aware of the sensitivity of this subject. The thought of the native majority receiving the franchise was anathema to the Afrikaner. "The subject of the black franchise can be delayed until after the implementation of self-government. I am sure the franchise could be managed to secure the just predominance of the white races."

Botha was greatly relieved to hear that. They went on to cover many important topics such as the use of the Dutch and English language in administration and schools, the payment of war debts and financial grants for the reconstruction of farms; pleasingly there appeared to be much overlapping and agreement of ideas. There was a short break for lunch when they were joined by both staffs. Conversation was restrained and stilted, but given the circumstances, the atmosphere remained affable.

When once again alone, Botha raised what he knew to be a contentious subject, "There must be a general amnesty for the Dutch colonials from Natal and the Cape who joined the Boer Republics in our struggle," he insisted.

"These men are subjects of the Crown who took up arms against their own government," pointed out Kitchener. "In the eyes of the law they are rebels guilty of high treason. However, I would imagine that all but the leaders would be pardoned, perhaps with the loss of their franchise. The leaders would be subject to the law, although I would not envisage the implementation of the death penalty."

"Let it be understood," stressed Botha, "these are men who have fought by our side for our freedom and independence, and we will not abandon them."

Kitchener nodded his understanding.

As the two Generals negotiated throughout the afternoon, there developed a growing respect between them: men of mutual understanding, sharing a common profession, serving their governments and people. Finally, after a long day Kitchener brought the discussion to an end,

"Let us submit our agreed proposals to our respective governments and await the outcome."

"This way gentlemen." Watson sensitively coaxed the Generals into the garden to join their waiting staffs, and arranged everyone for a photograph. He knew that Kitchener was unhappy about this, but he had been able to convince him of the necessity to record such an important event for future generations. Everyone looked stiffly towards the camera mounted on its tripod. The photographer disappeared beneath his black cloth to peer down the lens; he reappeared, "Kindly be still gentlemen." And with a flash of magnesium and a cloud of smoke, the moment was captured for posterity.

Botha and Kitchener shook hands with something akin to warmth.

As the sun waned, Watson conducted the Boers through the British lines back into the fastness of the veld. He saluted as the white stallion cantered towards the horizon.

••• • •

Kitchener met with Milner in the railway station at Bloemfontein to discuss the terms before despatching them to the British Government. Privately, Milner felt totally opposed to any peace terms with these bandits. There could be no compromise, only unconditional surrender. He visualised the creation of a new South African Crown Colony over which he would rule as an imperial pro-consul, just like Lord Cromer in India.

Whilst there was general agreement between the two men, much to Kitchener's chagrin, Milner watered down several of the negotiated terms, such as substituting loans for grants for farm reconstruction. But most telling of all was his insistence that the Afrikaner rebels from Natal and the Cape be tried as traitors under the full weight of law. "To do less," he maintained, "would have a deplorable effect in Cape Colony and Natal." Kitchener was dismayed when the British government subsequently endorsed Milner's stance.

****

The heavy sense of desolation and hopelessness which had permeated Botha's feelings over recent weeks, lifted like a bright sun following a tumultuous storm. He received news from the Orange Free State that De Wet had escaped the clutches of pursuing columns, and was once again on the offensive. In the Eastern Transvaal the great drive against his commandos had sunk into the mud following days of torrential rain, which heralded the collapse of the British supply chain. The majority of his burghers had managed to slip through or around the chaotic British lines, and safely occupied the empty spaces behind the enemy. Further, he had been sharply censored by President Steyn and De Wet for even talking with Kitchener, and many of his commanders had made it clear that they were not ready to give up their goal of independence for a vague promise of self-government sometime in an uncertain future.

He studied the document forwarded to him by Kitchener which outlined the British Government's conditions for peace. They demanded a complete cessation of all Boer actions before official negotiations could begin – a smoke-screen for unconditional surrender. And how could they abandon their compatriots from Natal and the Cape to be tried as traitors? Honour demanded that they stood by them. He called one of his aides, "Prepare gallopers; shortly I will have messages to be delivered to Lord Kitchener and my field Generals." He began to write, firstly to his Generals:

"Lord Kitchener's proposals contain nothing more, but rather less than what the British Government will be obliged to do should our cause go wrong. Since nothing worse than this can befall us, it is well worth while to fight on ... Let us, as Daniel in the lion's den, place our trust in God alone; for in His time and in His way He will certainly give us deliverance."

****

Maxwell knocked on the door of Kitchener's office and sidled in. He handed over the eagerly awaited letter from Botha. Kitchener slit the top of the envelope with a bone letter-opener and silently read its contents:

"I, and the Boer Governments to which I have communicated the terms, do not feel disposed to accept the proposals."

He could not contain his disappointment and frustration.

183

Angrily he stood up, his chair scraping noisily across the floor as he pushed it back. He paced the room, "I did all in my power to urge Milner to change his views, which seemed to me very narrow on the subject … Milner's views may be strictly just, but to my mind they are vindictive. I do not know of a case in history where, under similar circumstances, an amnesty has not been granted. We are now carrying on the war to be able to put two to three thousand Dutchmen in prison at the end of it. It seems to me to be absurd."

CHAPTER 16

Cruelty in war buyeth conquest at the dearest price.

Sir Philip Sydney – Poet, Scholar & Soldier 1554 -1586

MIDDLEBURG CONCENTRATION CAMP

Every breath brought sharp pains to his chest. He was racked with violent spasms of coughing, and spat out bloody phlegm. He felt increasingly light-headed, dizzy, and became prone to fainting. His injured leg swelled beyond use. Within two days of arriving at the camp, Boaz was dead.

Ruth joined the queue of distraught women outside the superintendent's office by the main gate, and when her turn came requested a coffin and transport to the cemetery. The clerk was sneering and unsympathetic.

"We don't 'ave any coffins. But I can sell you some wood and you can pay one of the orderlies to knock one up for you."

"And transport to the cemetery?"

"You can 'ave use of a cart, but you'll 'ave to pull it yerself, or …," the clerk paused for a moment as if gathering a helpful thought, " … for a small fee I can arrange the hire of a hearse from Middleburg … cost three pounds."

So Boaz was placed in a rough coffin made from bits of candle and soap boxes bought at exorbitant prices. The family and near neighbours from Witberg, solemnly followed the hearse to the nearby temporary cemetery, which was quickly filling up, and laid him to rest in his beloved veld. There was no minister of religion available and no formal service. Ruth borrowed a Bible, and by the grave-side read scriptures familiar on such occasions:

"To every thing there is a season, and a time to every purpose under heaven:

185

*A time to be born, and a time to die: a time to plant,
and a time to pluck up that which is planted;*
*A time to kill, and a time to heal; a time to break down,
and a time to build up:*
*A time to weep, and a time to laugh: a time to mourn,
and a time to dance ..."*

The food in the camp was totally inadequate, and even more so
for the likes of the Van den Bergs, for with their menfolk "on
commando" they were classified as "undesirables" and only
qualified for half of the already minimal rations. A local
contractor supplied the food and was motivated totally by
profit with callous disregard for the welfare of the camp
inmates. The flour was adulterated and a habitat for beetles and
weevils; meat was butchered from sheep which were so sickly
and thin that they resembled lean greyhounds – frequently it
was putrid and had to be thrown away; so-called coffee was
ground acorns, and the sugar was sweepings from the
warehouse. The only other item provided was a little salt.
Nutrition levels were low; diarrhoea was prevalent.

Fortunately, Ruth had some money with which to supplement
these meagre rations from a store established in the camp for
those who could afford to do so - prices were at least double
the norm. But the funeral had been costly and their nest-egg
would not last forever. The face of the future was all around
them as they watched the penniless starve and die.

It was almost impossible to stay clean. Soap was not issued,
and on enquiring she was brusquely informed: "It's a luxury
article. Besides, it's not even issued to the soldiers." She
pointed out that that was a matter between the soldiers and the
War Office, and did not reflect its necessity for women and
children. She was yelled at for her impertinence and noted as a
troublemaker.

Ruth and Anna took it in turns to do the washing. At the
prescribed time they gathered by the gate to be escorted in
batches of about one hundred to a nearby stagnant pool. They

only had the clothes in which they had been evicted from the farm, and so warm days were best, for more clothes could be discarded. During the allocated thirty minutes, they would scrub vigorously, but the brown waters did little to clean, and even added new dirt.

Shortly after arriving, Ruth found herself in trouble with the authorities. On returning from the pool she hung her washing on the wire perimeter fence for lack of a line.

"Take it down!" ordered a sentry as he patrolled on the outside.

"I'll take it down when the Superintendent provides a line for the washing. Are we expected to spread it on the bare ground?" she retorted.

Retribution was quick to follow. Shortly afterwards the Superintendent appeared flanked by guards. He ordered her arrest, and gloated as she was unceremoniously dragged through the camp, out of the gate and incarcerated in a small enclosure - an empty tent surrounded by coiled barbed-wire and under armed guard. And there she stayed for thirty-six hours in solitary confinement, her only furniture a galvanized bucket. Without bedding she shivered on the cold, dirt floor during the night, and throughout the day she sweated in the hot, airless space. Her only nourishment was rice-water.

Ruth feared for her family's health, but particularly for that of her young siblings. Many children were becoming sick, and she blamed the deplorable sanitation arrangements together with the poor food and cold. The latrines were on a trench system with no proper seats, but simply logs thrown across the holes. Many ignored the precarious latrines, and the surrounding ground was heavily fouled. On warm days the noxious stench was unbearable, and nearby tents unfit for occupation.

One day, Ruth, Anna and the young children were sat on the ground sifting through the flour removing the weevils and mouldy clots. It had become a weekly ritual following food distribution. Hundreds of women and children were engaged in the same laborious task. Ruth decided that she had had enough.

"Let's put all these weevils and clots into a bag and demand replacement flour to the same weight," she said to Anna. "And not just us. Let's get all the other women to do the same."

"You know that you are already considered to be a troublemaker. This will only make things worse," pleaded Anna.

"I don't care about me. People are starving. This injustice must be stopped!"

Ruth set off to visit neighbouring tents and to enlist like-minded protesters. Unexpectedly, she released the suppressed anger and despair of the inmates like an erupting volcano – at last here was a way to get justice and fairness! Quickly the scheme spread; the camp began to buzz. Families shared scarce sacks and quickly filled them with the offending insects, then marched resolutely to the superintendent's office.

The crowd of enraged women, with many children, chanted: "Hungry! Hungry! Hungry!"

The clerk emerged – a weasel of a man, thin faced with sunken eyes - but he quickly withdrew amidst threatening shouts demanding the Superintendent to appear. Finally, the Superintendent tentatively opened the door and stood in its frame at the top of the steps: a short, rotund man, puffed-up, stony-hearted and indifferent to the welfare of his charges. He was clearly shaken by the demonstration. "This is a riot!," he shouted above the noise. A quiet descended. "I could have you shot!"

"And no Boer would rest until you hanged."

"Who's that?" He tensely searched the sea of scowling faces for the speaker.

"This flour is inedible. We want replacement flour to the same weight as these filthy weevils." Ruth, from her place at the front of the crowd, held up a wriggling sack.

On cue, dozens of others held their living sacks aloft.

"It's what the contractor provides," he claimed lamely.

"You pay the contractor. How much do you pocket whilst he gives us rubbish? Would you give this to your children?" challenged Ruth.

Angry mutterings swirled amongst the irate women; at last they felt empowered and able to influence their lives in this bleak place.

The Superintendent sensed the tangible fury of the women. He needed to restore calm otherwise his superiors would hold him responsible for any resulting disorder – and perhaps his arrangement with the contractor might come under scrutiny.

"All right. Tomorrow there'll be a fresh issue of flour to all inmates, and thereafter I'll personally ensure that the flour is of good quality. Now disperse and return to your tents."

It was dark when the guards came for Ruth. She expected them and did not resist. She was dragged by rough hands and thrown sprawling onto the hard, dirt floor of the punishment tent. This time she remained for forty eight hours.

****

As he approached the camp, Rodger became aware of a stale, putrid, unhealthy odour which pervaded the air. He had known it once before; it was the smell of disease-ridden Bloemfontein.

The guard saluted Rodger, ushered him through the gate and directed him to the superintendent's office. He climbed the few steps, opened the door and entered a front room. A young, bespectacled man was sitting behind a rough, wooden desk. He glanced up at Rodger's entrance, then ignored him, returning to the scrutiny of a document in front of him. Rodger stood quietly for a few moments waiting for the man to raise his head and acknowledge his presence. Nothing. He felt the anger welling up inside him at such discourtesy; "Excuse me ... excuse me," he said curtly. The man looked up. "I've come to visit the Van den Berg family. I understand they're in this camp."

"I need to see your pass," responded the man officiously.

"I don't have a pass. I'm in the area for a very short time and just wish to visit a family."

"No pass, no visit."

"And who are you?" enquired Rodger losing patience.

"I'm the camp clerk."

"Then I'll speak with the Superintendent."

"Mr Schultz isn't here. Won't be back 'til this afternoon. But I know the regulations, and without a pass no-one's allowed in the camp."

"And where do I get a pass?"

"From the Town Commandant in Middleburg."

"I don't have time to fight with bureaucracy, I'm too busy fighting the damn Boers! Now let me tell you, you arrogant, ill-mannered little weasel; I'm going to visit the Van den Bergs and I don't need your permission. And don't think you can get the guards to stop me. I carry the Queen's commission and they'll obey my orders. Now tell me, where do I find them?"

The clerk was taken aback by the anger and authority in Rodger's voice. He decided it was best to be cooperative, "Half way down the third row of tents in from the fence."

Rodger stormed out deliberately slamming the door causing the frail, wooden building to shudder.

He picked his way between the tightly packed bell-tents carefully avoiding guy-ropes and pegs. He stopped as four young boys carrying a stretcher came towards him. He watched as they halted at a tent. A woman, sobbing bitterly, stepped out and gently laid on it a little bundle wrapped in a railway rug. He stood aside to allow the boys to pass, and noticed that their burden was a young girl, perhaps five years old – what he could not know, was that this was the second child that the tormented mother had lost in a fortnight.

As he walked through the lines of tents he became increasingly disturbed by what he saw. The women and children – for there were only a few elderly men – were inadequately dressed for the encroaching cold weather - many had summer clothes, torn and in need of repair. Their faces were pale and gaunt, pinched and hollow-cheeked; skin ingrained with dirt. He looked into one tent to seek directions and was shocked to find a young mother watching over two emaciated children lying on a blanket with sunken eyes and stick-like limbs. She stared back at him through haunted eyes: quiet, enduring, resigned. The sight reminded him of the famine-stricken children of Calcutta.

He instinctively recognised her. His heart raced. His nervousness churned inside. She was crouched by a small clay oven outside a tent, desperately trying to ignite kindling and dry manure. The wood was green, the task virtually impossible. He held back, watching silently. She became aware of a presence, raised her head and turned. For a tense moment nothing was said; then:

"What do you want? Why are you here?"

Rodger had imagined this moment endlessly. He had rehearsed his lines until he was word perfect, but now his mind was empty, scrambled. Words wouldn't come. Before him was the woman he had thought about, dreamt about, felt guilty about; but now what to say? What to do?

"Why are you standing there? Have you come to gloat?"

His words were hesitant, stumbling, "I'm staying at Middleburg for a night and wanted to see that you and your family are all right."

She stood up and looked at him defiantly, "Do I look all right?"

He had long carried her image in his mind: an alluring young woman with marbled face of smooth, olive complexion; long black hair swept back into a high bun; eyes sparkling. He was appalled at the change. She had lost weight, her skin had a strange yellowish pallor, her face was lined, she had black circles under her eyes, her clothes were worn and ragged like Grimm's Cinderella.

"I didn't expect the camps to be like this," he stuttered. "I understood that everything would be provided."

"Is that your excuse for not even allowing us time to pack the bare essentials, and for cruelly destroying all that we had? I saw you watching. You were too ashamed to face us after the care and Christian love we showed you. Well, this is what we are reduced to: living like animals; dying like animals. You think this will cause our men to stop fighting; you're wrong! They will fight all the harder to avenge the deaths of their wives and children!"

Rodger was cowed and burdened by the horrors of what he was witnessing, "I'm so sorry," he murmured almost inaudibly. "So sorry."

At that moment Anna appeared with Hannie and Adrian. The children were barefoot and dressed in clothes crudely fashioned from blankets; they were carrying water in battered kerosene cans. All were breathless from their exertions.

"Lieutenant Borthwick, what a surprise. Can we help you?" Anna's voice was respectful but distant. She too looked haggard, unkempt and exhausted, but she faced him proud and challenging. The children he noticed were thin and weak, they complained of aching legs and he detected blood on their lips – scurvy? Adrian made as if to approach his one-time friend, but Anna held his hand firmly.

"I wish to help," he said, reaching into his pocket and producing his purse. He held it out to Anna.

"Thank you Lieutenant," she responded, "but we don't need your help. We are managing satisfactorily."

Rodger hesitated; his hand remained outstretched, frozen, awkward.

Ruth snatched the purse. "Mama, we have to think of the little ones. They need food and clothes and shoes. Winter is approaching. Are they to die of starvation or disease because we are too proud. Besides, this is small payment for all that the English have taken from us." She turned to Rodger and stared at him defiantly, "Understand, we don't want your charity, this is simply a down-payment on all that you owe us. It's a matter of life and death for the children." She didn't offer thanks.

Rodger nodded, turned and walked slowly back through the lines of tents. He was disgusted at the treatment being meted out to the innocents of war by his own people. He felt dejected, emotionally bruised. He quickened his steps anxious to escape the heavy pall of noxious smells and imminent death. He couldn't help but bring to mind Dante's infamous inscription on the gates of hell: *"Abandon all hope, ye who enter here."*

CHAPTER 17

We think caged birds sing, when indeed they cry.

John Webster ("The White Devil" 1612)

THE BIRDS

It was a warm balmy night. Maxwell had been up since 3 a.m. routinely deciphering and sorting through the plethora of telegrams received during the night from the column commanders in the field. He spread them on the dining-table in appropriate piles in anticipation of Kitchener's appearance.

He stopped suddenly. Down the hall, from the direction of Kitchener's bedroom, he could hear a loud commotion. He dumped those papers in his hands, and rushed to investigate the disturbance. As he approached Kitchener's room, he was joined by the Military Secretary, Colonel Hubert Hamilton, who burst from his room adjacent to Kitchener's. They stood together listening at the door; from within came the sound of crashing furniture and excited shouts. They were concerned for their boss' safety. Hamilton knocked sharply on the door, and without waiting for a response he flung it open and barged in.

There was a pause as the two men stood in the doorway trying to absorb the scene. Kitchener, dishevelled and in his night attire, was chasing two fledglings around the room in a hopeless attempt to catch them. In the process he had upset a chair and knocked the ewer and water-bowl off the washstand – the floor was littered with shattered porcelain; water slopped about making it slippery under foot.

"Young starlings ... fell down the chimney," gasped Kitchener in explanation. Then having recovered his composure, "Close the door and help me catch the blighters!"

So began a merry dance. The three officers stalked the young starlings, flinging themselves at them every time the birds came to rest, but without success. Finally, Maxwell grabbed a

194

towel which hung by the washstand, and flung it over a stationary bird. "Got it!" he declared triumphantly. Using this proven tactic, the second starling was soon captured.

"Put them somewhere safe," directed Kitchener.

"The pigeon house?" queried Maxwell.

"Yes, the pigeon house. That will be fine," affirmed Kitchener. "And make sure that you take good care of them. Ensure they get properly fed."

Kitchener hurried through the morning's routine sending instructions to his column commanders, conducting interviews with departmental heads, and even hosting a session with representatives of the press - he detested speaking with reporters, but accepted that he needed to humour them. As he once expressed to Hamilton: "The newspapers inflate skirmishes into battles, and unfortunate incidents into atrocities." He did not trust them.

On his way out for his afternoon ride, he diverted to the rear garden to inspect the starlings. He was unhappy, "Fetch me "The Brat"!" he demanded of a servant. Soon Maxwell appeared, flustered and wondering what the crisis was all about.

Kitchener confronted his young ADC, "These birds are starving!"

"I've tried to give them tiny pieces of meat, but they haven't learned how to eat by themselves. Besides, the pigeons wolf down any food put in for the youngsters," explained Maxwell.

"Worms! That's what they need. Worms!"

"Yes, sir. I'll find succulent worms for the birds," promised Maxwell in utter disbelief.

Temporarily satisfied, Kitchener sought out his horse and left.

It was early evening when Maxwell was again abruptly summoned to the garden. It was Kitchener fussing over his new charges, "Have you fed them?" he enquired, less agitated but still concerned for their welfare.

"I tried worms without success, but the good news is that the parents, having spent time flying around in some distress, have become emboldened enough to feed the youngsters through the wire. I believe they're fine now."

The following morning Kitchener unusually deviated from his regular routine and visited the garden before joining his staff at the breakfast table. Solemnly, he announced, "I have been to inspect the starlings. I'm saddened to find that one has died during the night. However, I see that there is another one hopping about which is attracting undue attention from its parents to the detriment of that in the pigeon house. "Brat, you are to catch it and intern it with the other ... it will have a companion ."

Maxwell was taken aback, "Sir, how am I to catch a strong-on-the-wing young bird in an open garden?"

"A young fit man like you; it shouldn't be a problem," he insisted.

"But, sir! ….."

"I'm not interested in your excuses. Catch the damned thing!"

Maxwell left the breakfast table inwardly chuntering at the impossible task given to him by Kitchener. As he entered the hall he was struck with an idea. Standing there was a four foot high statue of a stork. Surreptitiously, he whipped it away and placed it with the pigeons before losing himself in the depths of the house. But it was not long before a servant found him, and he was standing in the garden next to Kitchener staring at his handy work. He waited for the bomb to explode.

Kitchener stood taut and seemingly angry. He did not even look at the culprit. Then, uncharacteristically, he laughed, "You, Brat, are an impertinent beast."

Maxwell relaxed. Emboldened, he decided to seize the opportunity to press a point in the hope of getting rid of this irritating distraction, "Sir, from my observations the parents have become quite callous and have stopped feeding their offspring. Soon the young starling will starve to death as he can't feed himself. Would it not be a kindness to release him into the wild?"

As he spoke the young bird paddled up to a fat worm placed there for his nourishment and swallowed the whole length – Maxwell later swore that it winked.

· ·

Kitchener took some of his staff on a visit to units in Pietersburg, leaving Maxwell and Hamilton to run the Headquarters. They enjoyed the opportunity to get on with their work free from demands and interference. But it wasn't to last.

The starling was now the occupant of a large, roomy cage, and its every need was met through the begrudging care of a burly Scot from Kitchener's bodyguard of Cameron Highlanders.

Hamilton was working in the dining-room, engrossed in his paperwork which was spread across the table. There came a timid knock on the door.

"Come in!"

The door opened slowly, and the broad-shouldered bird-orderly stood in front of him, anxious, trembling.

"It's the bird, sir."

"Bird?"

"Yes, sir, the wee starling."

Hamilton sensed disaster, "What of it man!"

"It escaped."

"Escaped!"

"I was feeding it and it slipped out of the door."

"My God!" uttered Hamilton. "This is dire!" He rushed out into the garden gathering up Maxwell as he went. They stared in silence at the empty cage.

Eventually Maxwell sighed with a satisfied grin, "Good riddance. Now we might get some peace instead of our lives

197

revolving around the antics of a damned bird."

"This will have consequences," bemoaned Hamilton.

"This bird already brings consequences," retorted Maxwell. "The Commander-in-Chief of some two hundred thousand men spends half his day watching a bird fluffing worms and chirping at it through the wires. For God's sake, we're at war!"

Hamilton chose to ignore this derogatory outburst, "Deploy every available member of the house staff and see if we can recapture the thing!"

An uneasy atmosphere settled over the headquarters as the staff anticipated Kitchener's wrath. Finally, Hamilton could stand the tension no longer, and he summoned Maxwell, "How goes the search?"

"Nothing. We're looking for the veritable needle in a haystack. I've called it off. There's work to be done."

"Look, I think we should break the news to the Chief while he is away so that he can get over the shock before his return. I want you to send him a wire to break the sad news gently ... cheerfully."

"Me!" protested Maxwell. "But you're senior."

"Kitchener is far more tolerant of your indiscretions and cock-ups. And as you so clearly point out ... you're junior."

Maxwell sat at the corner of the dining-table and decided to try and defuse the situation; he wrote:

"C-in-Cs humming bird, after being fed by a Highlander this morning, broke cover and took to the open. Diligent search instituted: biped still at large. Military Secretary desolate; ADC in tears. Army sympathises."

There was no reply.

Two days later Kitchener returned. He made no reference to the circumstances of the escape, but summoned his military staff and instructed that every member of the household be mobilised to find the bird. He allotted personnel to areas and delegated tasks as if it were a military operation. He perfunctorily signed off the papers confirming the execution of two Boer rebels, and then, like every good commander, he led from the front. He crawled under bushes and scoured flower beds in pursuit of the escapee. Lunchtime came and went and still the search pressed on. It was 7 p.m. when at last a triumphant shout rent the air. The poor bird was found, less its tail, cowering in the chimney of a neighbour's house.

Kitchener was overjoyed and remarked breathlessly, "I've never been so fond of that bird since it's been loose."

CHAPTER 18

A voice was heard in Ramah,
lamentation, and bitter weeping;
Rachel weeping for her children
refused to be comforted for her children,
because they were not.

Jeremiah chapter 31 verse 15

ESCAPE

With the approach of winter the number of camp deaths increased alarmingly, particularly amongst the children. Measles assumed epidemic proportions.

Hannie was the first to display the tell-tale rash. The itchy red spots started on her head, and over the next few days spread slowly to the rest of her body. Her eyes became inflamed, she developed a deep hacking cough and boiled with fever. The nurse visited and examined the inside of her mouth; the white spots confirmed the diagnosis.

"You can bring her to the hospital, although we're very crowded," offered the nurse. But Anna declined. Stories were rife of children dying alone as heartless doctors refused parental visits. No. She would nurse her own children.

Two days later Adrian also caught the disease.

Ruth had spent the last of their money acquiring a straw-filled palliasse on which the children huddled together. When it rained the water seeped under the tent canvas and wet the straw, but still, it was an improvement on the muddy ground. A few blankets had been distributed with the on-set of winter by a women's committee from nearby Middleburg - one each. Thankfully, the "undesirables" were now on full rations after the British Government had been shamed by the protestations of foreign consuls, which had precipitated a fierce row in the

200

House of Commons.

The pitiful moans of the two children joined the chorus of pain and sorrow which permeated the whole camp. Their muscles ached; their throats were sore; their noses streamed; they refused the porridge cooked by their mother in the rain using precious fuel. When the rash began to fade there was hope that the worst was over, but the fever intensified and the children coughed up blood-stained phlegm. In their weakened state their frail bodies were incapable of fighting off infections - the new enemy was pneumonia.

Anna and Ruth relinquished their blankets in an attempt to bring some warmth to the children. Under the regulations, sick children were entitled to condensed milk, but instead of the tin being given to Anna, the nurse brought the diluted liquid in a jug and it quickly turned sour. Anna and Ruth felt helpless, desperately inadequate. They squatted on the damp, chilled ground and held the children's hands. They prayed softly; earnestly: "God in your mercy, spare these little ones."

"Candles is a luxury; you've no entitlement." The words of the heartless Superintendent echoed in Ruth's ears. It was only through the sacrificial giving of a neighbour that she could now see the fearful, tearful eyes of her young siblings.

When dawn broke, Hannie and Adrian were still and deadly cold.

The tattered skirts of the weary, shattered women wafted against thin, dirty legs as they pulled and pushed the cart with their draining strength. On board were the bodies of their children, six in all, including Hannie and Adrian. The old cemetery was full; the new was almost a mile away. There was no longer any money for coffins and hearses; today the children were wrapped in coarse army blankets and conveyed on a rickety old cart.

The Boer orderlies had dug the graves and more, in preparation for the day's grisly harvest - up to thirty were expected. The women strove to lower the small bundles into the holes with a semblance of dignity, and then stood holding hands for mutual comfort. Tears ran silently down faces; some shook unashamedly with unrestrained sobbing. Ruth stood stoically, watching rivulets of soil dribble into the graves from the surrounding piles of spoil. Tears would not come. Anna clung to her for support; prayerfully she pleaded, "O Lord, how long?"

······ ································

During the issue of rations, the Superintendent loudly decried the recent spate of attacks on the railway line to his captive audience of hungry women. Ruth was fed-up with this arrogant, overbearing, officious bully.

"The railway was built with Boer money," she shouted. "We Boers have every right to destroy what is ours." She knew that such insubordinate behaviour could have only one result, but as she sat on the cold, bare floor in the punishment tent, she drew consolation from the fact that the period of solitary confinement gave her time to hatch her escape plan. She would join her menfolk on commando.

The sky was heavy, the autumn rain relentless. Ruth lurked between the tents nearest to the main gate, waiting for the late afternoon funeral party. Tiny bodies wrapped in grey army blankets were laid lovingly by tortured mothers into the back of an open, four-wheeled carriage. It would normally be drawn by two horses, but routinely none were provided. Black Native police rudely herded the mothers together, conducted a quick headcount, and waved to the guards to open the gates. Some women grasped the vehicle shafts and pulled like beasts of burden, others pushed from the rear. In the ruckus of negotiating the gate, Ruth slipped unnoticed to the back of the carriage and heaved, keeping her head down.

The women strained to manoeuvre the carriage over the rutted track the mile or so to the cemetery. They were drenched, muddied. They slipped and slid; tore clothes; were bruised. Tears of grief, anger and frustration mingled indistinguishably with the raindrops which trickled down their soiled cheeks. But despite their weakened state, they were determined, driven to gargantuan efforts.

As they passed a group of Native women, the latter scooped up hands of mud and threw it at the tormented prisoners. The attackers laughed and shouted insults at the whites now reduced to rags and manual labour. The escorting police made no attempt to intervene, instead they smirked and gloated over the misery of their charges.

How painful was the familiar routine as Ruth helped the mothers carry their pitiful bundles to the gravesides, and to lovingly place them into the dark, muddy holes. Then they stood looking down onto their children, distraught with emotional agony and tearful memories.

"It gets dark! Time to go!" shouted the policemen. They had remained in the area of the carriage huddled under capes in a forlorn attempt to remain dry, and now they beckoned the grieving mothers who returned slowly, reluctant to leave their children.

"Quickly! Quickly!" encouraged the policemen.

Ruth judged when the policemen were not looking towards her, and dropped into an empty grave. It was child-size; she crouched. She listened as the headcount took place, and then to the sound of squelching footsteps and the fading creaks of the carriage as it rumbled back to camp.

For half an hour or so Ruth could hear the sound of the cursing orderlies as they filled in the graves, but with the approaching darkness, quiet descended. She was alone in this sad place. She scrambled from the hole pleased to stretch her cramped limbs. The rain had stopped; the cloud was lifting; soon the stars would shine to aid navigation.

Ruth knew that she must get as far away from the camp as possible before daylight and the prospect of her absence being noted – unfortunately, her notoriety amongst the authorities meant that she would quickly be missed. She could walk, but in her reduced state she might hope to cover eight at most ten miles. The better option was to ride.

The horses and mules of the camp officials were held in a kraal outside the camp perimeter, not far from the main gate – she had noted its position and layout during her laundry trips. Rarely had she seen police or armed guards in the vicinity. She surmised that it was probably regarded as being a safe area, and hopefully security would be at a minimum. In fact it may only be watched by Native grooms and wagon drivers, and they were infamous for their laziness and lack of diligence.

Cautiously, she skirted around the camp until the kraal came into view. She crouched by an ant-hill using it for cover, and observed intently. By the kraal gate were two Natives with blankets draped over their shoulders; they threw wood on a camp-fire and huddled around the flames for warmth – an all-consuming occupation. But she noticed in the vicinity a couple of horses grazing; they were knee-hobbled to restrict their movement. Probably mounts belonging to visitors and left in the charge of the watchmen. She presumed that the owners would soon return.

Carefully she approached the nearest animal; she advanced head-on making eye contact and whispered gently, soothingly. The horse stood still, head raised, ears pointing alertly. Ruth's movements were slow, deliberate, her utterances calming, until she could stretch out and gently take the halter. She patted the horse's neck to win his confidence. Slowly, she untied the rope and quietly led the horse away from the flickering fire-light and into the thickening darkness.

As Ruth galloped across the veld, the night skies cleared and the Southern Cross became acutely visible. In the east arose Orion then Sirius, and by their light and guidance she went on. Suddenly a sharp point of light glinted in the east; was it an enemy camp-fire? No. She recognised it as the morning star – Venus? – which heralded the wakening dawn; soon the rising blood-red sun tinted the eastern horizon. She must find somewhere to hide and rest during the coming day.

To her left she noticed the silhouette of a farm and rode towards it. From afar it looked fairly intact, but as she drew close the skeletons of numerous sheep were an ominous sign. On arrival she could see that the destruction was complete. The house walls were punctuated with black borders marking the missing doors and windows; the corrugated-sheet roofing lay scattered about, blackened and twisted by the heat. The tops of trees in front of the house were scorched, and a vine lay half torn from the wall against which the owner had trained it. As she trudged through rooms she picked her way over heaps of ashes; but most cruelly of all, dead sheep had been tossed into the devastated rooms; their putrefying carcases stank.

Attempts had been made to destroy the outbuildings, but a grain-store remained virtually untouched. It was apparent that sacks of corn had been cut open and paraffin poured over them and set alight, but the conflagration had burned out before consuming the crop and building – most of the roof was intact and the interior was dry.

The farm dam was contaminated by dead livestock, but she found water in a damaged water-butt, sufficient to refresh her horse and for her own needs. She tethered the horse outside the store and fed him with salvaged grain, then, with a rusting shovel in hand, she sought out the vegetable plot. Soon she had dug up the few remaining vegetables: potatoes, carrots, onions.

One of Ruth's finds in the saddlebags of the stolen horse was a tin containing a packet of Bryant & May matches. Quickly she made a fire, concealed within the store walls, and soon produced a nourishing soup. Exhilarated by her new-found freedom, Ruth lay down to sleep, bone-weary but content. For the first time in many months she was no longer ravaged by the penetrating pangs of hunger.

Through her half-sleep she heard the restless neighing of her horse, and awoke to find a man standing in the doorway, back-filled by the sunlight. He pointed his rifle at her, "What are you doing here?" The harshness was tinged with curiosity.

"I've escaped from the concentration camp at Middleburg," she explained, throwing off her blanket and rising unsteadily to her feet.

"So where are you heading?"

"To join my father and brother on commando."

"And which commando would that be?" He lowered his rifle and stepped inside. His face was now out of shadow; Ruth could see that he was a few years her elder: slim built, weather beaten, scruffy beard, slouch hat pushed back revealing thick, brown, matted hair.

"The Witbergers," she confirmed.

"Don't you know that Botha has decreed that families can't go on commando any more?"

"How am I supposed to know what Botha has said when I've been incarcerated for the last four months. Besides, I'm not just family. I'm someone capable of riding and fighting like any burgher."

The stranger smiled, "I don't doubt that."

Tensions dissipated. They were Afrikaners together.

"The last I heard the Witbergers were well to the east near the Swaziland border. I can try and get word to your father and let him know that you're safe, but for the moment I think you should join up with a women's laager."

"Women's laager?" she queried.

"During the Khakis' drives, some of the women managed to pass around their flanks or even through their lines back into the devastated areas. They move about the veld hiding and avoiding capture and internment. I can take you to one about a day's ride from here, but not now. First I must rejoin my friends who are waiting for me in the donga by the kopje," he gestured with a hand to the right. "We're on our way to cut communications. Be ready at dawn tomorrow when I'll collect you on our way back. And by the way, don't light your fire during the day; it was the smoke that attracted my attention. Wait until its dark and only burn your fire inside the building."

He smiled, "Take care Miss Amazon, and I'll be back for you."

She stood still, listening to the hoof-beats as they disappeared into the distance. Why couldn't it have been Henry? Suddenly she felt very alone, vulnerable. Wearily, she lay once more in the depression which she had scooped out of the grain, covered herself with her blanket and tried again to sleep. What if her rescuer became a casualty or was captured? Restlessly she dozed, robbed of her certainties.

CHAPTER 19

"As for fighting, the men of all races are pretty much alike ... but, for the grand, essential composition of a good soldier, give me a Dutchman – he starves well."

Daniel Morgan, American pioneer and guerilla leader in the American Revolution.

ON COMMANDO

Kitchener's first great drive disintegrated with the collapse of the logistic tail in the face of persistent rain and swollen rivers. On reaching the Swaziland border, the English columns turned about and retraced their tired steps across the high-veld back to Middleburg. Jan, Jacobus and Henry, in concert with the other burghers, seized every opportunity to snipe and harass the weary, dispirited soldiers. As the columns disappeared into the defensive perimeter around the town, it was apparent that the offensive was over - at least for the time being. But in its wake the countryside lay devastated with blackened ruins and trampled fields. A silent, unpeopled waste.

"It'll take weeks before the English are ready to renew the offensive," Pretorius addressed the Witbergers. "General Botha has degreed that everyone is to take two week's leave. We are then to reform in small groups and remain dispersed for easier provisioning until a general muster is called. We'll gather again in Witberg."

A good thing too, mused Jacobus. Botha knows his men well. In the absence of leave this citizen army would seek out their families anyway, and the commandos would simply disintegrate.

....

As they neared home, a scavenging flock of white-backed vultures scuttled noisily into the air with flapping wings and high pitched squeals. The half-picked carcases of hundreds of sheep littered the fields. The farmhouse was reduced to scorched, skeletal walls, and all around was evidence of a frenzied orgy of wanton destruction. As they crossed the yard they stepped carefully to avoid the rotting corpses of pigs and chickens, and on entering the ruins found decaying sheep in each room. The air was polluted with the rancid odour of putrefying flesh. Vainly, they covered their nostrils with their hands and hats against the penetrating, nauseous smell. Everywhere, scattered about in dreadful confusion, lay simple reminders of a lost, once-happy life. They stood speechless, in shock, gazing at the debris: broken furniture, ripped pillows, torn books, plates, pots, clothing ... an endless list, now trammelled and filthy in the mud; a family's life publicly desecrated.

A silence descended which magnified the furious, indignant mood.

Eventually, full of concern, Jan voiced everyone's thoughts, "Where do you think they've taken Grandpa, Mama and my brother and sisters?"

"Probably to a garrison town ... perhaps even Middleburg," suggested Jacobus. "I worry for them." He paused, then continued, "But if the Khakis intend to destroy all the farms, then perhaps unwittingly they are doing us a favour by caring for our families. We don't have to be anxious about their welfare and can focus on the fight."

They all drew some comfort from these thoughts.

They searched the area and recovered a few useful items such as a kettle and a couple of cooking- pots, before mounting their horses and heading off to the agreed rendezvous.

....

It was only May, but already the weather was wintry –

209

foreshadowing an unprecedented long spell of cold. By day clouds of dust and biting winds drove across the bleak plains, and at night the burghers lay shivering beneath thin blankets listening to the crackle of unseasonable ice forming on pools. Sleep was fitful.

The autumn weather became increasingly stormy, and the exposed burghers suffered severely from the cold and intermittent rains. This evening the weather was pleasantly mild. Earlier, Jan and the others had broken twigs from surrounding shrubs, and had spread an ox-skin on them to make a mattress on the soaked ground.

Jan lay fully clothed beneath his blanket with his saddle behind his shoulders acting as a wind-break; above was a canopy of heavenly stars. He was desperate for sleep. About midnight he woke to a peculiar sound, as of something soft falling on his blanket. It was snow. Soon it lay two inches thick. After a couple of hours, the snow turned to rain and he was wet to the skin. Once again, sleep was impossible. Cold, tired and disgruntled, he threw aside his wet blanket and decided to make a fire. He retrieved the twigs from beneath the hide-mattress and struggled to light the damp wood. He used his improvised tinder-box made from flint, and for tinder the fluffy substance found inside the pods of a common bush. Eventually the twigs began to crackle and the flames to dance. Out of the gloom he was joined by his father and Henry. Stoically, they crowded around the fire, miserable, pinched, shivering and despondent.

The incessant wet weather softened the horses hooves until they cast their shoes. Jan and Henry's mounts became lame, and they had no alternative but to lead their tired, sore animals on foot.

One day they came upon a kraal which by its dilapidated state and absence of occupants indicated that it was abandoned.

"Let's take a look," Jacobus led the way. In one of the huts they found a number of bull-hide shields. "Gather them up,

I've got an idea," he urged.

That evening when the laager was established, Jacobus sought out old Ben Zeederberg; he was the cobbler from Witberg, expert in making the traditional veld-shoes from bullocks' hides. "Can you do anything for the horses with these?"

With a knowing grin, the rustic peasant searched out a few tools from his saddlebag. By the light of a wood fire, he cut the leather into moccasins which, when soaked, could be tightly stretched over each hoof. With their horses re-shod, they could ride again.

At first food was plentiful. There was a variety of game on the veld, for even the English could not denude it of all animal life. When left in peace long enough, the Van den Bergs and their neighbours hunted antelope and varied game, jerked it and made biltong. Despite the trampled fields, there were still enough mealies to glean, which they boiled, roasted, ate raw, made into porridge and ground into flour - even toasted and made into ersatz coffee. Odd sheep roamed the veld – escapees from the massacres.

But eventually these sources became exhausted. The burghers began to suffer from hunger.

The dry stubble of the rainless, winter months provided little nourishment for their mounts. With the passage of time, both horses and burghers began to show signs of distress. Animals and men alike looked increasingly thin and gaunt.

Eventually, the burghers resorted to shooting their pack-horses for food, but whilst a fat horse is very nutritious, fine-grained and well-flavoured, a starving horse is stringy and tasteless and almost worthless as food.

Jan threw more wood onto the fire. The meat, cut from their last scraggy pack-horse, was roasting nicely on an improvised spit. However, he knew – they all knew - that no matter how much of it they might eat, within hours intense hunger would return.

Henry watched Jacobus with fascination as he placed the horse's head on a flat stone.

"The last bit of nourishment in a starving animal is the brain," explained Jacobus nodding knowingly to Henry. Then with a heavy, sure blow of a short cleaver, he split the skull in half. Carefully he extracted the lobes from inside the scull and proceeded to cut them into small pieces. He threw them into a saucepan, and being composed mostly of fat, on contact with heat they spurted and sizzled; within minutes they had browned nicely.

Without a word, but with a knowing grin, he passed the saucepan to the others. Jan and Henry stuck their knives into the fleshy chunks and ate warily.

"Good?" queried Jacobus.

"Excellent," the two agreed.

The problem of clothing remained unresolved. Due to the rains, boots rotted and clothes wore out and all manner of improvisation developed. Jacobus and Jan draped a rough, sheepskin overcoat over tattered jackets and trousers, whilst Henry opted for a home-made leather suit which he bought from a burgher. But others were reduced to a wardrobe consisting merely of a blanket, or a maize sack – they joked that the better class of grain-bag was tightly knit and without names and advertisements on it. Even women's dresses were worn, scavenged from desolate farms. Many wrapped cloths around their feet in the absence of conventional footwear.

Desperate tobacco addicts smoked horse dung calling it "Wayside Mixture".

The relentless English drives meant that the Witberg Commando, like all the others in the Eastern Transvaal, had to shift almost every night - rarely did they sleep in the same place on two consecutive occasions.

They were all aware of their deteriorating physical and mental condition. Tempers frayed. As old Mr Zeederberg never grew tired of reminding everyone; "A hungry man is an angry man."

Each evening the devout gathered, sang psalms and heard preaching. They clung on to their simple belief that God would bring them through these trials to ultimate victory.

···

All the railway lines were protected by the small tin forts linked together by trenches and barbed wire barriers, and now the tentacles of the blockhouse system stretched across the veld – about eight thousand blockhouses each manned by a section of seven soldiers - more than fifty thousand men. One obstacle line ran directly north to south from Standerton to Middleburg, thereby cutting the Eastern Transvaal into two segments. As these barriers were strengthened, it became increasingly difficult for the commandos to move freely.

With the ubiquitous English columns once again active in their area, the Witberg Commando was under pressure to move on. Jan and Henry were tasked to ride ahead to reconnoitre the blockhouse line in order to find a suitable crossing point. Skilfully, they used the folds in the ground to approach their objective, and as dawn broke they reached a small group of jagged kopjes. It was a beautiful morning. With borrowed telescope they could survey several miles along the snaking obstacle.

Throughout the day they watched as bored Tommies lounged outside their airless, hot, claustrophobic blockhouses, chain-smoking the addictive Woodbines. Some tended their tiny gardens – petunias planted in bully-beef tins – or sat in the shade writing letters home. A number of animals were evident – pets - which demanded the attention of their owners: dogs, goats, even a pig. But more menacingly they saw yet other soldiers strengthening the defences. These Khakis unravelled barbed wire and wove it into the already thick, metal, protective tapestry. Then they attached tins with pebbles inside which would rattle should the wire be interfered with.

Jan almost felt sorry for these soldiers and their terrible, tedious lifestyle, broken only by visits of the occasional supply convoy.

"If we had a gun, we could blow the blockhouses to bits," observed Jan.

"But we don't," countered Henry. "So long as they stay inside they're fairly safe." He further scrutinised them, "Now they've surrounded the blockhouses with wire we can no longer get close and fire through the slits."

There followed a short period of reflection. Jan spoke, "Can you see the best place to cross?"

"There's a slight depression between those two blockhouses," Henry pointed. "We're likely to be in dead ground. I think that's our best chance."

Jan agreed. "Let's get some rest ready for tonight. I'll take first watch while you sleep."

As darkness descended, the pair stole away and rode the few miles to the waiting Commando. A quick kriegsraad was summoned by Pretorius, and a plan of action agreed. A crossing by stealth would be attempted, but if foiled then a small herd of slaughter cattle, recently requisitioned from a Bantu kraal, would be driven at speed into the wire between the blockhouses and so force a path through. Appointed burghers were detailed to fire at the flanking blockhouses in order to neutralise them.

The Commando approached the kopjes unseen. The moon drifted in and out of cloud casting meandering shadows across the veld. Jan and Henry, with a couple of neighbours, crept forward on foot and slunk into the hollow between the chosen blockhouses. Each pair grasped a strand of wire and carefully placed a piece of cloth over it. They cut through the wire with nippers - the cloth dulled the snapping sound. They worked undetected: snip, snip. Inevitably, pebbles rattled gently in hanging tins, but not loud enough to be heard within the blockhouses, perhaps four-hundred yards away. Only the muffled talking and the occasional guffaw of unwary soldiers broke the silent stillness. The wire-cutting progressed well, until a bell hanging on the obstacle was disturbed and tinkled ominously. They froze.

Jan was alert to a change in the sounds coming from the left blockhouse: silence, agitated discussion, commotion, and finally a single shot, soon followed by a hail of rifle fire from several slots. The adjacent blockhouse came alive with shouts and firing, and soon the contagious fear rippled down the line with scores of blockhouses erupting with nervous, wild, ineffective shooting. The night was filled with flashes, noise and the zip! zip! of bullets cutting through the air. Moments later a red signal-flare whooshed into the sky exposing the scene under a ruby glow. Fortunately, the shallow depression saved Jan and his friends from direct fire.

The loss of surprise was the cue for the Commando to gallop forward spearheaded by the bellowing cattle. With manic shouts and frenzied screams the Boers drove the cattle into the partially cut gap. Barbs cut deep into flesh and some cows were hit by bullets, but the sheer force and momentum of these frightened, distraught animals was unstoppable. They crashed through the wire opening the way for the horsemen to follow. Simultaneously, the nominated burghers fired rapidly from the saddle at the flanking blockhouses.

Jan and Henry desperately sought out Jacobus who was acting as their horse-holder. They crouched clear of the seething mass and called to him anxiously as his figure emerged through the black night and swirling dust. As he came level, they jumped onto their mounts, and lying low on the backs of their horses, joined the forward crush.

It was momentary bedlam, but the ruction was over in minutes. Jan looked back to see several cattle writhing in the gap, but it seemed as if the Commando had escaped without any serious casualties. They rode on into the night exchanging self-congratulatory banter and laughing loudly, giving relief to their tensions. Behind them the racket continued unabated as scores of block-house dwellers fired fearfully into the empty night, accompanied by the occasional colourful distress flare.

● ●

It was the second week in September. The warmth of the spring sun was welcome following a long cold winter.

A black mass of cloud rose in the west, and with its approach they knew that soon everything would be wrapped in shadow. The deep rumbling of thunder grew louder as it drew closer; nearer and nearer like the mighty voice of God. Great drops splashed onto the dry earth announcing torrential rain. Henry and the others held out their capes, mackintoshes, anything to catch the precious drops, and then primitively sucked up the liquid. It rained for two hours and everyone was happily drenched.

The passing of the storm heralded a beautiful morning. The sun rose in glittering splendour over the refreshed earth. Once again this annual miracle would quickly turn the dry stubble of the South African veld into verdant grazing lands.

To the Boers, it brought renewed hope and vitality.

CHAPTER 19

Death pays all debts.

Shakespeare: Henry IV part I

THE "JOINER"

The cold of the night made for a disturbed and sporadic sleep. Ruth heard the arrival of visitors as they entered the laager; from beneath her blanket she sensed them dismounting from their horses, and listened to the commotion that followed: hurried, strong male voices. Then they galloped away.

The Commandant cracked his great whip as loud as a rifle shot: "Upstandt! Upstandt!" he shouted. "The Khakis are coming! Upstandt!"

Ruth stopped him as he passed, "What's happening?" she asked anxiously.

The Commandant paused for breath and leaned heavily on his walking-stick, "Burghers have just warned me that a khaki column is moving east towards Ermelo. We must trek south towards Standerton to avoid their line of march." With that he hobbled off to rouse his charges.

Their black servant rolled from under the wagon and quickly started a fire on which to prepare the coffee. Ruth stirred the sleeping oxen, and with the others tied them to the trektow by a great band of rawhide. The light pole yokes were laid over their necks and secured in place by two wooden keys about sixteen inches long. With practised skill and little fuss, within thirty minutes the wagons were packed and oxen inspanned. As they waited for the off, they dipped their cups into the kettle of steaming coffee and relished the hot liquid as it permeated every fibre of their bodies - an essential bulwark against the bitter cold.

Another crack of the whip signalled the order to trek. Each wagon in turn moved into line with much lashing of whips and

217

long resonant cries as the drivers abused and encouraged their animals. Women, young and old, took the reins or walked leading the ox-wagons; babies cried in the bitter cold of the winter morning; boys as young as ten years of age herded the loose stock behind. The ponderous oxen meandered across the dreary plains at the usual pace of three miles an hour – this rhythm once broken could not be recaptured - passing the black remains of burnt farms and the numerous skeletons of massacred sheep picked clean by the vultures. There was no forage available for the oxen and little nourishment in the dry grass; their weakened condition was increasingly evident in their sunken eyes and shrivelled frames.

The laager consisted of about thirty wagons and a dozen or so assorted carts. It was a transient home for almost one hundred women and children under the care of two elderly Boers: the Commandant, a child of the Great Trek and veteran of the Native wars, now bowed down with age, but of unquenchable spirit; and a retired, enfeebled predikant of the Dutch Reform Church, who remained resplendent - albeit tattered and dusty - in black frock-coat buttoned tightly to the neck, trousers to match and a felt hat with wide brim and low crown. Fear of the concentration camps and a growing awareness of the suffering and high mortality rates there, encouraged many families to choose a nomadic existence in the veld – anything not to fall into the clutches of the despised English!

Ruth found herself absorbed into a small family. It had not been intentional. She had just drifted towards helping a young mother and recent widow, Ezra, with her two young boys: Jacob eight years old and Amos six - a younger girl had died three years previously from measles. Although Ezra was almost ten years her senior, to Ruth this age gap seemed insignificant as they struggled together to survive the incessant hardships.

The Commandant scouted ahead. As the sun began to dip below the horizon at the end of a long day's trek, he galloped back to the lumbering wagons, and circling them like a sheep-dog pointed vigorously to a group of kopjes now visible a couple of miles ahead. It was almost dark as the wagons arrived.

Ruth was now well versed in the routine for establishing a laager, and dutifully drove her wagon into its allotted place. The Commandant, with his many years of experience, tactically sited the laager between two parallel lines of kopjes to provide concealment and give advantage should an attack be made from front or rear. Ruth drew her wagon across the open gully along with others, to create a framework for defence - the same manoeuvre was undertaken behind. In this way the perimeter was established. Ezra and the boys outspanned the oxen and allowed them to graze within the limits of the encampment, whilst Ruth unhitched her horse from the rear of the wagon and led it up the hillside. There she hobbled it and left it to feed as best it could. She returned to help heave the wagons close together, and to secure them to each other by rope. Brushwood was cut and crammed between wheels and trektow to solidify the breastwork. Not only were the English columns to be avoided, but the increasing number of marauding gangs of armed blacks were to be deterred.

Those women who were to act as sentries quietly took up their positions amongst the shrubs and rocks on the hills in front and rear of the laager. Ruth watched them go: mothers and mere girls looking so incongruous in their sweeping skirts, each with rifle in their right hand, a bandolier full of cartridges over a shoulder, and a scanty blanket tucked under the left arm.

Ezra and Ruth worked together to stretch a tarpaulin over a temporary ridge pole, whilst the boys cut brushwood for mattresses and laid blankets over it to provide beds. Ezra had managed to retain one black servant who instinctively cut kindling for a fire which he supplemented with dried cattle-manure pressed into bricks. Soon the dense smoke curled lazily upwards filling the air with a pungent odour. It was not long before the acorn-coffee and the meal of maize porridge were ready.

"It's time for bed," announced Ezra to the two boys. After a tiring day there were no protests. There was insufficient water for washing or night-clothes to put on. The boys simply scrambled beneath a couple of blankets and huddled together for mutual warmth.

Ezra picked up a torn, threadbare dress and sat on a box by the fire, "It's hardly worth repairing," she sighed. But despite the apparent hopelessness of the task, she began to sew.

Ruth took the Mauser rifle from the store box at the front of the wagon and joined her friend. Only ten rounds of ammunition remained, but she was intent on keeping the rifle in good condition. This weapon cleaning had become a nightly ritual - a virtual obsession. Competently, she removed the bolt and magazine, and using a pull-through she cleaned the inside of the barrel. Meticulously, she wiped the metal-work with a lightly oiled rag before carefully reassembling the parts.

From another area of the laager could be heard the strident voice of the Predikant reading from the Bible to a group of women who listened attentively, reverently. He then offered earnest prayers for God's protection over them all, his voice booming through the still night air, before a final hymn was sung and the congregation dispersed. The two friends rarely joined this nightly assembly; emotions from the recent loss of loved ones were still raw, challenging their once unshakable belief in an omnipresent and loving God. Silently their hearts screamed: "God, where are you in all of this?" They waited for an answer.

Soon the camp was wrapped in sleep, and nothing could be heard but the snorting of horses, the lowing of oxen, and the occasional barking of a dog.

Throughout the night, at regular intervals, women rose silently from the ranks of the sleeping, and noiselessly, like flitting ghosts, disappeared into the deep shadows of the kopjes; whilst other women, equally silently, slipped in from the posts they had been occupying, and stretched out to snatch sleep whilst they could.

•••

The commandos were increasingly active in the area making it difficult for the English to venture out in daylight other than in strong columns. It had become safer to conduct operations under cover of darkness. Black Native spies had brought information that a group of Boers were occupying the ruins of a burnt-out farm, driven into shelter by the intense cold, and with several of them suffering from illness. Pieter rode at the head of a strong force of mounted infantry, intent on destroying or capturing this group.

It was a freezing cold night. The frost lay heavily on the brown grass and crackled beneath the horses' hooves - the wet indentations clearly marked their progress. It was not long before the mist was swirling thickly, greatly reducing visibility. Pieter slowed the pace to a gentle trot as he sought to maintain direction – without stars to guide him it became more a case of instinct and intuition rather than precise navigation. After a couple of hours the officer in charge became restless:

"How much further?" he demanded.

Pieter resented the harsh, contemptuous tone of the question. He knew that many of the English disapproved of the volunteers – they saw them as collaborators; necessary allies, but loathsome.

"Almost there," encouraged Pieter. "We follow along this donga for about a mile to a drift. The farm is a few hundred yards on the other side."

With this reassurance the column pressed on.

As the mounted infantry cautiously negotiated the drift, a volley of rifle fire suddenly ripped through the night. There was panic; pandemonium; soldiers were cut down by the scything metal. Horses shied emptying their saddles, others slumped heavily to the ground riddled with bullets, spilling their riders. It was an ambush.

Pieter felt his horse shudder as a bullet struck home. He pulled hard on the reins and coaxed the animal back out of the drift and clear of the killing zone. He withdrew rapidly into the gloom of the mist. Miraculously he was unhurt, but his horse was wounded. He quickly examined it and found that a bullet had passed through his saddle-bag and into the flank of his horse - she would not last long. But he needed to get as far away as possible to evade capture and almost certain death at the hands of his countrymen. Desperately, he cajoled and coerced his failing mount to carry him to safety. For an hour she fought courageously, trotting on, until eventually she slowed to a halt, head drooping, wheezing painfully. He dismounted and held her by the halter. The right thing to do was to put her out of her misery, but any shot would give away his location. He took off the saddle, stroked her neck comfortingly, and set off on foot. He heard the clump as she collapsed to the ground; he did not look back.

He considered his options: it was too far to make it back to Standerton on foot in what was left of the night, and with daylight he would be exposed on the veld; not too far away was a group of kopjes where he might hide during the day, and then complete his journey the following night. He opted for the latter.

He was confident of his navigational skills, and was soon rewarded as the grey kopjes peered through the misty darkness and gradually solidified as he drew close in the revealing dawn.

"Wie kom daar! Wie kom daar!"

Startled, he stood still. To be challenged in Afrikaans was his worst fear; and was that a woman's voice?

"Wie kom daar! Wie kom daar!"

He turned to run. A shot rang out; the bullet zipped past his head. He lurched forward; tripped; fell. As he scrambled to his feet he felt a sharp pain in his ankle: damn! He'd twisted it. He stood up, staggered forward. He heard the dull retort of a rifle: zip! He sensed people running after him. A woman screeched: "Stop or I fire!" Other voices joined in the clamour. The next shot was fired from much closer, the voices just behind him. Realising that he could not escape he halted and turned about to meet a posse of women closing in on him, several armed and waving their rifles in his direction.

"I thought you were an English encampment," he stuttered unconvincingly. "I was out scouting for my commando when my horse took ill ... horse disease. I've been left stranded on foot."

The women approached warily.

"Look at his hat!", shouted one. "The blue band!"

"A joiner!" screamed another.

"A traitor!"

The whole laager was woken by the disturbance and alarmed by the shots. The women hurriedly scooped up their children and ushered them behind the wagons. Those who owned rifles grabbed them and assumed rehearsed positions ready to fight, but soon the message filtered down that a joiner had blundered into the laager and was now securely tied to the wheel of the Commandant's wagon. The children were excited:

"Can we go and see the joiner?"

After much badgering, Ezra reluctantly agreed. The children skipped off eager to see this curiosity. They soon returned disappointed. "He's just ordinary!" declared Jacob.

It was mid-morning when a group of a dozen or so burghers arrived. Ruth was to learn that they had set a trap for the English and had ambushed the Tommies a couple of hours' distance away. With the dawn they had followed the trails of some who had escaped, one of which led to the laager. Apparently, they had been loud in their compliments of the women's actions, and then incensed when they realised the captive was not a Tommy, but a joiner. Seemingly, he was roughly treated by them, and it was only the predikant's intervention which stopped them from shooting the prisoner outright:

"The punishment must be determined by the proper authority, and the verdict delivered to me," insisted the Predikant.

"He's a traitor, and the crime is high treason. There can only be one verdict. Why waste time?" protested the group leader, a Field-Cornet.

"Because we live by the rule of law ... God's law. If anything less then we are but animals," countered the Predikant in a shaky voice. "Bring me the verdict in General Botha's own hand and then, and only then, will I give the prisoner to you."

"We could take him now," threatened the Field-Cornet.

The old Preacher looked unflinchingly at his opponent: "*The fear of the Lord prolongeth days, but the years of the wicked shall be shortened.*"

Chastened, the burghers rode off promising to be back in two or three days.

It was as she was making her way to the hillside to check on her horse, that Ruth saw the figure seated on the ground leaning back against the wheel with stretched hands secured by ropes to the rim. At first she could not believe it. How could it be? But as she drew closer it was unmistakable.

"Pieter! My God! Pieter! It's you!" Her heart sank; her insides turned; she felt nauseous. She ran to him, and crouching hugged him with tear-filled eyes. She pulled back and stared into his battered face, "Why? Why?" she screamed at him. "How could you?" Confusing, tangled emotions flowed through her body: anger, disbelief, anxiety, fear, love. Once more she threw her arms around him. "O God! God!" she sobbed.

He said nothing. Eventually, with Ruth kneeling on the cold, hard ground in front of him, he said quietly, "I'm sorry; so sorry. I did it for the best."

"The best! How could it be for the best?"

"I just wanted the war to finish quickly ... to bring an end to all the killing and destruction ... to go home ... to be left alone."

"You know what you've done? You know what they'll do to you?"

He nodded in silent understanding.

Ruth leant forward and placed her head on his chest; she

224

cried quietly.

Ruth returned to her wagon where she warmed some broth and made fresh coffee. She gathered up her two blankets, and with the refreshments went back to Pieter. She wrapped him up and fed him, then sat with him, her hand touching his body in reassurance.

"It may be that you'll be sentenced to a lashing," she said.

"They'll shoot me."

"You don't know that."

"Yes I do. I always knew that that is what would happen should I be caught. I know the consequences of my actions." A pause, then, "I fought my fight a different way."

"Against your own people!" she burst out instinctively, then immediately regretted the bitter accusation.

"For my own people," he stressed.

Ruth could not understand his logic and motivation; all she knew was that she loved her younger cousin.

"Promise me something," he asked.

"Yes, if I can."

"After this is over, find me and bury me in the family cemetery beneath the poplar trees ... with my parents and brother."

"It won't come to that."

"Promise me!"

Sadly, she whispered, "I promise."

As they waited for the verdict, Ruth devoted herself to his care. Day and night she stayed close to him bringing food and hot drinks, feeding him with a spoon and holding a cup to his lips. During the frosty nights they huddled together beneath her blankets; never warm, mostly chilled and shivering. In the morning the blankets would be white and crisp with frost.

They talked in hushed voices guarding the intimacy of their conversation. They reminisced over their younger care-free days when they would roam the veld together – with her brother Jan and Pieter's twin brother Hans - shooting antelope and sleeping under the large star-filled skies. An idyllic existence rudely shattered by adulthood and war. Solemnly, they reflected on their enthusiasm to fight the Khakis; and now, where was the glory? Their way of life destroyed, their family decimated, and no end in sight. There were long periods when they sat quietly, united in a pain for which they had no words.

All this time Pieter was under constant guard. The women and children gathered intermittently throughout the day to gawk at the condemned man like vultures around a corpse. They kept a discreet distance, but made no attempt to hide their hatred and anger: "Judas! Judas!" they jibed. One tearful woman, unable to contain her hatred, taunted: "Look carefully young man, look at the sun; tomorrow you might not see it again."

Ruth became aware of a growing hostility and resentment towards her as she moved about the camp.

"Why are you doing this?" questioned Ezra on one occasion when Ruth was preparing food for Pieter.

"You know why ... he's my cousin ... he's kith and kin ... my blood."

"He's a joiner, a traitor. It's Christian to keep him alive until they shoot him; but you're coddling him."

Ruth placed a dung-brick onto the fire ignoring her friend.

"You know Esther in the next wagon," persisted Ezra, "it was the likes of him who guided the Tommies to her farm. They cast her and her young daughter out into the freezing night in nothing but thin night-clothes. If it wasn't for a passing commando they would have frozen to death. What kind of people are they?" she demanded rhetorically. "Scum!"

No one had been more damning of traitors than Ruth; but this was Pieter.

It was the third night, as the hymn singing ended and the flickering fires died down, when the burghers galloped noisily into the laager. There followed a short discussion with the

226

elderly leaders, after which the visitors dispersed amongst the women seeking hot coffee and food.

The Commandant hobbled across to Pieter and Ruth; he was dejected and desolate. With hushed voice he declared formally, "I have the verdict from General Botha. You are found guilty of high treason and are to be shot by firing squad as quickly as circumstances permit. I have agreed with the burghers that it's best for everyone that we don't delay. Your execution will be at first light. Until then may God comfort you." He paused, then added, "Young man, would you wish me to call the predikant?"

"No. Just my cousin to be with me."

The Commandant withdrew. Ruth fetched a Bible and an oil lamp and read, occasionally pausing, taut with tears:

"The Lord is my shepherd; I shall not want.
He maketh me lie down in green pastures: he leadeth me beside the still waters.
He restoreth my soul: he leadeth me in the paths of righteousness for his names' sake.
Yea, thou I walk through the valley of the shadow of death, I will fear no evil: for thou art with me; thy rod and thy staff they comfort me ..."

"Will they forgive me?" probed Pieter.

"My parents and Jan?"

"Yes, my family?"

Ruth could imagine their outrage and horror at what Pieter had done. Would they forgive him? "They love you," she replied shakily. "Of course they'll forgive you."

Pieter felt his convictions crumbling. Had he been right? For the first time he was filled with doubts: shaken, tense, agitated. Suddenly there was much he wanted to say, but the power to speak drained from him. His tongue cleaved to his plate with fear. His eyes grew wet with tears.

As the hours rushed by they were unable to sleep; tormented by physical discomfort and the approaching terror. Eventually,

227

through sheer exhaustion, they dozed spasmodically.

Immersed in their own traumatic world, Ruth and Pieter failed to notice two black Natives slip quietly out of the laager and disappear behind the kopje. They each carried a shovel.

....

A long, low arc of light suffused the eastern sky with crimson. The two elderly Boers approached followed closely by the Field-Cornet and three of his men. The clergyman placed a compassionate hand on Pieter's shoulder:
"Your time has come … be a man."
Ruth could contain her raw grief no more; shaking and sobbing loudly she hugged Pieter tightly, willing this nightmare to pass.
He nuzzled into her breast, "You've been the mother I never had. I love you." Reluctant tears filled his eyes, "Now you must let me die with dignity."
"Ruth, Ruth, stand clear", gently the Commandant pulled her back.
With this, two of the burghers strode forward and released Pieter from the wheel. They pulled him roughly to his feet and bound his wrists behind his back.
"You'll treat this young man with compassion as befits God's people," ordered the predikant firmly.
The two men paused and looked to the Field-Cornet for instruction; he nodded slowly. With a burgher firmly holding each arm, the party left the laager as it stirred into life. A small group of women watched the procession from a tactful distance – no one came to comfort Ruth in her distress.
As they walked, the predikant spoke comfortingly to Pieter, "My son; God promises that there will be a new heaven and a new earth. He read from his Bible:

"And God shall wipe away all tears from their eyes; and there shall be no more death, neither sorrow, nor crying, neither

shall there be any more pain: for the former things are passed away. Then shall the dust return to the earth as it was: and the spirit shall return unto God who gave it."

They turned a corner to see the two Natives leaning on their shovels by a hole surrounded by heaps of freshly dug earth. Pieter blanched. Until that moment he had been suppressing the reality of the situation in his mind, almost as if he was living a dream, but now the self-deception was cruelly shattered. His hands trembled; his teeth chattered. Fear tugged at his knees. He staggered. Unsympathetic arms propelled him forward. He was placed at the head of the grave.

"Do you believe in God?" asked the predikant.

"Yes," replied Pieter weakly.

"Remember the two robbers hanging at Jesus' side and his words to them: *"Today shalt thou be with me in paradise."* It's never to late to call on God's mercy. Do you repent of your actions?"

Almost inaudibly Pieter replied, "Yes. I repent."

"Then today you also will be in paradise; in God's eternal care. Be brave for just a moment longer."

The Field-Cornet moved forward and applied a blindfold. He stepped back from the shivering figure – was it from the cold or fear?

Pieter began to recite the Lord's Prayer. The accompanying burghers lined up and silently took aim. As Pieter came to the "Amen", the Field-Cornet struck a shovel with a stone; they fired. With a convulsive jerk, Pieter pitched backward into the grave. The Natives hurriedly scurried forward and covered the warm body with soil.

Ruth stood as if impaled to the ground, unmoving as she watched her cousin and escort disappear from view. She waited, stomach tight, heart pounding, tense with fear. Eventually the muffled sound of the volley drifted towards her on the breeze. Now, drained of emotion, empty, broken, she

229

turned and walked back silently towards her wagon, defiantly passing through a gauntlet of stern, unfriendly, uncomprehending women.

She knew that she could no longer stay. She had to find the Witberg Commando. She fetched her horse, placed scant food and her few belongings into a corn bag and saddle bags, tied a blanket to the front of the saddle, and waved a reluctant goodbye to the sad, bewildered boys.

CHAPTER 20

Boots – boots – boots -boots – movin' up an' down again!

Rudyard Kipling

"DRIVES"

It was 4:30 a.m. The bugle sounded "reveille". Rodger half-welcomed the end of a cold restless night. He threw off his blanket, stood up, stamped his feet and rubbed his hands to encourage the failing circulation. He was chilled to the marrow, stiff-limbed and pretty miserable. His soldier-servant soon brought him a mug of tea which he eagerly grasped with both hands to absorb the heat. With clumsy fingers he threw on his equipment, picked up his rifle and sought out his platoon.

Before long, the darkness dissipated and the glorious sun burst over the horizon, melting the frost which sparkled like a million diamonds on the long grass of the veld.

The column was on the move acting in concert with others to sweep across the undulating plains and flush out Johnnie Boer.

Rodger still found the sight of a well-ordered column awe inspiring, with each element smoothly performing its allocated task. Firstly, a long extended line of cavalry scouted ahead searching every nook and cranny for traces of the enemy. Then came half a battalion of infantry with companies extended on each flank. The light baggage wagons, drawn by mules, followed with their designated close escort of infantry. Next the guns with their ammunition train, and behind them the slow-moving ox-convoy carrying provisions and general stores. Finally more infantry, with cavalry as a rearguard. The column numbered over three thousand men and stretched over a distance of five miles.

Rodger marched at the head of his platoon over the unchanging terrain, aware of their grousing and good-natured banter. At 10:00 a.m. the column halted.

"Sergeant Mellish!"

"Sir."

"Take two men and collect the rations from the Colour-Sergeant."

It was not long before Mellish returned and issued the daily food: for each man a packet of "hard-tack" biscuits and a tin of bully-beef.

"The men are to eat and rest. We move out at 3:30 p.m."

Everyone welcomed the opportunity to snatch deprived-of sleep in the scant warmth of the winter sun.

The ponderous column renewed its manoeuvre, crawling over the barren veld, once the home of enormous herds of game, before being sparsely settled by the Boers with their six thousand acre farms. There was little to relieve the monotony except the occasional Native kraal with its small patch of mealies, and the blackened shells of farmsteads, their environs littered with rotting animals. The stench was disgusting. Rodger and the others held their noses as they hurried past, leaving the vultures to finish their gruesome feast.

Shortly after dusk the column halted. Rodger circulated around his men as they lit small fires and brewed tea; painfully they eased off their boots and inspected their damaged feet. "Here, apply this to the blister." He tore a piece of surgical tape from a roll which he always carried in his pack and handed it carefully to a sufferer. "My uncle is a doctor and he swears by it," encouraged Rodger.

Soon the weary soldiers were wrapping themselves in their blankets in pursuit of illusive sleep.

Another typical day, thought Rodger. We move at the speed of the slowest beast – the oxen – and on a good day cover twenty miles; a distance the Boers can cover in a couple of hours. No wonder we barely see the enemy. Increasingly, he perceived an element of futility in their aimless wanderings, but would never share that opinion with his men.

Another night, another day.

The column swept through and around a deserted town. As Rodger advanced down its dusty main street he was saddened to see the roofless houses with doors hanging drunkenly and shattered windows. Only the wooden church, with its commanding bell tower, was left unscathed.

"What town is this?" asked a curious soldier.

"Bethal," responded Rodger, "and there are plenty of others like it on the high-veld."

A rider passed down the column informing officers as he did so: "Scouts have located Boers a few miles to our front. We're going to close on them."

They marched on through the low rolling landscape; from the summit of one rise another loomed tantalisingly in the distance with monotonous repetition, seemingly beyond reach. They marched unrelentingly.

A wind developed, growing stronger with each passing hour. Soon blinding showers of sand and dust stung their faces making marching arduous and tiring. Mile after mile they marched, half covered in dust and parched with thirst. No water; feet swollen and bleeding in the stiff, unforgiving leather of issued boots; eyes bloodshot with fatigue and penetrating sand; faces begrimed with a thick layer of dirt. They plodded along mechanically like automatons; strength failing; spirits low.

"They're marching us to death," complained a soldier with rasping breath.

Mellish would have none of it, "Stop yer whining and keep going or you'll 'ave me to deal wi.'"

The forced march continued through the night with little concession given to their fatigue.

Rodger tried to motivate his weary men, "The Boers will camp for the night and expect us to do the same. We'll catch up with them during darkness, and in the morning they won't know what's hit them."

By the time dawn broke they had covered thirty miles with little rest and no food.

The air was filled with the whip-like crack of the Mauser. The cavalry screen fell back and the guns trundled forward. The smoke-filled roar of the 15-pounders was followed a few seconds later with the burst of brownish-green lyddite on a line of low kopjes about a mile ahead.

"Move forward! Into extended line!" Rodger positioned his platoon ready for the assault on the kopjes. He searched for the signal from his company commander. There it was - the vigorous wave of an arm.

"Advance! Advance!" His exhausted men stumbled forward, first across the open ground, and then up the slope through thickets of prickly mimosa bushes. At this point the artillery fire stopped for fear of hitting their own men.

Surviving Boers poured fire down on the assaulting infantry. Next to Rodger was his runner; he dropped to the ground with a stifled groan. Instinctively, Rodger stopped to give assistance. A quick examination showed that a bullet had entered the soldier's head just in front of the left ear, and, following the contours of the skull, emerged at the back of the neck. Miraculously, he was not dead; but Rodger knew he could not linger, "We'll be back Armstrong, just as soon as we see off the Boer." He had to lead his men from the front.

"Fix Bayonets!" Forward movement stopped momentarily as bayonet studs found their locking lugs. "Charge!" As he topped the crest of the kopje he was met with the sight of dozens of horsemen galloping away into the emptiness of the veld, at liberty to fight another day. Surprisingly, the guns had caused few casualties; he could only find the shredded corpses of three enemy. He quickly returned to Armstrong to find that he was dead. Two other of his men were slightly wounded.

The column needed rest. As Rodger led his men to their

allocated space in the camp, he passed a conductor who was placing his pistol behind the ear of a collapsed ox; he shot it dead. He looked up, and unsolicited remarked in frustration and bitterness, "Forty-two oxen dead in twenty-four hours. That's what this damned chase has cost us; forty-two oxen."

Rodger was dead-beat; he could find no soothing words for the distressed conductor and passed by silently.

Dutifully, Sergeant Mellish sought out the Colour-Sergeant for the platoon's rations. He returned with a flour sack thrown over his shoulder, his face red with anger and annoyance, "No bloody biscuits! The Commissariat Department say they've run out, so we've been issued flour and told t' make wor own bread."

"How'd we do that, Sergeant?" enquired a hapless soldier.

"Don't ask me. I'm no bloody baker!" And with that he poured each each man's portion into his mess-tin.

Rodger was surprised at the ingenuity of some of his soldiers as they experimented with the flour. Some mixed up a dough and baked it on a fire – for some the paste was too thin, for others it burnt on the outside whilst remaining raw on the inside. Others simply added a little salt, tied it in a handkerchief and boiled the mixture into a sort of dumpling.

There was also time to mend clothes using the small, issued, cloth pouch which contained useful items for make and mend such as buttons, needles and thread. And time also to fight the uneven battle against the ubiquitous lice secreted in the seams of their rags by burning them with cigarette ends.

In this way Rodger and his platoon spent the dry, cold months of a South African winter. The column plied incessantly backwards and forwards across the veld, rarely encountering an illusive enemy who fought only at his time of choosing - shadowy silhouettes which forever drew them into an unending vacuum. The column's progress was plotted by the flames and spiralling smoke of any building which had previously escaped destruction.

On one occasion, as they squeezed a group of Boers against a blockhouse line, the latter used a favourable wind to set the veld on fire. A gentle breeze fanned the flames, and within an incredibly short time acres of grass were ablaze. The flames travelled with remarkable speed emitting a roaring sound which reminded Rodger of the sea breaking on the rocky Northumberland shore. Soldiers fought the flames with blankets, waterproof sheets, wagon tarpaulins, whatever was to hand, to beat out the menace. The veld glowed like a furnace. In the ensuing smoke and chaos, the Boers melted away.

It was early September when the usual clear, blue sky blackened with a great mass of dense, threatening clouds. Rodger stood looking into the distance as a high bank of cloud raced towards them, travelling with an amazing rapidity, and a primal howl. Suddenly it fell upon them. Thunder crashed overhead and a terrible lightening of magnificent brilliance lit up the gloom. As a spectacle it was grand, majestic - an awesome display of nature's power. At first the rain splashed on the ground in "pieces" - Rodger thought "drops" inadequately described it - but then came down in torrents. Soon he was soaked; water ran down his back. Where once the ground had been dry, gurgling streams surged past. The roar rumbled into the distance, now returning, reverberating overhead in a deafening roar, a mind-stunning din. All the while the lightening blazed about them; great lurid flashes of flame lighting up the veld.

Rodger welcomed the spring rains; the air was deliciously cool and bracing, and after the rains everything seemed to revive. Soon the brown grasses of the veld would be replaced by new fresh green shoots wholly changing the face of nature. But it also heralded danger. The new growth would provide nourishment for the Boers' hardy ponies, and instead of them lingering on the defensive, it would restore their far-ranging mobility.

CHAPTER 22

With women the heart argues, not the mind

Matthew Arnold Merope 1858

"THAT BLOODY WOMAN!"
(October 1901)

Lord Ripon, as Chairman of the Distress Fund, approached the War Office with the suggestion that ladies should be sent at once to South Africa to ascertain the true situation in the concentration camps. He offered Emily Hobhouse as a suitable candidate. The Government was facing approbation from foreign governments, bruising criticism in the House, as well as public rallies and demonstrations at home – the country was roused. The Government had to be seen to be responding.

Emily was not surprised when she was excluded from the Ladies Commission of Enquiry which departed for South Africa. St John Broderick had been very frank in his letter to her:

The only considerations which have guided the Government in their selection of ladies to visit the Concentration Camps, beyond their special capacity for such work, was that they should be, so far as is possible, removed from the suspicion of partiality to the system adopted or the reverse ... It would have been impossible for the Government to accept your services ... as your reports and speeches have been the subject of so much controversy ...

She scrutinized the Government's latest published statistics from the camps which showed that in August there had been

1,878 deaths, of which 1,545 had been children. Far from improving, she was dismayed to see that the situation was deteriorating. She had done all she could to inform and alert public opinion at home, now, despite Government objections, she determined that it was time to return to South Africa; on this occasion with a companion.

....

Lieutenant Colonel Birdwood knocked tentatively on the door before entering Kitchener's office. It was going to be a difficult meeting. He stopped before the desk waiting for his boss to finish writing. A few moments elapsed before Kitchener looked up and laid down his pen. He leaned back in his chair, relaxed but expectant, "What is it Birdie?"

"We've just received a signal from Sir Alfred to say that Miss Hobhouse has sailed from Southampton on the *Avondale Castle*. She's due to arrive in Cape Town a week Sunday, that is on 27 October."

Kitchener thrust back his chair and jumped to his feet, "That bloody woman! Hasn't she caused enough trouble!"

Birdwood had anticipated this explosion. Now he watched as the Commander-in-Chief paced the room.

"Haven't we enough to contend with without this damned Ladies' Commission tramping unchecked through the camps. On top of all this, that interfering troublemaker is to return. I blame Milner. He should never have given that woman licence to roam in the first place. Wasn't it her letters exaggerating the problems, and her emotional rantings on return to England which created a furore and gave the Liberal opposition a stick with which to beat the Government? What was it the Liberal leader, Campbell Bannerman, said of the camps: "Methods of barbarism". Didn't I forward the report written by Goold-Adams after his inspection of every camp in the Orange River Colony, in which he stated that all the people were well looked after and completely satisfied with all we are doing for them?"

His anger flowed, "Hobhouse belongs to the radical wing of

the Liberal Party – pro-Boer; everyone of them! This agitation over the concentration camps has been raised by an unsexed, hysterical spinster who is prepared to sacrifice everything for notoriety!"

He paused, his face red with outrage. "The Colonial Secretary should have known better than to send a bunch of do-gooding society ladies to poke around the camps as if my word was not sufficient. This Mrs ... erm"

"Fawcett, sir," prompted Birdwood.

"Exactly ... Fawcett, has reported sickness amongst the inmates." He rushed to a side table littered with documents, and after a moment's frenzied shuffling of papers lifted up a file. "Here is the report from Dr Woodroffe, the medical officer from the camp in Irene." Kitchener began to read aloud: "The habits of the people in general are such as would be a disgrace to any European nation ... napkins for babies are seldom used. They are allowed to mess their beds, which lie for days without being washed or aired, and the tents absolutely stink of decomposing urine etc."

He searched again, and amid a flurry of papers produced another report, "From Maxwell, the military governor of Pretoria: "The camps are going well, the inmates are well cared for, and although the death rate amongst the children is excessive, it is in most cases the fault of the mothers themselves. There has been a severe epidemic of measles which only requires care, but women won't have anything to do with the doctors or nurses and prefer their own squalid methods."

"I, myself, am more than familiar with some of these Boer quackish remedies. Whilst we were providing excellent nursing for our soldiers during the enteric epidemic in Bloemfontein, Boer women would boil horse dung, strain it, and give it to their people as medication. Medieval! Unbelievable! And I have seen the habits of these trekboer women. They are accustomed to defecating in the open veld and shun the toilet facilities we provide. Is it surprising that there's disease!"

Birdwood watched his agitated boss, judging the right moment to interrupt, "Undoubtedly, the high mortality is due to the primitive habits of the Boer women and their inferiority as mothers."

Kitchener quietened with this calm affirmation.

"But," continued Birdwood, "we still have the looming problem of Miss Hobhouse."

"Doesn't the woman know that I will not allow her to visit the camps? She will be confined to Cape Town."

"Even there I fear she will be a provocation. A focal point for discontent ... many of the Cape Dutch are incensed by our scorched earth tactics and concentration policy. It would be best if she was not to disembark at all."

"That's simple enough, arrange for her to be immediately placed on the first ship back to England."

"At the moment that cannot be done, sir. She has committed no offence so the civilian authorities have no justification to act," explained Birdwood.

Kitchener screwed up his face in angry frustration.

"However," added Birdwood, "should you extend the reach of martial law to include Cape Town itself, then that would give you the authority to send her home."

"But the imposition of martial law in the capital would cause an uproar amongst the representatives of the Cape Legislature."

"Naturally, but we could weather the storm for the short time needed to rid ourselves of that woman."

"Excellent," concluded Kitchener.

....

In the warm autumn sun, Table Bay was at its most beautiful. With her friend, Emily leaned against the ship's rail and admired the calm, azure sea, the green hinterland, and the iconic Table Mountain in the distance draped with a white fluffy cloud.

As sweating Africans caught the thick hawsers thrown from

the ship, and pulled the vessel alongside the quay, they returned to their cabin to pack their few remaining items in preparation for disembarking. There was an officious knock on the door.

"Miss Hobhouse?" A young army Captain stood in the doorway accompanied by a ship's officer.

"Yes," confirmed Emily warily.

"It is my duty to inform you that you and your companion are not allowed to land, and that you must remain on board the ship. You may not communicate with anyone. In three days time you will be transferred to a ship leaving for England."

Emily was dumbfounded. She had never expected to be welcome in all quarters, but to be thrown out of the country before even landing! "Do you have a warrant for my detention?" she demanded.

"No; but Cape Town is under martial law and I have my orders."

"As I have committed no crime, you cannot detain me."

"Please, Miss Hobhouse, do not make things difficult. I would appreciate if you would give me your parole and promise to stay on board."

"No! I will not. And furthermore, the only way you will keep me from disembarking is to place me under guard. I want it to be clear to everyone that I am not remaining here by choice."

The Captain was flustered.

"And young man," she persisted, "you will take my letters to the Town Commandant and forward others to Sir Alfred Milner and to Lord Kitchener."

"Madam, I've explained that you are not allowed to communicate with anyone."

"Would you deprive me of the right of appeal?"

The Captain had never expected such fierce resistance and buckled under the pressure of this determined woman. "Miss Hobhouse, I am going to arrange a guard who will be posted at the gangplank. You will not be allowed to pass. When I come back I will take your letters and give them to my superior officer."

The following day the Captain returned, "I'm sorry Miss Hobhouse, but there is no change to the situation, you are to remain on board."

"Who has issued these instructions?" she demanded. "I wish to appeal."

"And to whom would you appeal?"

"Sir Alfred Milner ... Lord Kitchener."

"It is Lord Kitchener who has ordered your removal. There is no appeal"

It was as she had suspected. "Then place me in a prison on land."

"No madam."

She tottered unsteadily from side to side, before swooning into a nearby chair, "All this aggravation makes me feel weak. I could have a fever. I should see a doctor in the town."

The officer was unconvinced by this feminine display of frailty, "I will arrange for a doctor to come on board," he countered.

Finally, on the morning of the third day the young officer reappeared.

"Good morning Miss Hobhouse. It's time to leave. The troopship down the quay sails for England in an hour's time and you are to be on it."

"I am not leaving. I haven't packed," with a sweeping gesture she pointed to her belongings scattered about the cabin.

The Captain had had time to consider the various scenarios and remained unruffled. "I will arrange for a steward to collect your things, but you must leave with me now."

Emily sat in her chair unmoving.

"Miss Hobhouse, the ship will not wait for you, we must leave now."

"The summary arrest and removal of an Englishwoman bound on works of charity, without warrant of any kind or stated offence, is a proceeding which requires explanation."

The Captain was no longer listening. With the wave of his hand, he summoned two burly soldiers who were waiting down the walk-way. "Be careful now," he cautioned them as they brushed past him into the confines of the small cabin.

Emily was firmly, but gently, pulled up from the chair and bodily carried out horizontally.

"Wait!" called the officer to his soldiers. They stopped by the gangplank. Carefully he covered Emily's lower body and legs with a shawl for the sake of decency. "All right; take her away."

The soldiers proceeded down the gangplank and along the quayside to the waiting troopship. Her flailing legs and noisy protestations drew curious glances, but her departure was assured. Her companion followed compliantly, accompanied by a ship's steward bending under the weight of woollen carpet-bags.

CHAPTER 23

If you deal with a fox, think of his tricks

Proverb

NIGHT RAID

Josiah dismounted, left his horse behind a small kopje and scrambled up the rocks. Keeping low, he scanned the veld to his front. He had been following the spoor of a Boer commando since sun-rise, careful not to be seen. If captured, his summary execution was a certainty. This had happened to other black scouts, his friends - their bodies dumped on the veld as a warning.

About half a mile to his front was a Basuto kraal of five huts surrounded by a fence of woven mimosa branches. The Boers would have visited the occupants; he lay quietly surveying the kraal to ensure that none remained. Soon he was rewarded by the sight of a young woman who emerged with a twig-broom sweeping away the loose dust from within the enclosure. She was bare-breasted with a long, tattered chitenge wrapped around her waist which almost touched the ground; a couple of small, naked children skipped about oblivious to the morning chill. They were relaxed. It was free of Boers.

Josiah approached the kraal at a gentle trot. On seeing him, the young woman grabbed her children and hastily withdrew. She was replaced by a wizened, white-haired, old man who defiantly barred the entrance. They exchanged traditional greetings, and after Josiah had offered a gift of a small bag of mealies, suspicions eased and he was welcomed inside. The two men sat on low, wooden stools and drank maize beer brought by one of a number of women. The old man explained that his sons had left for the towns to find work with the English, and that their wives and children were in his care.

As soon as convention permitted, Josiah moved the

244

conversation to the passing Boers. At first the old man angrily recounted how they had tried to force him to reveal his cache of food, but of course he insisted that he barely had enough to meet his family's needs - his triumphant grin indicated otherwise. He commented on how badly dressed were some of the Boers – wearing grain sacks and even a woman's dress – and on how hungry they were. Josiah probed gently to see if they had indicated their destination. They both knew that any suspicion of collaboration with the English would invite violent retribution, but his host seemed ready to help, "They're tired, and as they were leaving the leader said that they would rest soon." He paused before adding, "There's a broad depression where men and horses could hide." He pointed to the east.

Josiah thanked the old patriarch for his hospitality, and once again cautiously followed the trail of the commando. He was familiar with the place indicated, and after half an hour he again dismounted and continued cautiously on foot, leading his horse by its reins. He stopped short. A wisp of smoke spiralled idly upwards from beyond the next rise. He quietly withdrew.

It was late afternoon before Josiah reached the camp of Flying Column Number 3, where he reported to the Intelligence Officer, Major Aubrey Wools-Sampson. Wools-Sampson was an eccentric uitlander born in Cape Town: ex-gold-miner; ex-conspirator who had been imprisoned after the abortive Jameson Raid; ex-Commanding Officer of the colonial Imperial Light Horse – his exploits became so alarming that Kitchener cabled London to secure his dismissal. He had fought in the Zulu War and later in the First Boer War when he had been severely wounded. More recently, he was again wounded during the battle of Elandslaagte near Ladysmith. He possessed a pathological hatred of the Boer, but also had an intimate understanding of their psyche and behaviour. This, and his excellent knowledge of the Natives, their languages and the terrain, made him the ideal person to lead a team of African scouts – paid for out of his own pocket. Wools-Sampson spurned convention and rarely messed with his fellow officers. He would rather eat with his scouts. He was idiosyncratic and a loner. He always insisted on personally debriefing his "boys".

He sat around a fire drinking tea with Josiah who was recovering after his strenuous ride. Josiah was one of his best scouts: intelligent, educated, a fluent English speaker, had a good knowledge of the country, and was utterly committed to the defeat of the Boers as the precursor to better Native rights.

"So, how many in the commando?" quizzed Wools-Sampson.

"They were driving some cattle so it's not easy to be precise from their spoor, but I think between fifty and seventy."

"And the place of their laager; do you know it precisely?"

"Yes." Josiah went on to describe the ground in detail.

Wools-Sampson was reassured. "That's good," he affirmed. "Did you get any indication of their physical state and moral?"

Josiah recounted his conversation with the old man in the kraal and added, "They made no attempt to cover their spoor or deploy a rearguard. They are either careless or very tired."

"Either way, the advantage is with us," declared Wools-Sampson. "Now get some rest before you guide us tonight."

Flying Column Number 3 was led by Lieutenant Colonel Benson, an artillery officer of twenty years service in the army. He was a graduate of the Staff College, and a veteran of action in the Sudan and on the Gold Coast. A square-faced man with bushy eyebrows and generous moustache. He had been in South Africa since the early days of the war, and was now the most successful of the column commanders through his perfection of the night raid.

At dusk, Benson left his wagons, with their ten days of supplies, under the protection of his infantry battalion, and sallied forth with his mounted force of almost eight hundred troops: cavalry and mounted infantry.

The column moved at a regular canter with the occasional horse stumbling as their feet sank into the ant-eater holes which covered the veld, but there was no waiting for the casualties. It was a clear night; the sky carpeted with a dazzling array of stars. Josiah led the way accompanied by Wools-Sampson. There were no signs or tracks to follow, just estimated speed and the stars as navigational aids. After several hours of riding without a break, the shadowy kraal emerged from the greyness. It was with relief that he pointed it out to Wools-Sampson, "There! Over there!" He was always anxious at the weight of responsibility laid on his shoulders during the approach to these attacks. Thank goodness his navigation was accurate.

"Well done! We'll shake out here whilst you confirm that the Boers are still in their laager." With that Wools-Sampson moved off to meet the approaching column and to confer with Benson.

A halt was called which allowed everyone to draw breath after the hard ride; exhausted horses were replaced by fresh from the stock of led remounts. Only Josiah continued forward. After an estimated mile he dismounted, tethered his horse to a scraggy bush, and crept forward silently. After about ten minutes the ground began to slope down gently. He stopped. Ahead and below he saw the glowing, dying embers of half a dozen camp-fires, around them lay still, grey mounds; hobbled horses wandered about grazing idly. Wary of undetected sentries, he cautiously withdrew.

Benson greeted the confirmation of the Boers' presence with a triumphant grin. He ordered his men to deploy into two extended lines about a hundred yards one behind the other. A tremor of excitement ran through the attackers as they sat on their sweating horses, carbines in hand, waiting impatiently for the order to advance. It seemed an age before the first fingers of stabbing light broke the dark skyline. As the blood-red sun nudged into view, the order to advance at a trot rippled through the lines in hushed tones. The muted sounds of creaking leather and jingling accoutrements marked the ghostly advance. After a mile Benson stood in his stirrups to gain height and shouted at the top of his voice, "Charge! Charge!" The cry was taken up by the attackers as they accelerated into a gallop. There was no challenge from alert sentries. The riders came over the gentle rise to find the Boer laager lying at their feet barely eight hundred yards away. Spontaneously, the troops screamed and yelled with pulsating excitement as they bore down on the startled Boers. The latter struggled to their feet and began firing raggedly at the charging mass, but nothing could stop that momentum. The first line of horsemen smashed through the laager brushing defenders aside and rode beyond to capture any who might be fleeing. Then they turned to complete the encirclement. The second line swirled amongst the Boers, some fired indiscriminately ignoring raised hands, but as order was restored after the momentary chaos and exhilaration, the shocked survivors were herded together. Within minutes the fight was over. Four Boers were killed, twelve wounded and fifty-two taken prisoner for the price of one soldier wounded.

Benson drew his horse alongside Wools-Sampson's, "Another successful night raid, and a reasonable bag. Kitchener should be pleased. Pass on my thanks to your boys."

CHAPTER 24

Because I could not stop for death
He kindly stopped for me.
The carriage held but just ourselves
And immortality.

Emily Dickinson 1830 - 86

FLYING COLUMN NUMBER 3
(And the Battle of Bakenlaagte 30 October 1901)

General Louis Botha was relieved to arrive at Roodepoort farm, some four miles south of Ermelo, where he co-located his headquarters with Acting President Shalk Burger's token government. He was tired, disappointed and a little dispirited after several weeks of failure. His invasion of Natal had been thwarted by the heavy spring rains and resultant swollen rivers, and so he had turned his efforts to subduing two English strong points on the Transvaal – Zululand border. Despite his local superiority, the defenders of Forts Itala and Prospect had beaten back his burghers with heavy casualties. His actions had drawn down upon himself seven English columns from the Transvaal, and he had only managed to escape encirclement and capture by abandoning his supply wagons and riding fast through a closing gap as the noose tightened. Only a couple of days previously, whilst resting at a farm near Amersfoort, he had been surprised by a British dawn attack which forced him to flee precipitously leaving behind his hat and revolver as trophies for his enemies.

But it was not his nature to remain inactive for long. He summoned two of his staff, Piet Jooste and Fred Siemssen: "Go and find out what the enemy is up to."

The two men rode in a westerly direction without seeing any Khakis. By the third day they had covered more than sixty miles and were looking down on the burnt-out village of Trichardtsfontein.

"Look!" Jooste drew his friend's attention to a telegraph line with the wires seemingly intact - Jooste was a field telegraphist and always carried his vibrator with him. "Come on, let's see if it's in use."

They cantered across to a pole which Jooste climbed expertly. He connected his vibrator and listened carefully. The dominant noise was like the rushing buzz of hiving bees, but as he listened with a practised ear, in the background he could discern the rhythmic tapping of the telegraph key. He was amazed. Apparently, Kitchener was to their south in Standarton, and Benson was reporting that his refit was almost completed, and that he planned to leave Middleburg for the high-veld on 20 October with a force of fourteen hundred men and a large convoy.

"Botha needs to know this and quickly!" shouted Jooste as he dropped to the ground.

Botha listened intently to the news. Flying Column Number 3 was the scourge of his commandos; it struck terror into his burghers making them afraid to laager in the same place on two consecutive nights. In fact, his men now saddled up at 3 a.m. each morning, bracing themselves for the expected attack. Botha was determined to destroy this threat.

"One good thing has come from our failure to invade Natal," he told his staff. "All the English columns from the Eastern Transvaal which chased after us are still thrashing about far to the south-east. Benson will be alone on the high-veld." His plan was solidifying.

He took two of his staff and a heliograph and climbed a nearby kopje. Soon the clicking shutters produced flashes of sunlight reflected by a mirror; the Morse code signals probed the veld in search of General Coen Brits somewhere in the Standerton District. Botha scanned the distant horizon through his telescope hoping to see reciprocal flashes. A few minutes passed; "Got him!" He turned to his staff, "Tell him to advance on Bethal with all speed."

In the same way, orders were passed to his scattered commandos to facilitate the concentration of his forces. He spoke personally to the leader of the local Ermelo Commando, General Hans Grobler, "I want you to find Benson and to harass his column and slow him down until I reach you with our main force."

****

Josiah was always glad to see the end of the dry, cold winter months, and welcomed the warmer weather and life-refreshing rain. This year, however, the spring rains had arrived with a vengeance. Days of unremitting downpours had left the veld soft and sodden, and the dongas and spruits gushing torrents where previously they had been lazy trickles.

It had been an unproductive expedition. An early success had bagged thirty-seven prisoners, but thereafter it was apparent that the enemy were alert to the presence of the column – subsequent raids were like punching wildly in the air.

That evening Josiah was summoned with his fellow scouts by Wools-Sampson; he briefed them, "Our supplies are running low. The column is returning north to Brugspruit on the Delagoa Bay railway. Get what sleep you can. We leave at 4:30 am."

****

It was not difficult for Grobler to find a column of fourteen hundred men and three hundred wagons. They travelled slowly, and in their wake left an unmistakeable spoor. He deployed his men to snipe at flanks and rear and to destroy any patrols that came out to meet them. Occasionally, and at a safe distance, he would expose strong numbers of burghers on the skyline, threatening attack and building up uncertainties amongst his quarry, but then would melt away. At night he withdrew his main force several miles leaving only small parties to monitor the column at rest. He remained wary of Benson's night time raids, and had no intention of being ambushed himself. After three days of playing cat and mouse, the English column reached Zwak Fontein and made temporary camp.

It thundered, it poured, it blew, and a heavy mist covered the ground.

Throughout the day Grobler's burghers probed and prodded the stationery soldiers - like a child cautiously poking a cornered wild animal at arms length with a stick. Sometimes they excited warning shouts, sometimes the response to their presence was a bullet or even a volley. But the aim was achieved: the Khakis got little rest.

****

Benson was not surprised that his slow-moving column attracted the attention of the Boers, but he detected an unusual determination and persistence. They obviously did not have the strength to attack outright, but appeared to be exceptionally reckless and threatening. He felt uneasy. With the oxen rested, he would hope to reach Brugspruit and safety in three days. Tomorrow night they would camp at Onderwacht.

In the early hours of 30 October, in the dark and driving rain, the column continued its trek adopting its usual formation: the scout section roamed ahead, followed by the advance guard consisting of the wagons, protecting infantry, two guns and a pom-pom (37 mm quick-firing gun which fired a belt of ten 1-pound shells at the rate of one every two seconds); about an hour behind, as the rearguard, came the mounted infantry with a similar complement of artillery. With the passage of numerous wheels and hooves, the soggy ground was soon churned into a quagmire of glutinous mud.

Zip! … Zip!

Bullets cut through the air, fired blindly by the Boers as they

252

swirled around the clumsy column. Occasionally, the clinging mist wafted and parted momentarily exposing the attackers, but then swallowed them up in a ghostly haze.

Josiah and his fellow scout, Makao, searched the banks of the donga for a crossing place. The sides were steep and the water course about twenty feet wide - the brown, gurgling waters were in full spate and presented a real obstacle to the wagons. They trotted along the bank for about a mile before spotting a drift. There both banks of the donga had been graded by the efforts of a previous convoy, enabling access and exit. Cautiously, Josiah entered the surging water testing its depth – it washed the under-belly of his mount - and it quickly became apparent that the bottom was muddy and soft. But there was no alternative.

"You stay here and mark the spot. I'll tell the baas and bring on the wagons," asserted Josiah.

He soon found Wools-Sampson, and guided the vehicles to the drift. The oxen dragged the first wagon down the slope and plunged into the swell; the leading span was half way up the exit slope when the movement stopped. The wagon was stuck in the mud. The Native driver flicked his hide-whip and lashed the leading animals. With screams and curses he urged them onwards. The animals reacted, strained, and slowly, very slowly, the wagon nudged forward. The first one was across.

For a short while Josiah watched as more and more wagons negotiated the obstacle. Many had to be man-handled by soldiers of the vanguard, or double-teamed to drag them through the drift. Throughout, the rain was relentless and everyone was drenched and filthy. Wools-Sampson was joined by Benson who was worried at the delay. They moved a little distance from the hubbub in the donga; Josiah overheard their anxious discussion:

"How long before we get the wagons over?" quizzed Benson.

"Perhaps another hour," shouted Wools-Samson as he strove to be heard in the driving wind and rain.

"Too long," responded Benson. "The rearguard is under considerable pressure. They're falling back by rushes in good order, but they'll soon be here. The whole bloody column will be concentrated on this drift ... we've got to get moving and find a position we can defend."

"About three miles on is the farm at Bakenlaagte. It's on higher ground. We could head for there," suggested Wools-Samson.

"Good!" exclaimed Benson with a sense of relief. "Collect all the wagons which have crossed and head for the farm. I'll see the rest of the column over, and we'll retire on Brakenlaagte." He paused; then, "Keep your guns with you, but see if you can find an intermediate position for the rearguard guns."

The parley over, Benson dropped into the donga, waded through the water, and put his shoulder against a floundering wagon, heaving with his tired, sodden, cursing soldiers.

Wools-Sampson summoned his waiting Native scouts and explained the plan; he allocated tasks: "Josiah and Makao, I want you to reconnoitre Bakenlaagte to check that it's clear of the Boer. Pula and Mohato, you're to locate an area of high ground between here and Bakenlaagte where we might place guns to cover our withdrawal. Report back directly to Colonel Benson. Seetane and Metsi, scout west for a mile and see if it's clear of Boer." His gaze lingered for a moment on his motley collection of Native scouts with their ill-fitting jackets, baggy trousers, trilby hats and bandoliers full of ammunition criss-crossing their chests. He held them all in great affection. "Good luck!"

Josiah found the farm without incident, and then reconnoitred the area to the west where the ground rose slightly. With the knowledge that the location was Boer free, he and his companion returned to guide in the wagons. From the direction of the drift, the strong southerly wind carried the sound of a distant battle: the incessant "pop-pop" of rifle fire and the occasional muffled report of the 15-pounders.

****

It had been a hard ride. Botha and his reinforcing commandos had galloped more than seventy miles, the final thirty without stopping. But now the Boers had numerical superiority, and he was intent on destroying Benson's column before it could reach the safety of Brugspruit. He knew his men; they were dog-tired, but nonetheless eager for battle.

Botha sat on his horse waiting for his staff officers to bring news of the fighting; outwardly he exuded his famed calm; inwardly he was impatient and eager to strike.

"The English are conducting a disciplined withdrawal, but we are putting them under great pressure," reported a staff officer. "It seems that they are having enormous problems getting their wagons across a donga, and there's much confusion and congestion at the drift."

Botha considered the situation, and as if thinking aloud announced, "It's time to attack."

****

A wagon was stuck in the drift; all attempts to haul it out failed. Benson grabbed a trooper, "Ride fast to Major Wools-Sampson and tell him to send two empty mule-carts so that we can cross-load the cargo and get this wagon out!"

This took time.

Meanwhile, the rearguard, under Major F Gore Anley of the Essex Regiment, was in difficulty. The pom-pom had jammed and was useless. The two 15-pounder field guns could only fire blindly into the mist and were ineffective. "Get that pom-pom to safety!" he ordered. Then turning to the Battery Commander he shouted above the wind, "Get your guns across the drift and find high ground from which to provide cover!"

The Boers were growing bolder; more frequently now they worked in through the rain and mist: jabbing, poking, prodding, pressing; clinging to the column with the tenacity of a shadow. They fired volleys at the Khakis and retired, only to resurge again minutes later. The cold rain, driven by a southerly wind, made the work of the rearguard all but impossible. When they turned to face the enemy the stinging rain drove into their faces, blinding them and making it impracticable to see and take aim. Inexorably, Anley and his rearguard were pushed back to the drift.

Soldiers, officers, Native drivers and steaming animals sweated at the drift hauling out the unyielding wagons. Oxen staggered and strained, slipped and collapsed in their tracks though the whirling lashes still stung them. Wild curses and cries filled the air. The situation was electric with crisis.

In this bedlam of confusion, Anley sought out Benson, "The Boers are pressing harder and in greater numbers. Some are wearing cavalry cloaks and slouch hats adding to the confusion … it's difficult to tell friend from foe." He paused to gather breath; "I suspect they've been reinforced. We're in danger of being overrun."

"I've ordered Wools-Sampson to establish a defensive position at Brakenlaagte … it's about three miles north," explained Benson. "I've sent your guns with infantry protection to a ridge half way; if the mist lifts they can give covering fire."

"Colonel, without guns we can't hold back the Boers. What if we were all to retire at speed and make a clean break with the enemy? We could join the guns and even reach Wools-Sampson, and make our stand."

Thankfully, the last wagon was being hauled up the exit bank, but Benson was only too aware that some were still crawling across the veld towards Bakenlaagte farm, and that a quick withdrawal would leave them at the mercy of the Boers. But he hesitated only a moment, "All right, fall back on Wools-Sampson; I'll pick up the guns!"

It now became a race for the high ground. The rearguard, comprising the Scottish Horse and Yorkshire Mounted Infantry (YMI), splashed across the drift and galloped northwards. Elements of the Essex Regiment, who had been protecting the wagons, bent their heads before the fierce squalls and tramped fearfully towards the guns. Anley veered east with a company of infantry in tow and occupied a small kopje.

****

The Boers prodded the emptiness until it was apparent that the Khakis had broken off the engagement. Botha determined that the time was right for an all out pursuit and attack. He ordered his commandos into an extended line on a front of a mile plus, and shouted through the wind; "Attack! Attack!" A cry taken up by his subordinates. The burghers needed little encouragement. With kicking heels, they goaded their tired horses to best speed and pounded across the saturated ground, yelling and firing from the saddle in a frenzied state. A small group made for Anley and his detachment, but most swept towards the guns on the ridge, shooting-up labouring wagons as they passed and mercilessly riding down knots of tired, bedraggled soldiers.

****

Benson threw himself down near the guns and quickly took stock of his situation. Apart from the two 15-pounders and their small escort of twenty men, he had a detachment of YMI, a company of the Essex Regiment which was deployed on the slope facing the enemy, and a forward screen of Scottish Horse.

He looked back, and through a rift in the mist caught a glimpse of horsemen streaming over the veld - the air alive with yelling Boers. He watched as best he could, but also sensed the enemy as they galloped forward recklessly, smashing the Scottish Horse with overwhelming force; the infantry on the forward slope broke under the onslaught. Then the attackers disappeared into a hollow just below the ridge where they were out of sight in dead ground.

****

257

The Boers discarded their spent horses and crawled unseen to within forty yards of the defenders on the ridge. Unbeknown to Benson, a large group of enemy had occupied a similar hollow to the right rear of his position – they had the advantage of knowing the ground intimately.

****

A torrent of rifle fire swept the hill-top concentrating on the gunners. Benson watched as every man went down under remorseless volleys. He saw Sergeant Hayes who was wounded, the only survivor of his gun, crawl forward and reach up to pull the lanyard and fire a round before collapsing unconscious. Corporal Atkins, also wounded, reached up in an attempt to remove the breech block and so immobilise the gun, but a bullet passed through both his hands; he slumped down to the ground nursing his bloody wounds.

He saw the Battery Commander rush to the other gun and, bravely, but recklessly exposed, fire a round only to collapse mortally wounded. With his last gasps he summoned the limbers and teams waiting on the reverse slope of the ridge, to save the guns. Obediently they galloped forward only to be mowed down as they crossed the skyline.

Within minutes of the assault, the ridge was reduced to a shambles. Adopting a half-crouch, Benson moved amongst the survivors encouraging them to fight on.

Wham! When the bullet hit him it was as if someone had kicked the legs from beneath him. His left leg crumbled and he fell heavily to the ground; the pain was terrific. He looked; his knee was shattered; there wasn't much blood: "Damn!" He took his field-dressing from his top tunic pocket, and using his teeth ripped open the packaging. He crudely wrapped the bandage around his knee and tied it off. He then dragged himself towards two soldiers lying in a shallow hollow surrounded by protecting rocks; they were firing steadily at the Boers. He was only yards from their position when he felt a sting in his right forearm as another bullet struck home; helping hands pulled him roughly into the meagre cover.

There was a momentary lull in the firing. Out of the mist came a cry: "Surrender Khakis! Hands up!"

Before Benson could reply there came a terse, contemptuous shout, "We're Scots!"

As if affronted by the rebuke, some Boers rose to their feet to rush the position, but were sent scurrying back under a spontaneous volley.

The fight was renewed.

Benson grinned – he hoped encouragingly - at the soldiers, trying to infuse courage. He addressed one, "Trooper, I want you to take a message to Major Wools-Sampson. You're to tell him not to send the ambulances as the Boers will use the mules to drag away the guns." He looked into the frightened young face, the rain dripped from the rim of the soldier's helmet. "Do you understand?" he shouted amidst the noise of battle. "We mustn't let the guns fall into the hands of the Boers."

"Yes, sir."

"Good man!"

The trooper rose hesitantly, reluctant to leave the safety of the hollow; he was about to launch himself over the skyline; crack! He fell with a howl of pain and grasped his boot where a bullet had passed through, blood oozing through the eyelets. It was a few moments before he noticed his Commanding Officer; Benson was doubled up in pain, his hands clutching his stomach. The same bullet had ricochetted and struck him in the abdomen.

••

Everyone at the camp near Bakenlaagte was busy preparing the location to repel the anticipated onslaught. Cooks, officers' servants, Natives; all were employed digging trenches, laying barbed-wire and stockpiling ammunition. Wools-Sampson moved coolly to and fro encouraging and cajoling.

Occasionally the mist parted momentarily like drawn curtains through which they could see the battle raging a little over a mile away; hundreds of Boers were swarming over the ridge. They would be next.

Quartermaster-Sergeant Warnock of the Scottish Horse did not wait for orders. "All right you two, pick up the boxes and follow me." The unfortunates dragged an ammunition box in each hand by the short rope handle and took off after the burly, no-nonsense non-commissioned-officer (NCO). They staggered towards the ridge to their front keeping in the lee of the rise and out of sight of the Boers. After an exhausting twenty minutes, they reached the shallow donga where the horse-holders were sheltering, and then climbed the slope to the hellish maelstrom.

"Take the ammo over there! You, over there! Then Warnock crawled forward throwing bandoliers of fifty rounds to the surviving soldiers - he was so consumed by his own actions that he failed to see one of his two men jerk to a deadly halt. He kept the last bandolier for himself, picked up a discarded rifle, and calmly fired at the enemy whenever they exposed themselves – until he died riddled by three bullets.

....

"Sir! Sir!" Wools-Sampson was summoned by an agitated soldier. "Runner coming in!"

Trooper Grierson of the Scottish Horse tumbled into the camp, rasping and short of breath. "What is it?" urged Wools-Sampson, "You have a message?"

"Sir," Grierson fought to recover his composure. "Sir, from Colonel Benson. He says you're not to send the ambulances as the Boers will take the mules to carry off the guns. Also, he says that you are to fire shrapnel over the ridge to prevent the Boers reaching the guns."

"Are you sure about that? ... firing our guns I mean." He was alarmed at the consequences for survivors.

"Yes sir. Colonel Benson emphasised that it was an order."
"And what of Colonel Benson ... how is he?"
"Wounded sir ... badly."

Wools-Sampson moved away a little. He pondered the order and its consequences. Then he turned, "Get me the artillery detachment commander."

....

Benson remained conscious and in command despite his wounds. A soldier had propped him up against a boulder and applied field dressings to stem the flow of blood from his stomach, but the pain was excruciating.

Few of the almost two hundred men on the ridge remained unscathed. The summit was littered with British dead, dying and wounded; ammunition had been expended and the survivors waited for the inevitable final rush. It soon came.

As one, the Boers rose and directed a storm of indiscriminate fire on anything that moved, then they charged forward and seized the hill.

****

The trailing whoosh was followed by an ear-splitting crack as the shrapnel shells fired from the camp burst in the air. Mostly the hot, metal fragments peppered the environs of the ridge, but occasionally they struck the hill-top with an angry hiss.

It was a stalemate. The Boers withdrew slightly into the sheltering hollows; they were exhausted by their hard approach ride and the exertions of their attack. They could not remove the guns because of the artillery fire from the camp, and rifle fire from isolated, unsubdued strong points; the British were too weak to drive off the Boers.

With nightfall, Botha sent word to Wools-Sampson that ambulances could collect the wounded, and so began an informal truce.

With the cessation of firing, the burghers surged back onto

261

the ridge and began their customary looting. Benson watched helplessly as dead and wounded were unsympathetically stripped of clothes, boots and valuables. Wounded and prisoners were left shivering in the biting wind and unrelenting rain.

An elderly, mud-caked Boer with a long, straggly beard stood over him eyeing up his potential booty. Their stares met. The burgher was attracted by Benson's spurs, and ignoring the latter's helpless curses and painful cries, unceremoniously yanked them from his boots. He may have taken more, but he shrank back from the bloodied uniform and angry, condemning stare of his victim.

Occasionally, shouts and shots could be heard. Benson feared the worst for his men – tales of atrocities were to follow.

....

"He's 'ere! Colonel Benson's 'ere!"

Carefully he was lifted onto a stretcher and carried down the hill to a waiting ambulance. Through a haze of pain and grey consciousness he was transported to the makeshift camp at Bakenlaagte and laid in a tent.

"Thank God you've made it." Wools-Sampson knelt beside the stretcher. "The doctor will be with you soon."

"No! ... Only after the men have been seen to ... I'll be all right."

By the flickering orange glow of the storm lamp, Wools-Sampson could see the pain-squeezed, ashen face of his Commanding Officer; he was far from all right. "Then I'll call an orderly to dress your wounds until the doctor comes."

"No! ... No fussing ... I'll wait my turn." Distress was evident in his voice as he bore the agonizing pain. He had important orders for his Intelligence Officer, "Aubry." Wools-Sampson leaned closer, straining to hear the failing whispers. "I hand over command to you. You are not to surrender."

"I'll never surrender to these bloody Boers! You have my

assurance."

For a moment Benson's face seemed to light up; a veritable smile, "We shall do no more night marching; it is all day now. Good-bye. God bless you." His spirit slipped away.

Wools-Sampson lingered by the motionless body of his Commanding Officer and friend. He thought that he had become immune and cold to death, but for once he felt stricken by an unaccustomed sadness and aching grief.

The tent flap opened and a young Lieutenant stood in the entrance. For a moment he was shocked into silence and inactivity as he absorbed the scene.

"What is it!" demanded Wools-Sampson.

Gathering his composure, the young officer finally spoke, "General Botha has sent a messenger to say that we are to surrender immediately with all contents intact, otherwise he will attack tonight."

"Tell him that we won't surrender, and that we welcome his attack."

Wools-Sampson gave orders for the strengthening of the defences, whilst ambulances continued to bring in the wounded. Several of the men who had talked with the Boers whilst awaiting evacuation had learnt that Botha planned to attack at 3 a.m. Wools-Sampson summoned his Native scouts, "We are greatly outnumbered and may not be able to prevail. Should the Boers find you, they will shoot you out of hand. I'm giving you the opportunity to leave whilst there is still a chance. I don't believe the north is enclosed."

The scouts looked at each other; their expressions reflected their resolve. Josiah spoke for them all, "Thank you baas, but we'll remain with you."

A grin covered his face, "Then you bloody fools had better get digging."

Midnight came and with it the end of the truce. Wools-Sampson waited. Sporadic fire broke out at different points of the perimeter, but 3 a.m. came and went without a sustained assault. As dawn approached, all was silent.

****

"The burghers are exhausted and they don't have the heart for an attack against a fortified position."

Botha listened to the opinions of his commanders as they all huddled under capes for an impromptu kriegsraad.

"Besides," added another, "today we have suffered more than a hundred casualties; it's enough."

"The memory of the failed attacks against the prepared positions at Itala and Prospect are fresh and raw. There's little enthusiasm to repeat those failures," emphasised a third.

Botha could see that any zeal for continuing the fight had evaporated. He was conscious that he had driven his men hard and that they had achieved a remarkable victory, but there were limits as to how far he could push his citizen army before it disintegrated. He reflected that now the element of surprise and the advantages of mobility were lost. His generals were right; the English had quickly developed a strong defensive position and had retained the majority of their wagons and supplies. They could hold out for a long time. Little further was to be gained by pressing the attack. It was time to withdraw and disperse his commandos ready to exploit the next favourable opportunity.

He had made up his mind, "Hook up the two guns and the ammunition wagon and take them with you," he ordered Grobler. "How many badly wounded unable to travel do we have?" he asked his generals. They consulted: "We think about ten."

"Place them in the lee of the ridge out of the wind and rain. We leave them for the English to attend," instructed Botha. "We will withdraw south as a body for ten miles and then disperse to our own districts. The Witbergers will provide the rearguard. We must be clear of the area before dawn."

Ruth had been with the Witbergers for several months, and now she rode with her father, brother and Henry as part of the rearguard.

Small groups of burghers were stationed about a hundred yards apart in extended line, their task was to follow about a mile behind the main body of commandos to ensure that they were not surprised by pursuing English. The darkness and the drifting mist limited visibility. Knots of mounted guards whistled to each other in an attempt to maintain communication, but contact between flanking groups gradually broke down. The squalling rain gave way to an incessant drizzle. They huddled under the English cavalry cloaks which they wore, together with the distinctive slouch hats of the mounted infantry, but even these brought little respite from the penetrating wet. They were already sodden with the exertions of the past few days, and as they trotted along, conversation ceased and heads bowed in irresistible sleep.

They woke with a sudden start. Jacobus' horse uttered a tortured moan and fell heavily to the ground; Jacobus was trapped beneath the collapsed animal. The others jumped from their horses and together strained to pull him from under the heaving flanks. Henry and Jan took hold of Jacobus beneath the armpits, whilst Ruth comforted and coaxed the distressed animal, encouraging it to rise slightly enabling Jacobus to be eased from underneath. Jan instinctively examined the horse. The glassy eyes, foaming nostrils and swollen lips were unmistakable; the animal was stricken with the deadly horse-sickness from which barely one in a hundred recovered.

"He'll be dead within the hour," prophesied Jan.

"How badly are you hurt?" enquired Henry anxiously of Jacobus.

Movement brought sharp pains from Jacobus' left leg, hip and chest. He examined himself. "I can't find any breaks, probably bruised," he declared with his usual fortitude. With help he managed to stand, but it was clear that he could not walk any distance.

"You'll have to ride with me," announced Henry. With difficulty they both mounted his roan mare, but she was worn out and they made slow progress. Eventually, Henry dismounted and took hold of the reins, leading on foot.

"We're alone!" exclaimed Jan as the rising sun burnt off the opaque mist and visibility improved. They scanned the steaming veld; it was empty.

Jacobus considered for a moment; "I know this area. There's a farm a couple of miles to the west, belongs to the Kemps. It'll be a ruin like all the others, but you can leave me there where I can hide from the Khakis whilst you bring a fresh mount."

"I'll stay with you," declared Henry. "Jan; you take Ruth and fetch help."

"I'd like to stay," implored Ruth.

"It's best if you go together in case of problems," pressed Jacobus.

It was agreed. Brother and sister urged their flagging ponies towards the now distant commando, whilst their father and Henry sought out the farm.

****

With dawn the defenders peered over their improvised parapets, and in the welcome sun saw spread before them the debris of war and the scattered bodies of the fallen – six officers and sixty men killed; the aid station held several times that number of wounded.

The heliograph chattered hopefully, and was rewarded by an acknowledgement from the force at Leeuwkop under Colonel Barter, some thirty-five miles to the south. Help was on its way.

"I want you to reconnoitre the area and make sure that the Boers have really withdrawn and are not hiding to draw us out of our defences," Wools-Sampson briefed his Native scouts. "Josiah and Makao, you're to follow the spoor of their main force. I'm particularly interested in the movement of the guns."

The scouts were allocated the best horses available, and it was easy for Josiah and his friend to canter at speed and follow the tracks of two thousand horsemen. They had been riding for barely two hours when they came across a dead horse. They dismounted. Josiah examined the animal, "It's warm and the muscles haven't stiffened. It's very recent." He searched the ground and read the spoor. "We have two people on one horse," he remarked to Makao. "Let's follow." His curiosity was whetted.

It was not long before the tracks parted from those of the commandos and struck off westwards; now he detected one rider and another person on foot. After half an hour a farm came into view.

"Makao, you hold the horses and I'll go forward on foot." With that Josiah exploited the natural folds in the ground to edge closer to the farm; he found a cluster of ant hills which provided him with cover at a distance of about four hundred yards. He settled down to watch.

The sun was at its zenith in a cloudless blue sky. Josiah was tired; he had had no sleep to mention since striking camp at 4 a.m prior to yesterday's trek – more than thirty hours had passed. His eyes grew heavy in the soporific heat of the day; he felt himself slipping into a welcome doze.

There was movement! He shook off his lethargy and watched intently. A man half-emerged from the ruined buildings and looked around carefully before stepping out into the sunlight. He walked hurriedly to a small domestic dam a hundred yards from the farm, where he filled a couple of containers – probably water-bottles. It was when he turned to retrace his steps that Josiah recognised him; it was the American who lived with the Van den Bergs – Mr Barnham. An unexpected shock-wave ran through his body. Could the other person be a Van den Berg? The prospect sent his heart racing. He felt unsettled, troubled, even anxious; but as he gradually recovered his equilibrium, he reasoned with himself: these were the people who had denied him his freedom for the past four years;

he had worked without reward – a virtual slave. These are his enemies; people who would shoot him mercilessly without a second thought. It is the English who are his friends; the English who offer the prospect of freedom for himself and his people.

He waited until the man disappeared back into the buildings before cautiously returning to his friend, "There are two Boers in the farmhouse. I'll keep an eye on them. You go and fetch a patrol."

CHAPTER 24

"Do you not see that your country is lost?" asked the Duke of Buckingham.
"There is one way never to see it lost," replied William (of Orange), and that is to die in the last ditch."

THE TRIAL

Henry and Jacobus were led into the remains of a grain store. The mud and wattle walls were blackened by flames; only a few charred beams precariously spanned the gap where once there had been a thatched roof. There were no windows, just ventilator slots high in the walls. The door hung drunkenly from a single top hinge. To the sound of creaking groans it was lifted into place by the departing escort. They were alone. They heard a hurried conversation outside followed by the sound of soldiers leaving, and through the gaps in the door they identified certainly one soldier, possibly two, remaining on guard. They sank onto the grain-covered floor and leaned back against the wall. They were bone-weary.

Jacobus' left thigh and leg were causing him considerable pain. He had been surprised but grateful to the English soldier who had rendered first aid and then cut him a rough stick to act as a crutch - one moment the enemy, and next a compassionate helper - the English were full of contradictions; he couldn't understand them.

It was not long before the door was dragged open and a young officer entered. He stood in the doorway and looked towards the two prisoners. He spoke quietly, a little nervously, "I'm Lieutenant Dashwood. Tomorrow you are to be tried as spies by a field court martial. I have been appointed as your defending officer. I've come to discuss with you your plea and any mitigating factors that you would wish me to present to the court."

269

Jacobus and Henry were stunned by this announcement; could this be real? Henry noted the awkwardness and embarrassment of their messenger, and his grim facial expression – this was no joke.

"On what grounds are we to be considered spies?" enquired Henry incredulously.

"You were captured wearing British Army uniform. This is specifically forbidden under the Hague Conventions of 1899, and is punishable by death."

Henry was dumbfounded, bewildered, unnerved. This is ridiculous, he thought. What the hell are the English playing at? Is this some rouse to justify killing prisoners? He broke the tense silence which had descended, "Tell me Lieutenant, are you a lawyer?"

"No."

"Then how the hell can you properly represent us? You're not competent!"

Dashwood ignored the outburst and continued, "It is an indisputable fact that you are wearing the uniform of the Mounted Infantry. What we must do," he advised, "is enter a plea of guilty, and then I will put before the court any mitigating circumstance. For that I don't need to be a lawyer ... I have simply been nominated as it is your right to have a defending officer to speak on your behalf."

"And what if I choose to speak on our behalf?"

"I believe that the custom is that you speak through your defending officer."

"Then we'll have to change the custom!" asserted Henry angrily. "We have no intention of delegating our lives to someone who has absolutely no legal experience, and who has already decided that his clients are guilty. What is proposed is a travesty of justice. We'll represent ourselves in your kangaroo court."

Dashwood's hesitant voice betrayed his ebbing confidence and growing discomfort; he was unnerved by this resistance to procedures; "I'm sorry, but as I explained, you must have a defending officer."

"We'll represent ourselves; otherwise we won't participate in your sham. You'll have to shoot us without a trial. How would you explain that to the world? What would that say about British justice and fair-play?"

Dashwood was momentarily tongue-tied. This was not the response he had anticipated. They should be grateful that they are to have the benefit of a fair trial when they are so obviously guilty. The Boers are notorious for shooting captured blacks out of hand; at least we British scrupulously follow the rules of war. He was annoyed; "I'll relay your proposition to the Commanding Officer." With that he turned and left hurriedly; the straining door was hauled back into place.

Henry and Jacobus looked at each other in confusion; they were dumbstruck. Finally, Jacobus shrugged in his normal stoical manner, "We must see what the morning brings. Now we must rest and be fresh to meet new challenges: *Take therefore no thought for the morrow: for the morrow shall take thought for the things of itself."* Comforted by the scriptures, he wrapped himself in the army blanket provided and lay down to sleep. With a resigned sigh Henry followed suit. It was a long, restless night.

Probing light-shafts penetrated the damaged roof, banishing the piercing chill and heralding the new day. The door was hauled open. "'Ere yer are; 's not much, but same as what we get." With that the soldier placed two mess-tins on the ground containing bully-beef and a chunk of bread. A second soldier followed with two metal mugs of steaming tea and handed them out.

"Do you have coffee?" asked Henry innocently.

The soldiers guffawed loudly, "Yer'd think this was bloody Ritz! Coffee! Coffee!" Their sides shook with laughter as they left the prisoners to their breakfast.

Half an hour later they returned to collect the tins and mugs.

"I need to piss," pleaded Jacobus.

"Alreet, yer cum wi' me." The soldier pointed sternly at Henry, "And you stay put."

Tortuously, and with obvious discomfort, Jacobus leaned heavily on his crutch and moved unsteadily across a wide yard to what had previously been a pig-sty, but was now the designated toilet. He moved inside to relieve himself, whilst the lone guard lay his rifle against the outside wall and casually lit a cigarette. He puffed contentedly on his Woodbine. As he limped back to his temporary prison, Jacobus studied the farm layout: the sty was on the periphery of the buildings and was screened by a barn from the main complex; beyond and in depth he could hear noisy activity indicating the principal location of the Khakis – curling smoke confirmed his assessment. He noted that beyond the sty lay the open veld. He mentally stored this information.

Just before 10:00 a.m. an escort of four soldiers collected Henry and Jacobus and took them through the scorched and damaged outbuildings to the main farmhouse. A tarpaulin made a temporary roof where the tin sheeting had once been; blackened window frames bordered gaping holes which stared like skeletal eye sockets; the door had been replaced by a blanket now tied back for their entry. They passed into the main living room, stark and desolate, there to be confronted by three officers seated behind a table. The prisoners were directed to move slightly left where a box was indicated as a seat for Jacobus, whilst Henry remained standing. Another officer stood several paces to one side in front of his chair and also facing the table.

There was a moment of surprised recognition. Henry had last seen Rodger about ten moths ago lying wounded after the fight at Nooitgedacht, now it seemed his life was in Rodger's hands. Jacobus too identified the once uninvited guest; he noted the apparent alarm that their presence caused as Rodger stiffened and colour drained from his face.

Rodger was shocked to see the accused. He had learnt the

night before that two Boers had been captured and were to be tried by court-martial. He had been unhappy but resigned when detailed off for the Board, but never had he imagined that he would be facing people he knew. He was unnerved with indecision and uncertainty. Did his previous acquaintance compromise his position and possible judgement? Should he make his knowledge of the defendants known? He wrestled with his inner confusion. Henry and Jacobus made no sign of recognition and events moved on overtaking Rodger's procrastination.

The senior officer at the table spoke, "This court-martial is convened on behalf of the Commander-in-Chief, Lord Kitchener. I am Lieutenant Colonel Cowley, President of this court-martial. The other presiding officers are: on my right Captain Creamer, and on my left Lieutenant Borthwick. Captain Archibald," he pointed to the lone officer, "is the prosecuting officer." He looked directly at the defendants, "Kindly identify yourselves to the court."

Silence.

"If you refuse to cooperate with this court, then I shall have no alternative but to dismiss you both and try you *in absentia.*"

Henry played with the idea of walking away from the pantomime, but reasoned that their survival might ultimately depend upon their participation. He nodded affirmatively to Jacobus. "I am Henry Barnham, a citizen of the United States of America."

"Thank you Mr Barnham, and you?" He looked directly at Jacobus.

"I am Assistant Field-Cornet Jacobus Van den Berg, a citizen of the South African Republic, also known as the Transvaal." he snapped aggressively.

Cowley continued, "I believe that you have chosen to defend yourselves. I would like you to confirm that to the court for the record." He nodded towards a soldier-clerk who was scribbling on a pad.

"I will represent both myself and Assistant Field-Cornet Van

273

den Berg," asserted Henry, "but first I have a statement to make."

"You will have your opportunity to speak at the appointed time, but now I will make clear the charges against you both and hear the prosecution."

"The charges are irrelevant as we don't accept the jurisdiction of this court. It has no legal basis in law," interrupted Henry.

"And what do you know about law?" probed the President irritably.

"In my own country I am a qualified lawyer. I practised for three years in Boston, United States of America. I have a very good understanding of the law."

Momentarily the President was flummoxed; he suddenly felt inadequate; on unknown territory. Personally, he new very little about the law other than that contained within the Manual of Military Law, which empowered him to dispense summary justice amongst his soldiers. This situation was different; these were foreigners not encompassed by the Manual.

Seeing his opponent's hesitation, Henry seized the opportunity to strengthen his case and sow uncertainty. "This so-called court has no jurisdiction over me as a citizen of the United States of America. Neither does it have jurisdiction over my friend who is a citizen of the South African Republic."

There was a silence as Henry's declarations were absorbed. Cowley rested his head in his hands and stared at the table top. Slowly he looked up, and nervously twisted his waxed moustache between fingers and thumbs. He was only too aware that he was blindly following the directive that required him to execute Boers wearing British uniforms as a deterrent to others – it was an order from the C-in-C; there was no latitude. This underhand tactic of exploiting British uniforms to confuse our troops and close with and kill them had to be stopped; he was convinced of that.

The hushed court waited as he ordered his thoughts and arranged his arguments. The moment of indecision passed; his resolve stiffened. He spoke slowly with emphasis, "Sir, this court does not recognise you as an American citizen, but as a hireling fighting with the enemies of His Britannic Majesty. As for Mr Van den Berg, he will be aware that the South African Republic no longer exists, and that instead it has been absorbed into the British Empire as the Transvaal Colony. You, sir, are a foreign mercenary; Mr Van den Berg is a rebellious colonist. As for legitimacy under law, Great Britain is a signatory to the Hague Convention, and it applies throughout all her territories. I rule that this court has the proper and legal jurisdiction to proceed!" His equilibrium restored, he lent forward across the table and in raised voice asserted, "You are charged under The Hague Convention of 29 July 1899, and the Annex thereof; that is: Regulations Respecting the Laws and Customs of War on Land, Article 23, sub-paragraph f. This states: *It is especially prohibited to make improper use of the enemy's uniform.* How do you both plead?"

The two accused were silent.

Cowley turned to the scribe, "Record a not guilty plea. Captain Archibald, your submission!"

"Sir," he acknowledged briskly, then began to speak, "The two defendants were captured following the attack on Flying Column Number 3 on 30 October 1901. During this action the enemy, which includes the defendants, wore British Army uniforms and manoeuvred in formations deliberately designed to deceive their opponents as to their true identity. To verify this I call Sergeant Hinds as a witness for the prosecution."

A court usher called Sergeant Hinds into the room. He marched stiffly and made a parade-ground halt, driving his right foot noisily onto the floor. The water jug and glasses on the panel's table tinkled from the shock-wave. He saluted.

The usher placed a Bible in his left hand, "Raise your right hand. Do you swear that the evidence you shall give, shall be the truth, the whole truth, and nothing but the truth, so help you God?"

"I do."

"Stand easy Sergeant," ordered Archibald. "You are Sergeant Hinds currently serving with the Yorkshire Mounted Infantry?"

"Yes, sir."

"You were part of Column Number 3 when attacked on 30 October 1901?"

"Yes, sir."

"Now kindly tell the court what happened."

"I was with the rearguard. Johnny Boer was pressing us hard. It was chucking it down ... cats and dogs. We could hardly see each other. Then out o' mist came a mounted patrol; riding in formation and wearing our uniforms. Particularly distinctive was the slouch hats. We thought they was ours and let them come in close."

"And were they?" prompted Archibald.

"Well, no sir. They was Boers. We held our fire and called to them. They didn't answer, but came closer. Then suddenly they opened fire."

"Are you saying that the dress and behaviour of these Boers raised doubts and confusion, and that this delayed an effective response?"

"I am, sir."

Cowley leaned forward, "And tell me Sergeant, how many casualties were there in this engagement?

"Two of ours killed, young George Ogle and his mate, and one wounded, sir"

"And if there had been no confusion, how many casualties might there have been."

"None, sir. We would have opened fire earlier and shot the bastards!"

"Quite." The President turned to Henry, "Do you have any questions for the witness?"

"None."

"Sergeant Hinds, you may withdraw," indicated Cowley. With due noise and ceremony Hinds left the court room.

"Captain Archibald, do you have any further witnesses?"

Archibald moved slowly towards Henry and Jacobus and

with hostility pointed at them, "The accused are my next witnesses. Today, in this very court, we see the defendants still wearing the boots, trousers, shirts and jackets of the Mounted Infantry. Their guilt is undeniable. I submit that their dress and actions are in contradiction of the terms of the Hague Convention, which clearly condemns such behaviour in war, and which permits such perpetrators to be executed as spies."

Cowley nodded approvingly. He looked squarely at Henry, "Mr Barnham, kindly take the oath and offer your defence?"

Henry begrudgingly took the oath then began, "I point out that the South African Republic is not a signatory of the Hague Conventions and is therefore not bound by its terms."

"And I point out *again* that the South African Republic is defunct! Your defence Mr Barnham!"

There descended a contemptuous silence as the adversaries stared at each other unblinkingly. The air was thick with hate; almost touchable. The guards tensed ready to intervene.

Henry continued, crafting each sentence carefully, "I have recorded my objections to the proceedings of this pseudo court; however, I will offer an explanation as to why we are wearing khaki. For more than twelve months now, British forces have systematically destroyed the Boer farmsteads, crops and livestock, which represent the very livelihoods of tens of thousands of innocent civilians. Women and children are left to the mercy of vengeful black savages, or are forced into concentration camps from where we hear that many are dying from disease and neglect. Are these actions not against the terms of the Hague Conventions which supposedly serve to protect civilians?"

Cowley raised a hand to silence Henry and firmly interjected, "You were asked to respond to the allegations that you are spies, not to berate the court with a diatribe against legitimate British tactics."

"I was pointing out the arbitrary way in which British forces interpret and implement the Conventions, and that this fixation about uniforms is merely a smokescreen and excuse to justify your failure, defeat and tactical incompetence."

"We are deviating," asserted Cowley strongly. "Are you or are you not wearing British Army uniforms stolen from prisoners or the dead?"

"We are. But only because we have been left with no alternative following the barbaric destruction of our homes and the burning of our possessions, including our clothes. We have no wish to wear khaki ... we despise khaki! It is the uniform of our enemy and the symbol of imperialistic oppression! But we were reduced to wearing blankets and sacks to maintain our decency, and to find some protection from the cold and rain. Would you have us go around naked, or expect us to willingly die of exposure? Of course not! The only avenue you leave open to us is to wear the clothing of our enemy, and now you propose to murder us for that. As for acting like British soldiers in order to deceive and win advantage, it's laughable. Haven't your many defeats taught you that your tactics are discredited? Why would we want to copy your flawed manoeuvres? And why is it only now that you decide to focus on this particular Convention without even informing the commandos who are affected?" Henry stopped abruptly. He shook his head in angry frustration. He sensed that further explanation was futile.

Again silence. Eventually broken by Cowley, "Is that all you have to say Mr Barnham?"

"The truth is self-evident. I have nothing more to say."

Rodger watched as Henry fearlessly, defiantly, argued for his life. But that was the point! If found guilty then the death sentence was inevitable. And he, Rodger, was part of that decision. He held Henry's and Jacobus' fate in his hands. Of course, Ruth would mourn her lover's loss, but given time she would overcome her grief and could be open to his approaches. For a moment he visualised Ruth and himself walking hand in hand, laughing together, loving together.

But would she blame him for her father and Henry's death? Would the pain of loss forever exclude him from her affections?.

As he harboured these unsettling thoughts, his heart galloped uncontrollably.

Cowley addressed Jacobus, "Mr Van den Berg, do you wish to say anything in your defence?

Jacobus grinned contemptuously, "What is there to say? My good friend has spoken for us both. I have no wish to participate in these theatrics."

"And Captain Archibald, would you care to summarise your case?"

"Sir, the defendants admit to wearing the uniform of their enemy. We have heard how this understandably raised doubts and confusion amongst our soldiers, and undeniably delayed the time of an effective response. This led to unnecessary deaths and injuries amongst our men. I submit that the accused are guilty as charged and should suffer the appropriate penalty for this dishonourable and despicable crime."

Cowley spoke, "The court has heard the submissions for the prosecution and for the defence, and will now consider its decision. Remove the prisoners to their holding place."

Cowley waited until the room had emptied before turning to Rodger, "It is customary for the most junior member of the court to express his opinion first." He waited for Rodger's contribution.

Rodger was in turmoil. Should he declare an interest at this late stage? What was the required protocol? Would a failure to disclose his past acquaintance with the prisoners nullify the court's outcome?

"I presume you have formulated an opinion Mr Borthwick. After all that is why you are here." said Cowley sneering.

"Er ... yes, sir. It is undeniable that they are wearing British Army clothing, but having listened closely to their defence, I believe that there are vital mitigating circumstances. What alternative is open to them ... to go naked? I ask myself, what

279

would I do in similar circumstances? And we have no evidence to prove that these particular Boers set out deliberately to confuse, that is to make improper use of their enemy's uniform as expressed in the Hague Convention. Perhaps that was the inevitable result, but I don't detect premeditation, only necessity."

"So your recommendation?" prompted Cowley, clearly irked by Rodger's unpatriotic perspective.

"Clearly they are guilty of wearing British uniform, but compelled to do so by the essential requirements of circumstances, and not a calculated tactic to deceive and confuse. I don't believe they are spies. We should show leniency."

This was not what Cowley wanted to hear. The muscles in his face grew taut with restrained anger. He spoke pointedly, "And what is your opinion Captain Creamer?"

Creamer was not out to rock the boat. His father was a retired Brigadier who had great expectations of his son, and he was not going to disappoint him -.his very inheritance might depend upon it. He needed every possible recommendation to advance his career. He had twice failed the entrance exam for the Army Staff College and had reluctantly exchanged a comfortable job in the War Office to seek opportunities and accolades in the field. His understanding was clear and focused, "It is indisputable that they are wearing our uniforms. The confusion sown by this practise has cost and will continue to cost British lives until it is stamped out. We are not here to examine their motives – premeditated or not – just the facts. They dress to infiltrate our defences, to my way of thinking this makes them spies."

"Thank you Captain Creamery." Cowley sat back in his chair and waved his arms in an expansive gesture, "I have listened carefully to all the arguments, and am also of the opinion that the wearing of British uniforms is a deliberate act, and one which is forbidden under the rules of war. That it causes confusion in battle is undeniable and is the natural consequence of this deception. This must surely be foreseen by the perpetrators and in that sense indicates premeditation. Mr Borthwick, you ask what alternative do they have? Quite simply, to give up the fight. By a majority of its members, this court-martial finds the defendants guilty and recommends the death penalty. I will telegraph HQ for confirmation of sentence. Gentlemen, you are dismissed from this duty."

Henry and Jacobus waited for the verdict. Henry was angry, agitated, incensed at the injustice of their treatment; Jacobus remained calm, stoical. It was the following afternoon when the decrepit door was pulled open and a khaki figure stepped inside. It was Rodger.

"I'm sorry to see you here," began Rodger.

"We're not too pleased either," quipped Henry. He remained, like Jacobus, sitting propped up against the wall. "How are you? Fully recovered?"

"I'm plagued by headaches ... not surprisingly." Instinctively, Rodger thought about sitting with them; of being relaxed and informal, but that would be inappropriate considering the news he had to deliver. He remained standing at a discreet distance, "I've never forgotten your kindness, Mr Van den Berg, and that of your family. Even in the midst of some pretty awful times, I've always known that the Boers' motives are pure. I find this situation all very difficult. When I was wounded and vulnerable, you took me in and cared for me, eventually released me back to my own. Now the circumstances are reversed and I can't repay that debt." He paused. He needed to make something clear, "I want you to know that I did all I could to fight your corner ... to get them to understand the necessity for you to wear our uniforms. I know you're not spies."

Henry sat upright. He didn't like the drift of this conversation; Rodger's dejected look; the apologetic tone of voice. "You have the verdict?"

"I'm afraid it's guilty ... majority decision. The finding was sent last night by telegraph to Lord Kitchener for confirmation … we've just received his reply."

"So when do you shoot us?" asked Jacobus almost indifferently - he had anticipated this outcome.

"It's a little more complicated," stuttered Rodger.

"What's complicated about a firing squad?" enquired Henry sarcastically.

"Lord Kitchener has a proposition which he wants delivered to General Botha with all speed. He has ordered that one of you is to be released with a strong mount to carry the despatch."

"And the other?" Jacobus quizzed.

"The other will be executed tomorrow at first light."

"So who lives and who dies?" Henry gestured with a wide sweep of his hands.

"That is your decision."

"How the hell can it be our decision?" yelled Henry jumping to his feet and squaring up to Rodger.

The guards, responding to the raised voices, rushed through the doorway, rifles lowered horizontally ready for action. Rodger held up his hand, "It's all right. I can deal with this. Wait outside for me."

When the soldiers had withdrawn Henry continued, now composed, "How can you expect us to decide? For the love of God, make the decision!"

"How can I?"

"We're your enemies. Which of us is to die?" taunted Henry.

"I volunteered to bring this information because I needed to face you in order to say how sorry I am. But don't ask me to play God. I won't!"

"Thank you Rodger." It was Jacobus now rising unsteadily to his feet. He leaned on his crutch and offered his right hand. He spoke in a measured, calming voice, "We much appreciate your attempts to help us. We can understand that you have little influence in this situation. I pray to the God of Abraham that when this is all over, you will return safely to your family. Now please leave us alone."

Rodger took the extended hand and shook it firmly, lingering, feeling the warmth and emotion flowing from the firm grip. He turned to Henry; the latter's body still taut with anger. They looked at each other in silence before Rodger held out his hand again. They shook.

"I will never forget you both. As long as I live this grotesque episode will remain with me." Furtively, Rodger placed a book that he had been carrying on the floor, and hurried from the shed. The door closed behind him.

The two prisoners slumped onto the floor and again leaned against the wall.

"You must take the message," stated Jacobus emphatically. "This is not your war; it's not your country. I once doubted your commitment to us and our fight, but now I want to thank you for all that you've done for us." He smiled, "I believe Ruth is waiting for you. I give you both my blessing."

"That's not how I see it. I'm in this fight because it's where I want to be. I see the British as much my enemy as yours. I consciously chose to fight the evils of imperialism. My duty is no less than yours"

"The next thing is that you'll suggest we draw straws ... I understand that you're a gambling man?"

"Was."

"I've never gambled, instead I put my trust in God."

The conversation stopped. The conclusion uncertain. Each wallowed uneasily in their own secret thoughts.

There was a fluttering above. A dove alighted on a blackened beam, and with expanding chest confidently uttered its distinctive coo ... coo ... coo - calling to its mate. Henry studied the black-speckled necklace across its cinnamon breast. How he yearned for the simple freedoms of a bird. He watched it enviously.

Jacobus stretched forward and retrieved the book left by Rodger; it was a Bible. He sat down and contentedly flicked through the pages; "Let me read a psalm to you," he said:

"The Lord is my light and my salvation; whom shall I fear?
The Lord is the strength of my life; of whom shall I be
afraid?

"Henry, do you believe in Almighty God? ... you don't attend our services."

"I think I do. When I was young I went to church with my family, but the services were long and boring, and in winter the church was bitterly cold. It became a bit of a ritual which I was glad to shake off when I went to college. But I see how you and your people put God at the very centre of all you do. I used to think that God was only available to be reached on Sundays ... He was so remote, impersonal. I was convinced that He wasn't relevant to my life; now I don't know."

"Surely it's frightening to think that when you die you won't be allowed into God's house; that eternity in hell is your only option."

"I haven't got that far in my thinking ... not until now, anyway."

They sank into their personal worlds, their lives passing before them; neither wanted to talk any more. Both had determined that this was their last day alive. There was much to ponder. Henry closed his eyes, lulled by Jacobus quietly murmuring as he read the Psalms; the words indistinct.

••

"Guards! Guards!" Jacobus shouted loudly, "I need the latrine."

The door was pushed ajar and a guard peered around, "Piss in the corner."

"I need more than that."

The grumbling guards heaved the door open, "Alreet, cum wi' me."

Jacobus moved shakily towards the exit relying heavily on his crutch. He stopped at the doorway and looked back, "May

God bless you, Henry."

Henry detected a sadness; a resignation; a finality. Before he could respond, Jacobus was gone.

Slowly and unsteadily Jacobus wobbled across the yard into the pig-sty. His guard was a small, stocky soldier, perhaps in his mid thirties. He was moustachioed like most Khakis. When Jacobus moved behind the shoulder-high wall, the guard was quick to take off his helmet and lay it on top. He propped his rifle up against the outer wall, took out his tobacco pouch, and began to roll a cigarette. Jacobus crouched below the level of the wall and crept back to the opening. He sprang around, grabbed the rifle, and before the startled guard could react, he swung the butt mercilessly and smashed it into his face. The soldier collapsed, his face a bloody pulp. Jacobus limped out of the farmyard and into the open. Since shortly after his capture he had deliberately exaggerated the extent of his injury in the hope of reaping an advantage. He headed for the open ground knowing that the Khakis would soon give chase. One hundred yards on he passed three Natives busy digging his grave.

His leg and thigh were painful, and soon began to slow him down. He reckoned he had been running for about ten minutes when he sensed rather than heard the unmistakable rhythmic thud of galloping hooves. He cast about. There was no cover, but the heightened ground gave him a natural vantage point; he adopted a kneeling position. The Lee-Enfield holds ten rounds, but it was not possible to see how many were in the magazine. He operated the bolt pushing the first into the chamber.

A cloud of dust shrouded his hunters; were there three or four of them? He would need to engage at maximum range to allow time to reload, aim and fire. He took aim at about six hundred yards, eased the first pressure of the trigger and then squeezed gently but firmly. A distant figure rose up in his stirrups and then slumped over the side of his horse. There was momentary confusion as the riderless horse collided with another mount, but then the remainder came on. He operated the bolt and took fresh aim. The distance was now about four hundred yards. He fired. A horse reeled and crumbled throwing its rider heavily to the ground. Now there were two. He quickly reloaded. The riders began to fire randomly and ineffectively from the saddle. Jacobus fired again; a third soldier faltered, swayed and fell. But before he could further operate the bolt, he found himself overwhelmed by a mass of sweating, pulsating flesh which crashed into him, sending him flying like a rag-doll; he splattered in the dust. He tried to move. Nothing worked. His body was racked with pain as if every bone was broken.

The horse staggered from the impact; Corporal Winter fought to retain his seat, but finally brought his mount under control. He reigned in his mare and halted. He turned and trotted back; slowly he circled the moaning, writhing figure on the ground. He looked back in the direction from which he had come, and he saw three unmoving, dusty mounds of flesh which only minutes before had been his friends. They had been playing cards together – seven card brag – when the call came. They had laughed and joked as they hurriedly mounted, anticipating the brief and easy task of capturing a fleeing cripple. Now everything had changed. He stared down at his enemy with undisguised hatred.

The injured Boer turned on his side and looked up at him; not pleading, more in resignation. He showed no emotion as Winter raised his carbine and fired: once ... twice ... three times; until the twitching body lay still.

"That's enough! Cease firing!" Cowley arrived at a canter accompanied by Creamer. He had watched Winter firing into the helpless Boer, but considering his own casualties he was not of a mind to reprimand him. "Corporal, arrange for the collection of our casualties."

"Sir." Winter moved off to tend to his friends.

"How far did this invalid think he would get? It was stupid," remarked Creamer.

"To the real hero, life is a mere straw," muttered Cowley quietly.

Creamer strained to hear, "Sorry, sir?"

"Indian proverb." Cowley continued to stare at the dusty corpse. "This is exactly what he wanted. I believe that he was a brave man."

Henry heard a commotion: men running, frantic shouting and cursing. He thought he heard faint shots. Jacobus did not return. He received no food that night; the guards were unresponsive to his calls. At dawn he was hustled out of the shed and shoved onto a horse by angry soldiers. A letter was thrust into his hands by a surly sergeant. The mood had changed.

Get out o' 'ere! Good riddance, yank!"

CHAPTER 26

I hate that drum's discordant sound,
Parading round, and round, and round:
To me it talks of ravaged plains,
And burning towns, and ruined swains,(1)
And mangled limbs, and dying groans,
And widows' tears, and orphans' moans:
And all that Misery's hand bestows
To fill the catalogue of human woes.

John Scott of Amwell 1730-1783

(1) Country youth

TWEEBOSCH
(7 March 1902)

In the previous three months Rodger, with his platoon, had tramped across the veld chasing an elusive enemy with little to show for their efforts, and now they were on the move again. A few days earlier news had reached Vryburg of a devastating Boer attack on a convoy in which nearly two hundred soldiers had been killed or wounded, and twice that number captured. General Methuen - the most senior officer in South Africa after Kitchener – was determined to avenge this disaster, and hastily assembled all available troops in the town. This disparate, untried, ad-hoc force was mostly mounted, but it also included about eighty five ponderous oxen and mule supply wagons.

It was 3 a.m. when the slow-moving vanguard of ox-wagons left Vryburg, escorted by two companies of the Northumberland Fusiliers – the oxen trekked best in the cool of the morning before the sun reached its zenith. The main body of the column, with the mule wagons, waited an hour before following; it could move more quickly,

Following the recent rain, the ground was heavy and progress unexpectedly slow. In the first four days they barely covered fifty miles. The enemy monitored their torturous progress, and almost from the outset sniped at the vulnerable column.

The Boers, buoyed up by their recent success, grew bolder and mounted a concerted attack on the rearguard. The troops were badly shaken. It was only Metheun's personal intervention which saved the day as he steadied his half-trained yeomanry and unseasoned colonial irregulars – he quickly realised that the latter were better suited as scouts than as disciplined soldiers. He seized control and bolstered the defence with the fire of two guns. The Boers quickly dissipated under the threat of red-hot shrapnel. But the omens were not good. The General confided in one of his aides: "I found the men of the rear screen very much out of hand and lacking both fire discipline and knowledge of how to act. There seemed to be a want of instructed officers."

The wheel noise of the lumbering ox-carts temporarily drowned the pop-pop of distant rifle fire, but the boom of the guns could not be missed. They all heard it.

"Make ready!" shouted Rodger to his platoon as they plodded by the side of the wagons. Every man cocked his rifle and applied the safety catch. They waited tensely for the expected assault.

A galloper rode out of the morning half-light screaming as he passed down the line: "Halt! Halt!" He found the vanguard commander, Major Knox, "Sir, from General Methuen; the column is split into two. You are to halt so that the rearguard can catch up and the whole force concentrate to beat off the attack."

The ox-convoy was in a hollow following the course of a dried stream. Already it was under intermittent sniper fire from the higher ground.

"Where's the yeomanry for God's sake!" screamed Knox. "They're supposed to be covering our flanks. The enemy should never have been allowed to get so close." He looked around, "Close up the wagons!" The order cascaded down the line.

Rodger turned to give instructions to the Native drivers, but they had already taken cover under their wagons. "Out! Out!" screamed Rodger at the cowed drivers. "Close up the wagons! Close up!" No driver stirred.

Sergeant Mellish grabbed the leg of a frightened Native and tried to pull him out, but he wriggled free and slithered to a more inaccessible place. "Cum out yer bugger!"

"It's no bloody good. They won't move!" reported Mellish, with angry, spitting contempt.

At that moment Methuen came riding in to assess the situation. He found the wagons halted in an untidy, extended line, with fusiliers intermingled amongst them exchanging desultory fire with Boer sharpshooters at a range of about six hundred yards. He dismounted by the three guns and spoke encouragingly to the crews as they readied for action.

Shortly afterwards an aide came flying in; he swung from his horse and rushed up to the General,

"Sir," he shouted above the noise, "sir, the screen has broken! The cavalry and mounted infantry have fled!"

Methuen was silent in disbelief.

The aide described what had happened, "The Boers came galloping in firing from the saddle and flung themselves on the screen. It just crumbled away ... it was every man for himself!"

"The guns?" enquired Methuen anxiously.

"Lost, sir; and the mule-convoy ... gone. The rearguard is finished."

The news spread amongst the fusiliers like wild-fire: "Cavalry 'ave buggered off. Just us and three guns against hundreds of Boers." The implication was clear; the Boers would now concentrate on destroying the ox-convoy with its sparse escort.

Soon heavy rifle fire was pouring in from the flanking heights and rear onto the beleaguered, outnumbered fusiliers.

Casualties mounted. Rodger noticed that the most intense enemy fire was directed at the artillery. Only a few shells were fired before the gun position began to resemble a slaughter house. Gunner after gunner fell serving his weapon, together with their faithful horses. Miraculously, Methuen was unscathed. He stayed by the guns until the last man fell with a bullet to the head. Only then did he leave the scene of carnage and walk calmly to join the fusiliers.

He stood barely fifteen yards from Rodger, careless of his own safety, when a bullet bore into his right side; he staggered, but remained standing. In shock and disorientated, he started to mount his horse. What's he doing? thought Rodger. Is he crazed? The horse shuddered as a bullet struck its leg. Hesitantly, dazed, Methuen dismounted. A second bullet hit him in the thigh; he fell. Thud! Thud! His horse was hit several times. It keeled over trapping its master.

"With me! With me!" shouted Rodger. Mellish closed up with a couple of soldiers. Together they strained to ease up the stricken horse. Mellish grabbed the General by the straps of his equipment and pulled him clear; his leg was broken. In a flurry of movement the doctor appeared and sank to the ground by the casualty. He pulled a field-dressing from his bag and ripped open the covering; but before he could apply the bandage, he slumped forward; dead.

With the guns silenced and the hapless defenders greatly depleted, the Boer General, De la Rey, sensed his moment of victory. "Forward! Forward!" The Boers charged firing as they ran down the slopes, disregarding the desultory fire of the British survivors. Three hours of unequal fighting was over.

．．

Her Majesty's train *Cobra* was Kitchener's personal train, heavily armoured and equipped with guns and search lights, and commanded by an admiral. As usual, when he was visiting his men in the field, it spent the night in a siding, closely guarded by his bodyguard of Cameron Highlanders.

It was barely 7 a.m. when the Commander-in-Chief mounted his horse and rode into the veld with Maxwell and a small escort. He was making an unofficial and unannounced inspection of his columns. After a fifteen mile canter, his party came upon a temporary encampment where they were challenged by an alert but astonished sentry. Kitchener ignored the soldier's salute, as was his custom, and trotted through the lines looking at the state of the horses, and speaking briefly to anyone who was about. He learnt that the commander was asleep, but he judged it to be well earned and did not disturb him. Satisfied, Kitchener turned his horse and led his party at a gallop back to the train.

Maxwell joined his Chief for a hearty breakfast as they travelled up the line for a couple of hours before stopping at another station. Once again the Commander-in-Chief galloped off to see the troops. He found a unit of New Zealanders, and delivered a much appreciated speech of thanks and encouragement.

Kitchener was pleased with the state of his columns and their improving effectiveness. "The Boers are growing very weak," he confided in Maxwell. "The constant drain of killed, wounded and prisoners is telling on them, but they won't chuck it hoping for something to turn up." He was feeling confident of ultimate success. He gloated, "They very rarely now let us get within four miles of them except at night, and they are generally off when we are twenty miles away."

He relaxed back in his armchair and sighed with an assured sense of relief and satisfaction. He was a man intoxicated by the scent of imminent victory.

Cobra hissed to a halt as it drew into Pretoria station. Kitchener and Maxwell transferred to a waiting carriage for the short journey to Melrose House after an exhausting few days. They left their horses to be unloaded and brought on to the stables.

Kitchener was followed into his office by his Chief of Staff.

He casually tossed his pith-helmet onto a side-desk and turned to face Hamilton; he was instantly struck by his glum appearance.

"What is it?"

"I'm afraid it's bad news, sir,"

"Tell me."

"It's General Methuen. He went after De la Rey following the destruction of Colonel Von Donop's convoy and has himself been badly cut up."

"How badly?" demanded Kitchener brusquely.

"Very. Apparently the yeomanry and irregulars suffered a major dose of funk and fled the field. Just the infantry escort and gunners fought on until overwhelmed."

"And Methuen?"

"The report says that De la Rey has sent a message under the white flag to say that he is badly wounded and is to be brought in to the garrison at Klerksdorp."

"And casualties?" enquired Kitchener despondently.

"First estimates about two hundred killed and wounded, and the same number captured."

Kitchener was visibly shaken by news of yet another disaster. "I just don't understand," he uttered in exasperation. "What was the purpose of moving out with such a force to pursue De la Rey? With unmounted men and a wagon train Methuen couldn't possibly give chase even if contact was made. The Boers in that part of the field are still capable of concentrating in large numbers and of picking off weak columns. Have we learnt nothing after more than two years of fighting?"

Hamilton hovered awaiting instructions. He looked at the Chief; his body visibly sagged; his head held heavily in his hands staring at the desk. Without raising his eyes he muttered in a subdued voice, "Thank you. That's all. Leave me"

Hamilton withdrew closing the door on a dejected, broken man.

That night Kitchener did not appear for dinner. "He may be

293

feeling tired and has taken his meal in his room," speculated Maxwell.

Kitchener failed to appear for his usual early operational planning session, and again for breakfast.

"I'll go and see if he's ill," volunteered Maxwell, excusing himself from the table. He knocked on the door of Kitchener's bedroom. Silence. He knocked again.

"What!"

"I've come to see if you are all right, sir. Is anything wrong? Do you need a doctor?"

"Go away and don't bother me," came the curt response.

For two full days and nights Kitchener avoided any contact. His worried staff covered his absence: "The Chief has a heavy cold and is taking rest. He'll be back at his desk in a few days."

On the third morning Maxwell was late for breakfast - the others had finished and dispersed about the headquarters. He opened the dining room door to find Kitchener sat alone. Maxwell said nothing and quietly hobbled to his seat.

After a pause Kitchener spoke, "What's wrong with your leg?"

"My horse kicked me a couple of days ago and caught my shin; It's bruised, but improving slowly," replied Maxwell. Convention demanded a reciprocal enquiry about Kitchener's health, but he reasoned that the Chief was not ill, and so he would not play to his self-pity.

Not receiving any inquiry, Kitchener confided, "My nerves went to pieces."

Not surprising mused Maxwell, for a man who has worked long days for several years under relentless pressure and carrying enormous responsibilities. For once he detected an unusual vulnerability in this normally self-assured and iron man. "It's the most natural result of forty eight hours of starvation," consoled Maxwell. "I believe that the antidote is a hearty breakfast."

The incident was never mentioned again.

CHAPTER 27

There never was a good war or a bad peace.

Benjamin Franklin

THE BITTER END
(31 May 1902)

Botha was alerted by his scouts to the presence of a young cavalry officer, accompanied by a small escort, who was roaming the veld under the protection of a white flag. Intrigued, he rode out to meet him. The officer halted as he saw the distinctive white stallion approaching, and waited for the rider to draw alongside him. He saluted.

"Sir, I presume that I am in the presence of General Botha."

"You are correct."

He handed over a leather wallet, "Lord Kitchener sends these letters for the attention of Acting President Burger."

"Are you to await a reply?" enquired Botha.

"No sir. My duty is done." He saluted again, turned his horse, gathered up his escort and cantered away.

Botha was curious. He carried the wallet to the Vice-President who was resting in the ruins of the farm where they were hiding. They emptied the contents onto a makeshift table and scrutinised the documents. They comprised copies of letters between the British and Dutch Governments, and when read chronologically told a story. The latter had suggested that the Boer European Deputation be given safe passage to South Africa to discuss the situation in the field with the Boer Generals, and so return to Europe equipped to enter into peace negotiations. The British Government had rejected what it regarded as foreign interference, and reiterated its opinion that all powers of government rested with the Presidents in the field: Steyn and Burger. However, the British indicated that a way forward might be if the Boer leaders in South Africa were to open talks with the British Commander-in-Chief. The nuance was clear to them both: whilst the British would not officially make the first moves towards peace, they had left the door wide open to approaches from the Boers in the field.

"This is all about saving face," commented Botha to his President. "Clearly the British want an end to this fight just as much as we do, but don't want to be seen initiating peace talks. Some would interpret such a move as a sign of weakness."

"Perhaps we should explore this opportunity for talks with the Free State Government, and then together we could approach Lord Kitchener with our agreed terms," observed Burger.

"I'll send a request to Kitchener for safe passage so that we can meet President Steyn and General de Wet. I suggest Klerksdorp. It's on the main railway line and would be an accessible location for us all."

....

"The Boers have responded," stated Maxwell as he handed a letter to his boss. Kitchener examined it, and with a satisfied grin ordered, "Organise the trains and arrange suitable accommodation for the Boer leaders to assemble at Klerksdorp." The plan was working.

The swirl of Highlanders' bagpipes greeted the Boer Government Parties as they stepped from their trains onto the rudimentary platform. They were conveyed with all courtesy in waiting carriages to their allotted accommodation – the Free Staters in the old town and the Transvaalers in the new. Botha had wondered just how they would be received, and felt appreciative of the genuine efforts being made to treat them with respect, and to make them as comfortable as possible. On arrival, once alone in his room, he grasped the opportunity to sit quietly and to write and post a letter to his wife who was now residing in the Cape having been expelled from Pretoria.

That same afternoon, the senior politicians and generals of the two Boer Republics met in a tent erected for the purpose midway between the old and new towns. The numbers were small: for the Transvaal seven members, for the Free State only six.

Botha sat quietly as Vice-President Burger welcomed his colleagues from the Free State, and then paused for prayers led by the Dutch Reform Minister and close friend of President Steyn, the Reverend Kestell. The formalities completed, Burger outlined the circumstances which had brought them together. He mentioned receipt of the letters and summarised their contents; he went on, "So in this light I requested safe conduct from Lord Kitchener to enable a meeting of our two Governments in order to have a conference and, if possible, to cooperate in drawing up a peace proposal to lay before the British Government. Before we begin to discuss the proposal, I invite the General Officers to explain the situation pertaining to our burghers in the field."

Botha rose to his feet and looked along the wooden trestle-tables around which his fellow Boers were seated. In the pregnant quiet, the tent canvas fluttered distractingly in a strengthening breeze. He addressed them in his usual, calm, deliberate manner, "I speak for the Transvaal. Our country is wretched and miserable. Many districts are so exhausted of resources that the commandos can no longer continue in them. The lines of block-houses severely restrict our manoeuvres. Food is exceedingly scarce, and in some areas the burghers are totally dependent upon the little commandeered from the Kaffirs. Everywhere horse-sickness is causing great uneasiness. Increasing numbers of burghers are without mounts and there are no replacements. The situation of the families is desperate both in the concentration camps and in the women's laagers which roam the veld." He sat down solemnly.

General de Wet was next to speak. A plain man in appearance: of medium height; stockily built; a short, black beard streaked with grey; dark eyes under a broad brow. But he was a ferocious leader, one not averse to wielding his sjambok to motivate the shirkers and faint hearted. Not popular with his men, but feared and respected because he was successful. He spoke of the situation in the Orange Free State, clearly things were better than in the Transvaal, and he announced his belief that he could continue the struggle for at least another six months if not twelve.

Different politicians offered their opinions, until finally Vice-President Burger rose to his feet and addressed the gathering, "From the correspondence, I detect a conciliatory spirit on behalf of the British Government, and a willingness to put an end to this war. I believe that now is the moment to lay certain propositions before Lord Kitchener, which may serve as a basis for further negotiations to bring about the wished-for peace."

There was a general nodding of heads and a subdued acceptance of the idea.

General De la Rey spoke up, a proud-looking old man with a hawk-like nose and fierce black eyes, "I must insist that before any meeting we draft a proposal to steer our discussions."

Everyone agreed. The Transvaal State Attorney, Louis Jacobsz, took up his pen and hurriedly recorded the various suggestions. He consolidated the ideas before reading them aloud for approval. So the way was clear for a "Treaty of Friendship" between the Boer Republics and Great Britain. The Boers generously offered the British Government such concessions as a mutual amnesty, arbitration of future disputes, a customs union and fixing of the franchise. It had been a good day's work; they were confident of success. That same evening they travelled to Pretoria in a train helpfully provided by Kitchener.

Botha and his Transvaal colleagues were quartered in the house adjacent to Kitchener's grand mansion. He found the British to be a confusing, enigmatic race. They could be friendly, hospitable and considerate, yet ruthless and callous, and they apparently saw no contradiction in their behaviour.

His reflections were interrupted by the loud, sonorous tone of the dinner gong summoning him to eat. He joined the others in the dining room and was served a generous dish of varied meats and vegetables. He felt uncomfortable as he anticipated this feast in the knowledge of his starving burghers and despairing families. Botha exchanged awkward glances with his compatriots. Guiltily, hesitantly, he took up his cutlery and slowly began to eat. The others sheepishly followed suit.

After breakfast, carriages conveyed them to Melrose House where they were met by respectful young officers and ushered into a large room. They mingled for a few moments exchanging observations on their hosts, when a door opened and Kitchener entered. He stopped, stood erect and inspected his visitors; then moved forward and courteously shook hands with each of them; "Good morning," he said with a slight nodding of the head. "Shall we be seated?" He gestured for everyone to sit around a large, highly polished mahogany table.

The Boers sat tensely, wary of their enemy. They said nothing.

"Let the work which has brought you to Pretoria begin," pronounced Kitchener. "As our initial negotiations are to be conducted informally, I propose that secretaries retire." With nods of affirmation from the Presidents, the scribes duly left the room, the door closing behind them.

"So, who will begin?" inquired Kitchener.

It was Steyn who replied; a physically big man of immense strength, but very gentle in his manner: refined, cultured, a man of unshakeable convictions. "I believe you should do so." he suggested.

Kitchener observed his audience with his cold, intimidating eyes, "I wish to say something concerning what had been reported as me having said during the negotiations in June 1901 when I negotiated with General Botha. In connection with those negotiations I have been misrepresented, wrong motives having been imputed to me. It has been said, for instance, that I contemplated the destruction of the Boers. I assure you that no such thing has ever been my intention. Those who said so greatly misrepresented me." He looked accusingly at Botha. He paused; then suddenly in a lighter tone, "But that is the past. I only say this because no official minutes are being kept, everything must take place informally in a friendly manner. So, I understand that you have something to propose. This can be done now."

Burger rose to his feet and addressed Kitchener, "Both Governments have drawn up and agreed a "Treaty of Friendship" for the consideration of His Britannic Majesty's Government. I shall read it. He held the document aloft and began, "Article one: there will be a customs union between the two Boer Republics and the English Colonies of The Cape and Natal. Article two ..."

Kitchener sat stiffly, expressionless, listening as the Vice-President listed the concessions being offered to his opponents.

"... Finally," concluded Burger, "there will be arbitration of all future disputes." He sat down.

Before Kitchener could respond, Steyn stood and spoke to him directly, "I wish to thank you for your readiness to meet our two Governments, and I assure you of our earnest desire for peace. I also wish to offer an explanation with respect to a misunderstanding which the British Government is apparently labouring under, with regard to the position of our Deputation in Europe and its relationship to the burghers here in South Africa. The Deputation still represents the Boers, and enjoys the full confidence of both Governments. Now coming to the matter at issue, the Governments and the people are very desirous that peace should be restored, but that peace should be a lasting one, that is why the proposals are of the nature presented. We have come to attain no other object than that which the people have fought for until this moment."

Kitchener drew up his shoulders, threw his head forward and declared incredulously, "Must I understand from what you say that you wish to retain your independence?"

"Yes!" replied Steyn with raised voice. "The people must not be reduced to such a condition as to lose their self-respect and be placed in a position that they will feel themselves degraded in the eyes of the British"

"But that couldn't be!" interjected Kitchener. "It is impossible for a people who have fought as the Boers have done to lose their self-respect, and it is just as impossible for Englishmen to regard them with contempt." He well understood that he was dealing with a proud race, and that he must avoid any sense of their humiliation. He continued in a quieter, calmer tone, "What I would advise is this, that you should submit to the British flag, and should now take the opportunity to obtain the best terms in regard to self-government and other matters."

Steyn was still standing glaring down at Kitchener. He challenged, "I would like to know from your Excellency, what sort of self-government it would be? Would it be like the Cape Colony?"

"Precisely," affirmed Kitchener.

"I thank your Excellency. I put the question merely for information." With that he sat down, seething.

Silence. Time hung in the air magnifying the contentious mood. The Boers were shocked into inactivity.

Kitchener seized the initiative to press home his argument, "Consider the British colonist. The colonists are proud of there own nationality. If anyone, for instance, asked a colonist in Australia whether he was an Englishman, then he would reply, "No, I am an Australian." And yet such a man would feel himself one with the British Nation, and be proud of being a British subject."

"This comparison does not hold." This time Steyn remained seated. "In the case of English colonies, one is dealing with communities which from the beginning have grown up under the British flag with all the limitations connected therewith. The colonists did not possess anything which they had to surrender, and having lost nothing, they had nothing to complain about. The Afrikaners in the two Boer Republics are an independent people, and should that independence be taken away from them, they would immediately feel themselves degraded and a grievance would arise which would necessarily lead to conditions similar to that in Ireland. The conditions in Ireland have arisen from the fact that Ireland is a conquered country."

"I am an Irishman!" asserted Kitchener, "and Ireland cannot serve as a parallel seeing that it never had self-government." He refused to be drawn down that line of argument. "Let it be clear; the British Government is contemplating self-government for the Boers, preceded by a period of military administration. That is indispensable at the commencement of peace for the establishment of law and order. As soon as this period ends, self-government will be substituted."

The Boers were deflated; they discussed amongst themselves in a disheartened spirit, whilst Kitchener sat, watching impatiently. Eventually Burger announced, "In accordance with our constitutions, we are not qualified to make proposals which touch upon the independence of our Republics."

Kitchener fidgeted. He saw that he was not making progress. In exasperation he declared, "If you wish I will telegraph your proposals to the British Government, but I can guess what their response will be, and it will not be that which you desire."

"That is what we want," confirmed Steyn, "and if our terms are not satisfactory, we wish to know what terms the British Government would offer to bring about peace."

The Boer delegates spent two restless days anticipating the British Government's reply. On Sunday morning they attended divine service held in the accommodation of the Free State Representatives, and afterwards enjoyed the freedom of Pretoria, albeit under the watchful eyes of discreet military escorts.

On the Monday morning their morale was shaken as the news of a Boer disaster filtered through. A commando under Commandant Potgieter and General Jan Kemp had been cornered by a massive British drive in the Rooiwal valley near

Klerksdorp. They attempted to break out. Potgieter, wearing a distinctive blue shirt, led a line of twelve hundred burghers on horseback in a charge against a strong defensive position, firing from the saddle. One senior British officer was to observe: "The charge of the Light Brigade was child's play to this." Potgieter fell with a bullet through his brain barely seventy yards from the centre of the Scottish Horse. Fifty other burghers died with many more wounded, and the British recovered their guns lost at Tweebosch.

In dark mood, they responded to Kitchener's request to return to the negotiating table.

When they were all assembled, the door opened and in strode Milner making a haughty and theatrical appearance wearing his usual frock-coat and peering through his monocle with his cold grey eyes. Kitchener introduced him, "Gentlemen, I would like to present the British High Commissioner in South Africa, Lord Milner ... I believe that he is already known to some of you. He has joined us in our negotiations as the Representative of His Britannic Majesty's Government."

The Boers scrutinised this much loathed figure. Burger and Steyn knew him well from the abortive pre-war talks in Bloemfontein, although since their last meeting he had grown thin, his hair was greying, and his forehead furrowed with wrinkles; he was pale and tired.

Milner opened the proceedings, "I wish to remove wrong impressions. It is said that I am not well disposed towards the Boers. That is incorrect. Let me assure you that I wish to promote the interests of the Boers, and I, like you, desire peace."

This preamble was met with stony disbelief. Kitchener thought it prudent to move the proceedings along; he stood, "I have received a reply from the British Government addressed to myself in response to your proposals which I forwarded as we had agreed. Let me read it to you:

*His Majesty's Government sincerely share the earnest desire of the Boers' Representatives, and hope that the present negotiations may lead to that result. But they have already stated in the clearest terms, and must repeat, that they cannot entertain any proposals which are based on the continued independence of the former Republics which have been annexed to the British Crown. It would be well for you and Lord Milner to interview the Boer Representatives and explain this. You should encourage them to put forward fresh proposals, **excluding independence,** which we shall be pleased to receive."*

He placed the telegram on the table and sat down.

Steyn pre-empted the discussion, "It is impossible for our two Governments to act in accordance with the wishes of the British Government. It has already been said that we are not qualified to discuss the question of independence before having first consulted the people."

"May I ask, Mr Steyn," interjected Milner sarcastically, deliberately ignoring the more respectful title of president, "will the prisoners of war also be consulted?"

"How can they be consulted ... they are civilly dead! And what of the practical difficulty: suppose the prisoners should decide that the war be continued whilst the burghers on commando that it should not ... what then?"

Milner laughed aloud, scoffing, "You raise a good point!"

Kitchener was keen to avoid verbal conflict, and strove to maintain some momentum in the negotiations, "I must draw your attention to the word *excluding* in the answer from the British Government. It renders any discussion of independence superfluous and negotiations should proceed assuming this."

With annoyance evident in his voice Steyn reiterated, "I must point out again that that it is beyond our power to do so. We have no right to make a proposal which assumes the exclusion of independence!"

Burger added despondently, "I am convinced that the people

will say with one accord: "We will retain our independence, and if England does not agree to this, we will go on with the war.""

"It is not," Milner insisted, "the responsibility of the British Government to make any proposals. It appears to me that we have come to a dead-lock."

Kitchener realised that this was a critical moment; the last thing he wanted was for the negotiations to collapse. This would be ruinous for his ambitions in India. Sensitivity was required, "Would the gentlemen not first consult about this privately? If so, Lord Milner and I can retire from the room for a while and the result of your deliberations can, when you are ready, be communicated to us."

This offer was accepted unanimously and Kitchener and Milner left the Boers to their private discussions. It was 3 p.m. when the meeting resumed. Steyn began by reading a prepared statement:

> *"The Governments of the Boer Republics, having taken the reply of the British Government into consideration, have concluded that they can make no proposal on the basis therein suggested; but as they are desirous of peace request that one of the European Delegates be granted safe passage to come hither, and an armistice be agreed to enable the Boer Governments to consult the people regarding the question of independence."*

Kitchener and Milner sat quietly, absorbing what they had just heard. It was Kitchener who responded with undisguised exasperation, "This comes as a surprise to us." He continued slowly, "We cannot allow a member of the Deputation to come over because this would be an exceptional mode of proceeding to which I cannot consent." He was silent for a moment saying nothing about the proposed armistice. Then, as if suddenly struck by an idea he continued, "I think it might be better for me to ask my Government to propose what compensatory

305

measures might be offered for the surrender of your independence."

Steyn and Burger glanced across at each other and nodded. "This is what we asked of you earlier. We agree," responded Steyn.

Almost a week passed without a reply from the British Government. The Boers became despondent. They were frustrated by the intransigence of the British, and weighed down beneath the defeat at Rooiwal. De Wet, particularly, became restless and impatient, and threatened to confront Kitchener before returning to the field. It was only the timely receipt of an invitation for the meeting to reassemble that saved the moment.

"Once again gentlemen, I have a telegram from the British Government," opened Kitchener. He waved it prominently. "They express surprise that you feel incompetent to discuss terms which do not include the restoration of independence. Let me read on:

This does not seem to us a satisfactory method of proceeding. However, to spare the effusion of further blood and to hasten the restoration of peace and prosperity, you are authorised to refer the Boer leaders to the offer made to General Botha more than twelve months ago, and we are still prepared to accept a general surrender on the lines of that offer."

At a predetermined signal from Steyn, the Boers filed out into the garden. Milner paced the room irritably, whilst Kitchener stood at the bay window, hands behind his back, watching the animated discussion – he couldn't hear a word, but the gesticulations and body language clearly indicated a clash of opinions. Gradually, however, the Boers grew calmer and a peace seemed to settle. He and Milner moved to their chairs ahead of the Boers returning to the room; they entered looking sombre and serious. Kitchener was conscious of President Steyn's deteriorating health, and noticed that he was growing weaker daily. The ailing President needed physical support to climb the steps from the garden to the conference room. His eyes were swollen, and he was having difficulty reading.

It was Burger who now took the lead and confronted his opponents, "We are again asking for a member of the European Deputation to join us in South Africa."

"No!" Kitchener was emphatic. "What good would it do? Nothing is happening in Europe that could help you here. European governments may offer you sympathy, but they are not going to confront the Royal Navy in an attempt to break the blockade."

Stony faced and determined, Burger continued, "We insist upon a general armistice so that we can consult our people on the question of independence and the terms on offer."

On this point Kitchener was more conciliatory. He wanted to keep up the pressure on the Boers in the field to give weight to his negotiating position, but at the same time realised that he would need to facilitate Boer consultations. "I cannot grant a general armistice and so potentially permit the commandos to rest and regroup. However, I will make available to your generals the rail network and telegraph facilities so that you can go to the people and hold your meetings. Wherever a meeting is to be held, there will be a local twenty-four hour armistice."

This was agreed.

The politicians withdrew leaving Botha, De Wet and De la Rey to work with Kitchener in drawing up a plan. Thirty burghers from each Republic were to be elected by the commandos, and provided with safe passage to assemble on 15 May 1902 in the small mining town of Vereeniging on the banks of the Vaal River.

•••

Botha rode into Vereeniging to find a large tented camp

providing accommodation for the two Governments and the sixty representatives, together with separate dining tents and a large marquee for the meeting. There was nothing to complain about – the English had granted every reasonable request.

A thick, dripping mist rose from the river and hung over the ground; it was cold.

Botha greeted long-lost friends as they filed into the marquee, but as he did so his understanding and belief solidified: the Boer cause was lost. These burghers were the pick of the commandos, but they were starving, ragged men, huddled in skins or sacking, their bodies covered in sores from lack of salt, their faces disfigured from malnutrition. These haggard, emaciated men had reached the limit of physical endurance, but he swelled with pride at their undaunted spirit. He knew what had to be done, but these were proud men who could not be driven. He must cautiously lead them towards the inevitable decision.

One of the last to arrive was President Steyn - his physical condition was declining rapidly. With difficulty he was helped from his spider-cart, and leaning heavily on De Wet, he shuffled into the marquee to take his place at the top table with the other members of the Republican governments.

Burger rose and invited the Reverend Kestell to open in prayer. The latter stepped forward with open Bible and read:

> *"I will lift up mine eyes unto the hills, from whence cometh my help.*
> *My help cometh from the Lord, which made heaven and earth.*
> *He will not suffer thy foot to be moved: he that keepeth thee will not slumber.*
> *Behold, he that keepeth Israel shall neither slumber nor sleep.*
> *The Lord is thy keeper: the Lord is thy shade upon thy right hand.*
> *The sun shall not smite thee by day, nor the moon by*

night.
The Lord shall preserve thee from all evil; he shall preserve thy soul.
The Lord shall preserve thy going out and thy coming in from this time forth, and even for evermore."

He closed the Holy Book and studied the grim faces before him: men sitting uneasily - some shivering - on the rough benches listening to God's word, yearning for spiritual reassurance. "This psalm," began Kestell, "expresses assurance and hope in God's protection day and night. He not only made the hills, but heaven and earth as well. We should never trust a lesser power than God himself. Not only is he all powerful, he also watches over us. We are safe. Remember; we never outgrow our need for God's untiring watch over our lives." He blessed his congregation and sat down. A contemplative silence descended.

Burger disturbed the thoughtful mood, "Let me explain the circumstances that have brought us together ..." He recounted how he had received the correspondence between Holland and England which resulted in the meeting of the two Governments in Klerksdorp, and the subsequent negotiations with Kitchener in Pretoria. He told how the British Government was insisting on surrender with the loss of independence, and how they had declared that it was beyond their constitutional authority to enter into such discussions. Kitchener had agreed that the two Governments should consult with the burghers. "You, the people's elected representatives, are now gathered here at Vereeniging to inform your Governments what is the will of the people. Firstly, I call upon General Botha to present a statement of the current situation".

Botha repeated his cheerless understanding of the situation as previously given at Klerksdorp. He was followed by De Wet and then by De la Rey. Others spoke, and the discourse went on late into the night. It became increasingly apparent that their circumstances were becoming more and more desperate. The country was devastated, exhausted and facing famine from the burning and destruction of farms and villages, the removal of cattle, the ruthless slaughter of sheep and the destruction of grain. Horses were becoming increasingly scarce through fatigue, lack of forage and disease – what was a burgher without a horse? Most concern was for the women and children, particularly since Kitchener was refusing to accept any more families into the concentration camps whilst continuing his scorched earth tactics. Women and children on the veld were in a pitiable state, almost naked and suffering from cold and hunger, and vulnerable to violation by the blacks - women were being found enslaved in Kaffir huts. Commandos were becoming weaker and weaker and their mobility restricted by the spreading tentacles of blockhouse lines. There was a growing understanding that the English could absorb their defeats with an apparent inexhaustible resupply of men and stores. And whilst they, the Boers, could not detain prisoners of war, their captured friends and neighbours were shipped off to the rocky island of St Helena or to Ceylon.

It was with heavy hearts that the saddened representatives confronted the realities as they sought out their tents for the night.

After breakfast everyone reassembled in the marquee.

"The British Government still adheres to the same proposals made to General Botha in Middleburg in March last year," explained Burger. "They demand a general surrender after which they would grant certain privileges, and as soon as possible self-government. The question now is whether or not we accept this proposal or reject it and fight on?"

"Independence or else fight on!" shouted a Free Stater from the body of delegates.

Burger scanned the troubled faces; he cautioned: "Let me warn those who would fight on, that they should not continue just for the sake of their own honour. You have no right to sacrifice a nation to your own ambition!"

Botha stood and spoke quietly, men strained to hear, "I cannot continue this struggle. For myself I could still go on. My family is provided for. I have a healthy horse. I want for nothing. But I dare not think of myself only. Constantly the question arises in my mind, "What will become of the people?" Without intermission an inner voice speaks to me saying that it is my duty, whilst it is yet possible, to do the best I can for my people. It is often declared that we should fight on until the bitter end." He paused and searched the gaunt faces; he challenged: "Where is that bitter end? Would it be when the last man lay in his grave or had been banished? Or is it when the nation has striven until it can do so no longer?"

De la Rey replaced the distressed Botha. He looked into a sea of anxious, confused faces. He sensed their yearning for guidance, direction, certainties, "The circumstances of my commandos in the Western Transvaal are better than those under General Botha. We are still able to continue with the struggle, but it is apparent to me that many others cannot, and if all cannot do it, then a portion cannot succeed on its own. From all that I have learned, I have come to the conclusion that the war should be discontinued. Fight to the bitter end! Do you say that? But has the bitter end not come?"

"I don't deny that conditions are appalling and that there is great misery everywhere, especially amongst our women," it was a young Field-Cornet from Lindley in the Free State, "but wasn't that the case twelve months ago? Didn't General Smuts report so in his telegraph to our European Deputation? And yet the struggle has continued. It has been the case in the past that some of our districts have been completely destroyed and subsequently abandoned, but these, nevertheless, were again inhabited and resupplied with cattle."

De Wet spoke in support of his officer, "Did we not begin this war in faith? Should it not be carried on through the same faith?" He became earnest, agitated, "In the past, times of depression have been surmounted ... they will be again! If there are those who cannot provide for themselves, then it is the duty of this meeting to do so for them, and to continue the war."

A cry came from the depth of the marquee, "Those who wish to continue the war should not only consult their hearts, but their common sense!"

Another shouted, "The war commenced with prayer and the Mauser. What has been God's answer to this prayer? Can you not see that the hand of God is stretched out against us?"

For several hours the Boers exercised their tradition of inclusive discussion, every man venting his view. With passing time the peace-makers gained support, but there remained two clear camps of opinion for and against continuing the struggle.

It was the Transvaal State Secretary, F W Reitz, who finally gained a rough consensus, "I propose that we negotiate a retention of limited independence. We will offer to relinquish responsibility for foreign affairs and accept the status of Protectorate of Great Britain. We will surrender contentious territory and conclude a comprehensive defence treaty. I further propose that we appoint a commission to negotiate with Lord Kitchener on any subject that might lead to a satisfactory peace, to submit, through Governments, the results of their labours to this meeting for ratification."

Both proposals were agreed by a show of hands, and a commission appointed consisting of Generals Botha, De Wet, De la Rey, Smuts and Hertzog. They left by train for Pretoria.

The train pulled in to the dimly lit station to be met by horse-carriages. The commission members were taken straight to Melrose House where Kitchener and Milner awaited them around the usual table; it was 10 pm. The unique steam heating warmed the room on that cold autumn evening.

Botha presented the Boer case reading from a letter hastily crafted during the journey:

312

"Your Excellencies, with the object of finally putting an end to the existing hostilities, we have the honour, by virtue of the authority granted us by the Governments of both the Republics, to propose the following points as a basis of negotiations over and above the points already offered in the negotiations of April last at Middleburg:

One. We are prepared to relinquish our independence as regards foreign relationships.

Two. We wish to retain internal self-government under a British Protectorate.

Three. We are prepared to surrender a portion of our territory

If your Excellencies are prepared to negotiate upon this basis, the above named points can be further discussed in detail.

We have the honour to be, Your Excellencies obedient servants."

All five delegates had under-signed.

Kitchener was the first to reply, "The difference between what you desire and what the British Government proposed is too great."

"I concur," declared Milner.

Botha protested, "But there would be no distinction in principle. The Republics would be independent no longer if England was to agree to the little we are asking for."

"We cannot agree," insisted Milner sharply. "The Boer Republics must surrender their independence completely!" He was stark and uncompromising.

"At least send our proposals to England for consideration." It was De Wet.

"No! To do so would only cause irritation and might well injure your cause," argued Milner.

Smuts, the young Transvaal State Attorney turned seasoned fighter and outstanding General, calmed the rising tension, "Kindly tell us what terms England is prepared to give in case the Republics surrendered."

Now it was Milner's turn to produce a prepared document. He read:

> *"The undersigned leaders of the burgher forces in the field, accepting on their own behalf and that of the said burghers the annexations proclaimed by Lord Roberts ... and accepting as a consequence thereof their status as British subjects, agree to cease from all further opposition against the authority of His Majesty King Edward VII ... "*

"Must we understand that our proposal is rejected?" asked Botha.

Milner was unequivocal, "Yes."

The Boers were shattered. Further protestations proved useless. They wanted to retain their own flag, but were willing to surrender all relations with the outside world; were prepared to submit to the protectorate of England; would even become territorially smaller. All they wished was to be independent, even if only partly so.

The meeting adjourned temporarily for refreshments. Kitchener drew Smuts aside and discreetly led him out onto the balcony. "I can only give it to you as my opinion," he spoke quietly, conspiratorially, "but my opinion is that in two years time a Liberal Government will be in power. It will grant you a constitution for South Africa."

Throughout the war many Boers had been deeply touched and were appreciative of Liberal support and sympathy for their cause and over the conditions in the camps. A Liberal government brought a real prospect of a quick move to self-government. Smuts grasped this unexpected lifeline and withdrew to consult with the others.

With Kitchener's comments to the forefront of their minds, the commission members finally bowed to the inevitable. They suggested that they elect a small sub-committee to work with

Milner to draw up a document in terms more acceptable to Boer sensibilities; this to address their major concerns and for submission to the British Government. The draft was expeditiously agreed and telegraphed to England on the 21 May.

It was a long, worrying week as they waited restlessly for the British Government's reply. At last, on 28 May, the meeting was reconvened.

Milner announced uncompromisingly to the Boers, "This is the final draft to be put before the representatives of the people at Vereeniging. There can be no further negotiation, only "yes" or "no". We require your answer by the end of Saturday 31 May."

He went on to detail the conditions in which the burghers in the field were to lay down their arms and desist from any further resistance. Immunity from prosecution was granted for war acts; the Dutch language would continue to be used alongside English in schools and law courts; military administration would be replaced by civil government and then self-government at the soonest opportunity; Boer receipts issued for the acquisition of provisions and stores during the war would be honoured; and a suitable amount of money given for reconstruction of the country. Importantly, the question of the franchise for Natives would be deferred until the introduction of self-government.

···

On the commission's return to Vereeniging, the two Governments gathered to consider its report. In deference to Steyn's worsening health, this preliminary meeting was held in his tent. The politicians listened attentively. Though failing, Steyn was quick to condemn the terms: "The proposal is objectionable and I am strongly against it!"

De la Rey spoke calmly to defuse the rising tension and carefully laid out their options: "We can do one of three things: we can continue the struggle; we can accept the terms; or we

315

can surrender unconditionally. The last course would not legally or morally bind us to any future actions, and we could resume the struggle subsequently when conditions might be more favourable."

"There is a fourth option," argued Steyn in a wavering, agitated voice, "to insist upon our cause being decided in Europe by persons empowered and sent by us, but I am like one who has been wounded to death. I can no longer take part in the struggle, and have, therefore, no right to speak any more." He paused to gather his fading strength. The others looked on respectfully, silent, full of concern for this gargantuan figure who personified all that was noble and heroic in the Afrikaner. Eventually he continued, "Today I must, of my serious illness, resign my position. Now the matter is in your hands and in those of the representatives of the people. I have authority to appoint my temporary successor. I nominate General De Wet as the President of the Orange Free State." He looked about with a sad weariness, "Now friends, kindly leave me to make arrangements for my departure."

Later that day, ex-President Steyn was gently helped into his cart by his personal driver. As he departed, virtually unnoticed, he could hear the sounds of lively debate drifting from the Marquee into the cold air.

Botha read out the terms of the draft document to the gathered representatives. A dark shadow of stunned disbelief wafted over the audience. Silence. Then there followed a sudden explosion of questions as burghers demanded an explanation of the various articles. The mood was angry, sullen, dark.

General Nieuwoudt, a Free Stater, jumped to his feet and demanded that the Governments hold a vote immediately on the three options. He judged that the heated emotions favoured his wish for continuing the war, but the leadership would not be cajoled into taking precipitous action.

The meeting was adjourned for that day to allow cool reflection, but the next days brought no obvious resolution.

Two opposing camps solidified either behind Botha, who recommended acceptance of peace, or De Wet, who urged that the war should continue.

"If we carry on the fight there is still hope of winning," argued the bitter-enders. "We shouldn't let our courage sink on account of passing through a dark hour. There have been dark hours in the past, but we put our trust in God and carried on the struggle. The fact that the English are ready to negotiate is proof that by persevering we can gain something more. Fight on! And the chances are that at each negotiation we will obtain better terms."

But there evolved a sense of realism, an understanding that the Afrikaner nation was on its knees. Even those who might continue on commando in their districts, began to realise that they could not achieve victory alone.

With the deadline approaching, De la Rey strove to bring the discussions to a conclusion, "You may say what you will, resolve what you will, but whatever you do, here in this meeting is the end of the war"

He was challenged by a burgher, "What will you say to future generations when they blame us for laying down our arms when we should have continued the struggle?"

"It is you who must decide, not for your own village, or for your own district, but for the whole nation," countered De la Rey.

Nieuwoudt stood up again and spoke in a strident voice, "I proposed that the English terms be rejected and that the struggle continue!"

"I second that proposal!" It was another Free Stater, General Brand.

"I offer a counter proposal," quickly interjected General Viljoen, a Transvaaler, "that the Boer Republics accept the terms of the British Government."

"I second that," asserted General Albert.

The four men stood, alternatively glaring at the top table and searching the floor for support. The tension in the marquee was explosive.

The youthful Smuts stood, and with a sense of resignation made a final appeal, "Perhaps it is God's will to lead our nation through defeat, through abasement, yea, and through the valley of the shadow of death, to the glory of a brighter day."

Botha was disturbed; the Afrikaner nation was split with seemingly Free Stater against Transvaaler. A vote now with feelings running high, would, whatever the result, invite anger, reproaches, the disintegration of his people. "Friends, please be seated." His quiet, placatory demeanour brought a respectful hush to the gathering; passions eased. He appealed, "The time for discussion is drawing to a close. Tomorrow we must give our answer to the English, but before we vote let us take a time to weigh up the consequences of this momentous decision on our families, on our nation." He searched the faces of his Government colleagues, "It is late. I suggest we adjourn until tomorrow when the vote will be taken." Heads nodded in weary confirmation. "Then let us go and reflect; let us search our hearts and pray. We meet again in the morning."

Early the following morning before the scheduled meeting, Botha and De la Rey visited De Wet in his tent. Botha opened the discussion, "Surely you must see, you must know in your heart that the struggle cannot continue. During the last winter drives we lost nine thousand men; irreplaceable losses. And winter is upon us again; the drought and frost will turn the grass brown. We will be unable to feed our ponies and will freeze into immobility. What of the starving women and children roaming the veld in their laagers, prey to belligerent, armed Natives? For the sake of the families, for the sake of the Afrikaner nation, we must find peace. We have been united in the struggle until now, it would be wrong to be divided at the end."

"My friend heed the Scriptures," said De la Rey: "*Every kingdom divided against itself is brought to desolation; and every city or house divided against itself shall not stand.*" He paused then gently pleaded, "We cannot be a nation divided. We must vote unanimously to avoid future recriminations and rifts. For the sake of our people we must all vote for peace."

De Wet, that unyielding, lion of a man, sat silently. Minutes, seemingly hours, crept by. In his heart he knew that the cause was lost, that the further sacrifice of life was futile and indefensible. At last he spoke, reluctantly accepting the inevitable, "I will speak to my burghers before today's meeting and recommend that they vote for peace."

Once again Viljoen submitted his proposal to the gathering: "I propose that we authorise the two Governments to adopt the terms offered by the British Government to end the struggle."

It was seconded. There were no counter proposals. Voting slips were collected.

The weary, stressed representatives waited impatiently for the result of the vote to be announced. The tellers handed Burger the ballot papers together with a summary of the result. He stood and spoke gravely, "The vote is fifty-four in favour of the motion and six against."

His pronouncement was met with a despondent, crushing silence - the gentle patter of rain on the canvas assumed thunderous proportion. He looked at the stern faces of the representatives, men who, until that moment, had been unbending. They stared as into empty space: is this the bitter-end of our sufferings? of our faith? of our pleadings to God? Men who had never flinched before the enemy, now had eyes welling up with tears. Lips trembled. Burger broke the stillness:

"We stand at the grave of the two Republics. For us there remains much to be done, and we must devote ourselves to it. Although we can no longer do so in the official capacities we heretofore held, let us not draw back our hands from doing what is our duty. Let us pray God to lead us, and to show us how we can keep our people together. Of the unfaithful ones

319

*also we must be mindful. We may not cast out that portion of
our people; let us learn to forgive and forget."*

Shortly before 11 p.m. the train pulled into Pretoria – just one
hour before the final deadline. Carriages awaited the Boer
party, and they were whisked away to Melrose House and
through to the dining room. They were kept waiting for a few
moments before Milner and Kitchener appeared. Everyone sat
around the dining table. The atmosphere was strained. Without
saying a word Kitchener produced four copies of the treaty
which he passed to Burger. The latter took his pen and signed
(11: 05 p.m. 31 May 1902). The documents circulated around
the table, each member of the two Governments signing in
turn. Finally, Kitchener then Milner added their signatures. For
a few moments all sat still; the Boer delegates as if rooted in
shock.

It was De la Rey who shattered the funeral atmosphere.
Looking around at the long faces and speaking slowly in his
heavily accented English he extracted pained smiles, "We are a
bloody cheerful-looking lot of British subjects."

Burger pushed back his chair and stood, indicating to the
other ex-officials of the now defunct Republics that it was time
to leave.

Kitchener jumped to his feet and blocked their exit. He
moved amongst them, passing from one to another, firmly
shaking their limp hands and insisting, "Now, we are good
friends!"

The Delegates left with broken hearts.

••

Botha returned to Vereeniging to collect his horse and personal
belongings. In the privacy of his tent, he withdrew a clutch of
papers from a leather pannier. He placed one on the ground and
lit it; as it burnt he carefully fed the other sheets, watching the
flames consume them and ensuring that only crumbling grey

ashes were left.

"What's this?" It was De la Rey standing at the entrance flap, having been attracted by wisps of escaping smoke.

Botha looked up, "You know that in every department of the English administration we had our people. The names of every burgher in the Transvaal who joined with the English were collated at the Headquarters in Pretoria, and subsequently a copy was conveyed to me. The time has come to destroy these lists."

For a moment De la Rey stared at the glowing embers as if mesmerized, then he spoke quietly with a suppressed anger, "There are men who voluntarily or for greed of gold took up arms against their fellow countrymen ... they are guilty of a crime ... there are no extenuating circumstances."

Botha was exhausted; he explained wearily, "My friend; it is better for the descendants of traitors not to know about the action of their forefathers during this war. To us God has given the task of rebuilding the Afrikaner nation. We cannot enter into our new circumstances as a divided race torn by dissension and mutual recrimination. There must be reconciliation, not revenge and retribution." Returning to his task, he placed the remaining papers onto the fire.

....

When Pretorious returned from Vereeniging to the Witberg Commando with news of the surrender, he was initially met with total disbelief. However, most accepted the outcome quietly; after all, it was no surprise. They were starving, dressed in rags, hemmed in by blockhouse lines and constantly pursued by Khaki columns. Moreover, they were haunted by the heavy death toll among their women and children. A few cursed and declared that they would never surrender, but quietened when told of their two remaining options: submit or leave the country.

The Commando rode to the town of Belfast where they had

been directed to hand in their rifles. The procedure was overseen by an English officer who sat at a table beneath a clump of trees – behind him at a discreet distance, but clearly in sight, loitered a large contingent of soldiers ready to intervene should there be trouble.

The officer instructed that ammunition and rifles were to be placed carefully onto designated piles, but Jan, Henry and Ruth joined with the others in firing off all their rounds into the air before smashing their rifle-butts against a rock. The English watched nervously, reluctant to interfere.

They joined the queue. In front of them was Pretorius who defiantly refused to sign the statement promising that he would abide by the peace terms.

"You understand that this will mean your permanent exile from South Africa?" explained the officer.

"Of course I understand," replied Pretorius scathingly.

"Join the group over there." The officer indicated in the direction of three burghers standing under guard about fifty yards to one side.

Henry was next. He flung his broken weapon onto a mounting pile of scrap metal, and sullenly read the document:

I .... adhere to the terms of the agreement signed at Pretoria on 31 May 1902, between my late Government and the Representatives of His Majesties Government. I acknowledge myself to be a subject of King Edward VII and I promise to owe allegiance to him, his heirs, and successors, according to the law

He signed.

Jan followed suit. As Ruth stepped forward, she removed her hat. Her long, black hair fell over her shoulders; the officer's expression froze in incredulity as he stared at this beautiful, shapely young woman. Without a word, Ruth signed.

Immediately, the three joined the rush to the concentration

camps as burghers sought out their families. By the time they had covered the thirty miles to Middleburg, the sun was already falling behind the horizon.

The camp gates were wide open; no guards in sight. They paused.

Ruth was seized by a gut-wrenching dread. The black memories flooded her very being: the filth; the disease; the life-sapping hunger; the degradation; the inhuman neglect. She could not hold back the tears as she relived the last hours of her two younger siblings. And her mother? The guilt at having left her alone in that hell. Was she still alive?

Henry drew alongside her. They exchanged looks. He smiled supportively, lovingly. She brushed away her tears with a sleeve; willed a laboured smile. They trotted on.

Anna and the other inmates had learnt of the peace several days earlier when gathered routinely to collect their rations. The Superintendent had made the announcement in a compassionate, magnanimous manner, respecting the women's feelings. He was a good man. Women wept with joy, or gathered to pray and sing hymns and psalms of thanksgiving.

Anna received the news with a confused ambivalence. She was relieved that her ordeal was over, that now she could escape the camp with its confinement, pestilence, frugal, regimented existence and haunting shadow of death. But her heart was pained. All the sacrifice, all the wasteful, needless deaths in camps and on the veld had not been enough to save the Republics, to secure freedom and independence. Simultaneously, she felt joyous relief and bitter disappointment.

And what of her family? She had encouraged Ruth to escape – what possible good could have come from her remaining a prisoner, particularly as she was branded a trouble-maker? Had she managed to join Jacobus and Jan? Were they all alive? Hurt? Prisoners?

She had no means of travelling home. She must wait and

323

pray in the hopeful expectation of being rescued by her husband and children.

As the menfolk began to arrive, a crowd of women gathered excitedly near the gate. There were loud, happy shrieks of reunion as husbands and wives shamelessly hugged each other. There were tears of bitter sadness as enquiring burghers learnt of the deaths of their children, or even of whole families.

As she entered the camp, Ruth was alert to the changes: the air was free from the polluting odour; the tents were wider apart in neat rows; the main thoroughfares were lined with white-washed stones; brick water-boilers were evident; there was even a newly constructed hut bearing the sign *school*. She had heard that a group of English ladies had inspected the camps as a result of which governance had shifted from the military to the civilian authorities. Apparently, many superintendents had been replaced and wide-ranging improvements introduced.

The three dismounted and carefully led their horses through the swelling, emotional crowd, all the time searching for Anna. As they emerged from the pressing throng, it was Henry who saw her first. He pointed her out, "Over there. Your mother."

They saw her; a frail figure. Her dress was patched with odd scraps of material and frayed at the bottom. She looked thin and gaunt, her skin an unhealthy grey. She had aged with the weight of suffering.

Anna stood as if in shock staring at her two children; unmoving.

Ruth and Jan dropped their horses' reins and fell into their mother's hugging arms. Tears flowed – of joy and pain.

When finally they released each other, Anna spoke softly with trembling voice, "Your father? He's not coming?"

"No, mama. He's not coming," confirmed Jan gently.

"Don't tell me now … later." Anna felt tortured with aching, debilitating hurt and suffering: Boaz, Adrian, Hannie and now the father of her children; her best friend; her only lover.

"We can rest the night here and leave for home in the morning. It's getting dark," suggested Jan.

"No! This is a place of death and bitter memories. I can't stay a minute longer," insisted Anna.

"What about grandpa and the little ones?" asked Ruth.

"They're at rest. There's nothing we can do right now. When we're stronger we'll return with the predikant and place them properly into God's hands. We must leave now."

CHAPTER 28

He that forgives gains the victory

African Proverb

DENOUEMENT

During his two years of luckless war, Rodger had passed through Pretoria on several occasions, but had never had the opportunity to absorb its delights. Now, as he strolled around the Capital, he thought Pretoria a charming place with its profusion of trees and shrubs and perfectly maintained public park. He was disappointed by the ex-President's poky, little, one-storied, tin-roofed house famously guarded by two stone lions, about the size of bulldogs, sitting on pedestals outside the steps. He was, however, impressed by the wide streets lined with fine shops, and the handsome public buildings around the central square. As lunchtime approached he gravitated towards the Transvaal Hotel, and there joined the crush of army officers demanding plates of beef from harassed waiters.

His Battalion was part of a tented encampment mushrooming on the outskirts of the Capital - thousands of soldiers impatiently waiting to return home. The men were confined to the camp for fear of swamping the town with licentious soldiery, but fortunately officers could escape the boredom and claustrophobic environment.

Rodger joined a table with friends, but with a migraine developing, ate quickly and then made excuses and left the noisy, smoke-filled dining room for the cool, fresh air. He wandered into the outskirts of the town and found himself by the beautifully groomed racecourse with the cemetery opposite. He turned right and ahead saw a Native suburb of traditional mud huts and temporary dwellings constructed from all kinds of miscellaneous materials. This crude, rudimentary settlement sat incongruously beside the elegance of the Capital, but Rodger knew that black residence was only permitted in order to provide the labour needs of the white inhabitants. A trickle of Natives wandered past him going to and from the town.

He decided that he had come far enough and was about to turn around when his attention was caught by one particular black African who strode purposefully towards him: a young man dressed in baggy, corduroy trousers, tight Harris-tweed jacket, and broad-rimmed hat. He thought he recognised that figure and gait. He waited until the young man drew close.

"Josiah? Is it you?"

The man stopped: startled; surprised; suspicious. He was unaccustomed to being randomly addressed on the street by a white army officer. But then, "Lieutenant Borthwick ... Rodger!" He allowed his hand to be grabbed and pumped enthusiastically.

"Are you well? What are you doing here in Pretoria?" asked Rodger warmly.

"Yes, I'm well," responded Josiah. "And I'm in Pretoria trying to obtain the release of my father."

"Oh yes, I remember he was detained by the Boers."

"And now he is detained by the English," he retorted fiercely. "All that the war has changed for us blacks is our oppressor: the English have replaced the Boer."

Rodger was taken aback by this unexpected outburst, and froze in embarrassed silence.

"Tomorrow I must leave Pretoria," continued Josiah. "The Pass Law is still in force, and the authorities won't grant me permission to stay. They have tolerated my enquiries only because I fought on your side and received a written commendation."

"Fought?" quizzed Rodger.

"I scouted for Flying Column Number 3."

"That was Colonel Benson wasn't it?" Rodger was impressed.

"Yes, Colonel Benson and others."

"Well done, fighting for your country," congratulated Rodger.

327

"My country! We blacks fought for the English in expectation of creating a different country, a different South Africa. A country based on non-racial principles; a country where we could enjoy the same political rights as other British subjects. We want the same access to education as the whites, and the repeal of laws which prevent us from acquiring land."

"But won't these things be granted now there's peace?" suggested Rodger naively.

"Have you seen the terms of the peace treaty?"

The newspapers had carried the terms in detail, but Rodger had only scanned the text barely absorbing the content. He was shortly going home, that was all he needed to know.

" ... I can see by your hesitation that you haven't. Well I have. Clause eight defers the matter of the Native franchise until after self-government has been granted to the Boers. The Boers will never give the franchise to us blacks. We outnumber them. The prospect of losing control to us savages frightens them." His face contorted with a sarcastic grin, "We believed that the British Government had a sense of fairness, of justice, that they would show sympathy to those robbed of their land and liberties. We've been betrayed. The tens of thousands of blacks who worked in the labour gangs, who repaired the railways, who drove the wagons, who manned the blockhouses or scouted with the columns; all betrayed."

Rodger felt awkward; cowed. Instinctively, they began to walk together towards the town centre. "What will you do now?" enquired Rodger tentatively.

"I'll return to my tribe before the authorities arrest me and force me into a labour gang. But I'll take up the struggle for Native rights, not violently. There is a newspaper in Natal, *Ipepa lo Hlanga,* which promotes the cause of the black franchise and political equality. I have exchanged telegrams with them and they've expressed an interest in me joining them."

"So, a journalist!"

"And hopefully a politician!" Josiah smiled bullishly. "I must leave you now, I have to buy stores for my journey home."

They stood still and looked at each other. "You know that I'll always be grateful to you for caring for me when I was wounded. I like to think that we became friends. That we are friends. I shall always remember you as such."

"In my heart you will always be my friend," responded Josiah sincerely.

They shook hands with affection and sadness, uttering mutual goodbyes.

Rodger watched until Josiah was lost in the melee of a bustling side street.

....

Rodger galloped over the veld at a punishing pace anxious to reach his destination. He led a spare horse enabling him to alternate his mounts so maintaining his pace. He was in a hurry. His battalion was under orders to return to England; there was less than a week until he was required to entrain for Cape Town.

There was no sense in trying to rationalise what he was doing. After all that had happened, why would the Van den Bergs even want to see him. He had destroyed their home and been complicit in the deaths of Boaz and Jacobus. It was ridiculous, nay absurd, for him to visit. His very presence might incite a violent reaction. But whatever logic might tell him, his heart, his very sense of compassion, justice, honour, integrity – affection? – drove him on, inexorably. He could not help himself. He was driven by an irresistible impulse. He had to see them, or rather Ruth, for one final time. He halted his horses by a spruit and waited for them to drink their fill. He consulted his compass, then quickly rode on.

It was mid-afternoon on a bright winter's day when Rodger reached the rim above the farm. He stopped. His mind jumped back to the last occasion he had stood at that very same spot. A day of ignominy, disgrace, dishonour. He shuddered. He was in a state of emotional chaos – misled by a deluded heart. He suddenly felt foolish; vulnerable.

He steadied his nerves, slowly regained control of his senses, and hesitantly surveyed the scene below. His gaze immediately settled on two white bell-tents standing about fifty yards from the burnt-out buildings. Then he noticed activity in the graveyard; four people: two women and two men. He peered through his binoculars. Jan and Henry were busy spading soil into a newly dug grave; Anna, in traditional white cotton dress and large bonnet, was huddled up to Ruth who was wearing her usual blouse and long dark skirt, but no boater – her long hair flowed alluringly. He watched, uncertain of his next move.

It was Anna who first saw the figure on the skyline as they slowly filed out of the cemetery. She gestured to the others, and for a short time they all scrutinised the visitor. Then Ruth detached herself from the group, untethered a pony, and rode out towards him. She halted short.

"I thought it was you. I never expected to see you again. What brings you here?"

Rodger instantly noted her placative mood; he did not detect any hostility. "I'm leaving South Africa in a few days … returning to England. I felt a compulsion to say sorry to your family and goodbye to you."

"Goodbye? Why goodbye? We were never friends."

"Perhaps not friends, but I thought I knew you quite well. You and your family have been a concern to me during this war."

"My family? Why should we be a concern?" She was genuinely puzzled.

"You treated me so well. The army treated you and your family so badly. Somehow I felt responsible. I should have done more for you all."

Ruth sank into a meditative silence. For a moment her thoughts were deep in the sorrows of the immediate past. Finally, she looked at him through sad eyes and spoke quietly,

"What you witness today is my cousin Pieter coming home. It was his last wish before he died at the hands of his own countrymen ... not the English. You see, we killed our own. It wasn't just you Khakis."

Rodger detected her eyes moistening as tears formed. She continued, "But Adrian and Hannie are not coming home. You killed them. In the concentration camp; you killed them."

He felt desolate. What to say?

Ruth reached into a pannier and brought something out; she offered it to him.

He took it instinctively. It was the whittling knife which he had given to Adrian.

"It's yours," she said assertively.

He held it lightly, reluctant to reclaim it; this symbol of a young life so cruelly taken. "I wish it wasn't," he stammered.

Ruth could see the pain in Rodger's face; the welling, unmanly tears in his eyes. His suffering was real. "Why don't you come and join us for a meal" she said kindly. "I'm afraid it won't be a feast. The war is over. Perhaps now it is possible for us to be friends."

AFTER NOTES

EMILY HOBHOUSE

Having been thrown out of South Africa, Emily Hobhouse went to France and there wrote a book: *The Brunt of the War and Where it Fell.* (a valuable contemporary source used for factual accuracy during the writing of this book).

At the end of the war she saw her mission as giving assistance to heal the wounds inflicted by the conflict, and to support efforts aimed at rehabilitation and reconciliation. With this objective in mind, she returned to South Africa in 1903 and helped to establish Boer home industries, and to teach young women spinning and weaving.

Due to ill health, from which she never recovered, she was forced to return to England in 1908. She did return to South Africa again in 1913 with the intention of attending the inauguration of the National Women's Monument in Bloemfontein. She reached Beaufort West, but due to her deteriorating health, had to turn back and was unable to attend the dedication.

In 1921 the people of South Africa raised £2,300 and sent it to Emily in recognition of the work she had done on behalf of their women and children. The money was sent with the explicit condition that she was to buy a small house for herself somewhere along the coast of Cornwall. Her immediate instinct was not to accept the gift, or to donate it to charity, but on further consideration she graciously accepted the money and purchased a house in St Ives.

Emily Hobhouse had been shocked by the lack of a positive response by the majority of her own countrymen to her revelations concerning the concentration camps. She had truly believed that the British public and government would rise up with righteous indignation when she told the truth about the horrors she had witnessed. A month before her death she wrote:

My work in the concentration camps in South Africa made almost all my people look down upon me with scorn and derision. The press abused me, branded me as a rebel, a liar, an enemy of my people, called me hysterical and even worse. One or two newspapers, for example the Manchester Guardian, tried to defend me, but it was an unequal struggle with the result that the mass of people was brought under an impression about me that was entirely false. I was ostracised. When my name was mentioned, people turned their backs on me. This has now continued for many years and I had to forfeit many a friend of my youth.

Emily Hobhouse died in London on 8 June 1926. Her ashes were ensconced in a niche in the National Women's Monument, South Africa, where she was regarded as a heroine.

NATIONAL WOMEN'S MONUMENT BLOEMFONTEIN

The Monument commemorates the suffering of the estimated 26,370 Boer women and children who died in British concentration camps during the Boer War.

It was designed by a Pretoria architect, Frans Soff, and sculptured by Anton van Wouw. It consists of an obelisk 35 metres in height, and low, semi-circular walls on two sides. A central bronze group statue, sketched by Emily Hobhouse and depicting her own experiences, is of two sorrowing women and a dying child.

The Monument was unveiled on 16 December 1913, attended by about 20,000 South Africans.

Also beside the Monument are the graves of General Christiaan de Wet, Rev John Daniel Kestell and President Martinus Steyn and his wife.

LOUIS BOTHA

Shortly after the signing of the Treaty of Vereeniging, Botha went to Europe, together with De Wet and De la Rey, to raise funds for the reconstruction of the defunct Republics. He was regarded as the leader of the Boer people and was prominent in politics, always advocating measures commensurate with the maintenance of peace, good order and the establishment of prosperity.

He was fundamental in forming the Het Volk (The People), a new political party dedicated to healing the rift between former Boer "bitter-enders" and "hands-uppers", to conciliation between Boer and Briton, and to obtaining self-government. When the Transvaal was granted self-government in 1907, he was elected Prime Minister.

On 1 June 1910, South Africa obtained dominion status. He became the first Prime Minister of the Union of South Africa – forerunner of the modern South African state.

General Louis Botha died of a heart attack following a dose of Spanish influenza on 27 August 1919.

An equestrian statue of Botha stands outside the Union Buildings in Pretoria.

LORD KITCHENER

Following the Treaty of Vereeniging, Kitchener hurried back to England to many honours and to the job for which he had aspired and schemed over several years, Commander-in-Chief India. He served in that position until September 1909, a period during which he introduced many important military reforms, and famously quarrelled with the Viceroy, Lord Curzon.

After a period of frustrations and gardening leave, he finally returned to Egypt in September 1911 as The British Agent and Consul-General – *de facto* Administrator. He ruled with a mixture of autocracy and benevolence.

Whilst on leave in England in the summer of 1914, war broke out and he was invited by the Prime Minister, Herbert Asquith, to take up the post of Secretary of State for War. He reluctantly accepted.

At the first Cabinet meeting on 6 August, Kitchener predicted that the war would last for at least three years and would be fought principally on the European continent. He announced his intention of raising a new citizen army of at least 100,000 men. His effectiveness as a recruiter was illustrated in his iconic poster: "Your Country Needs You".

At 4:45 p.m. on the 5 June, he set sail from Scapa Flow in severe weather in the cruiser HMS *Hampshire* for negotiations with the Russians. At approximately 8 p.m. she struck a mine west of the Orkney Islands and sank by the bow within fifteen minutes. He was one of more than six hundred killed on board the ship. Only twelve members of the crew survived.

SIR ALFRED MILNER

On conclusion of hostilities, Milner was made a Viscount in recognition of his services.

On 21 June Milner published the Letters Patent establishing the system of crown colony government in the Transvaal and Orange River Colonies, and changing his title of Administrator to that of Governor. He played a major role in the reconstruction of the new colonies in the period immediately following hostilities. To achieve this he provided a steady revenue by the levying of a 10% tax on the annual net produce of the gold mines. He devoted special attention to the repatriation of the Boer prisoners of war, land settlement by British colonists, education, justice, the constabulary, and the development of railways. To aid him in his task, Milner recruited a team of gifted young lawyers and administrators, most of them Oxford graduates, who became known as *"Milner's Kindergarten"*.

After several years his health began to deteriorate due to the incessant strain of work, and he decided to retire. He left Pretoria for England on 2 April 1906. On his return from South Africa Milner immersed himself in his business interests.

When at the height of the First World War, Lloyd George replaced Herbert Asquith as Prime Minister, he invited Milner to join his exclusive five-person War Cabinet as the Briton most experienced in the civil direction of a war. He was active in every aspect of war planning. On 19 April 1918, he was appointed Secretary of State for War, and subsequently became Colonial Secretary. Milner retired in February 1921 after long service, and at a time when his views on imperialism were waning in popularity. He died on 13 May 1925.

Found among Milner's papers was his *credo* – statement of belief - which was published to great acclaim:

"I am a Nationalist and not a cosmopolitan .... I am a British (indeed primarily an English) Nationalist. If I am also an Imperialist, it is because the destiny of the English race, owing to its insular position and long supremacy at sea, has been to strike roots in different parts of the world. I am an Imperialist and not a Little Englander because I am a British Race Patriot ... The British State must follow the race, must comprehend it, wherever it settles in appreciable numbers as an independent community ... "

ENTERIC (Better known as typhoid)

Enteric fever is a potentially fatal multi-systematic illness spread by eating food or drinking water contaminated by the faeces of an infected person. Historically this disease has ravaged armies, although by the time of the Boer War both its cause and prevention were understood. Unfortunately, the application and supervision of preventative measures was atrocious, and this poor hygiene discipline caused many unnecessary deaths.

By the end of the War more than 400,000 British, imperial, and colonial troops had passed through the South African theatre of war. Of those 5,774 were killed by the Boers; a further 16,168 died of disease, mostly from enteric.

ABOUT THE AUTHOR

William (Bill) McDonald

Bill McDonald was born in Rochdale, Lancashire when it was a thriving mill town. Almost without exception his family were mill operatives. He began his education in a small C of E school in a neighbouring village before attending the Secondary Technical School in the centre of Rochdale. On leaving school aged 18, he joined the Army and was a professional soldier for 24 years. He subsequently served with the Territorial Army in various full and part-time capacities for a further 10 years. He began his career as a soldier in the Lancashire Fusiliers, and retired in the rank of major with the Royal Regiment of Fusiliers. He saw service, amongst other places, in Germany, Northern Ireland during the "Troubles", and the Former Yugoslavia.

On leaving the Army he worked for a humanitarian organisation in Rwanda, Zambia and Burundi.

He is now retired and lives with his wife in Northumberland.

34812151R00200

Printed in Poland
by Amazon Fulfillment
Poland Sp. z o.o., Wrocław